Pelican Books
Democracy and Participation

John Randolph Lucas is a Fellow of Merton College
Oxford. He was Chairman of the Oxford Consumer Group
from 1961 to 1963. He was married in 1961 and has two
sons and two daughters.

J. R. Lucas

Democracy and Participation

 Penguin Books

Penguin Books Ltd,
Harmondsworth, Middlesex, England
Penguin Books Inc.,
7110 Ambassador Road, Baltimore, Maryland 21207, U.S.A.
Penguin Books Australia Ltd,
Ringwood, Victoria, Australia
Penguin Books Canada Ltd,
41 Steelcase Road West, Markham, Ontario, Canada
Penguin Books (N.Z.) Ltd,
182–190 Wairau Road, Auckland 10, New Zealand

Published in Penguin Books 1976
Copyright © J. R. Lucas, 1975

Made and printed in Great Britain by
Hazell Watson & Viney Ltd,
Aylesbury, Bucks
Set in Linotype Plantin

To S. K. L.

Contents

1 Introduction

'Democracy' is a noun, but should be an adjective. Because it is a noun, we tend to think that there is a thing – a particular system of government – which it refers to, and that all existing states can be put into some order of merit according to the degree they approximate to true democracy. Each country regards itself as a democracy, and is indignant at the pretensions of its rivals, which also describe themselves as democracies and maintain that every other country must be fraudulent in its claims. In the end we weary of the debate, and decide that the term 'democracy' is a meaningless one, an honorific title which each country applies to itself, in the same way as every residence on an estate agent's list is desirable. Even if we do not become cynical, the task of distilling an essence of democracy that is common to Britain and Russia, India and China, the United States and Argentina, East Germany and West Germany, Italy and Israel, Norway and South Korea, is a daunting one; and we may suspect that rather than look for a concept so dilute that communists and capitalists, liberals and socialists, republicans and Maoists can all call themselves democrats, we should do better to avoid the term and concentrate on those concepts which have content, and serve to distinguish one system from another. But this would be wrong. The idea of democracy, for all its imprecision, is an important one, which sways men's minds and influences political decisions. It will not go away merely by our deciding not to talk about it. Rather than ban the concept from our discourse, we need to try to come to terms with it. And the most important thing to do is not to think of there being some one system which exemplifies true democracy, but rather to distinguish different aspects of each system, and consider which aspects are, and which are not, democratic. Almost every system of government has some democratic aspect, and almost every system of government has some aspects which are not democratic. Monarchies characteristically contain some provision for popular acclamation of the monarch, and few people are such ardent democrats that they object to there being a chairman of a meeting, and his having authority to decide who shall speak next.

The word 'democracy' and its derivatives apply to decision-procedures. In its original Greek sense a decision is democratically taken if the answer to the question *Who takes it?* is 'More or less everybody' in contrast to decisions taken only by those best qualified to take them, as in a meritocracy, or those taken by only one man, as in an autocracy or monarchy. The word 'democratic' has secondly come to specify the way in which a decision is reached; it is an adverb, answering the question *How is the decision taken?* A decision is taken democratically if it is reached by discussion, criticism and compromise. And thirdly the word is used to characterize the spirit in which a decision is taken, as being concerned with the interests of all, instead of only a faction or a party. These senses are related, but are not the same. Ideally, it would be best, for the sake of clarity, to keep to the original sense. After all, meritocracies often engage in discussion, criticism and compromise before reaching their decisions, and monarchs often have the interests of all at heart. Unfortunately, the question *Who?* is not as simple as it seems at first sight, and we are forced often to replace or supplement it with the questions *How?* and *In what frame of mind?* As we transplant the term 'democratic' from simple, small, ideal societies to the complicated, enormous, un-ideal communities that we are obliged to deal with, we have to transmute the questions we ask in order to determine the applicability of the word in these more sophisticated contexts. In so doing we easily lose the unifying strands in a welter of detailed considerations, and often we feel cheated as simple ideals are compromised in the face of practical realities.

Many people are disenchanted with democracy, and in a sense they are right. Democracy has not delivered the goods. People thought it would eliminate injustice, abolish poverty and create a society in which everybody could play a creative and meaningful role. Our society is less than perfectly fair, contains many people who are poor and even more who feel under-privileged, and is woundingly impersonal and insensitive to the interests and aspirations of the individual. Those who had high hopes of democracy and fought for it in the expectation that it would answer all the problems that face our society feel cheated. It is only when we abandon high hopes and consider actual alternatives, that we are reassured that our efforts are worthwhile, and that our way of doing things, although far from ideal, is less imperfect than it well might be. Yet we should not dismiss idealism. Great expectations, although easily disappointed, enhance the vision and expand the heart. We cannot be inarticulately pragmatic, saying only that 'Whate'er is best administered is best', because whether any actual situation should be accounted well-administered depends at least implicitly on various standards and criteria of assessment which are formulated in terms of ideals. Ideals and practicalities are both important. They react on each other in a number of different ways, and give rise to many different arguments. There is no one single argument for democracy, any more than there is one single form of government that should be reckoned a democracy. Rather, there are different arguments, with differing degrees of cogency, bearing on different aspects, not all compatible, open to different objections and giving rise to different expectations and different disappointments. It is these we need to disentangle in this book.

2 Action, Argument and Agreement

Democracy is concerned with what we are going to do. It sounds very simple, but is not as simple as it sounds. Even the concept of *doing* contains unsuspected difficulties. Actions are 'homeostatic' processes. I am hardly aware of it as I bicycle, but my body moves to compensate for the pedalling of my legs, and as I approach a corner I begin to lean over in order that I shall be able to get round it when I reach it. If I wish to build a house, I make a number of varying responses to the local authority's refusal of planning permission, the architect's unwillingness to take account of my needs and wishes, the builder's dilatoriness and incompetence, the building society's reluctance to grant me a mortgage; unless I take compensating action to circumvent difficulties, I shall not achieve that state of affairs which was my original goal. From this it follows that actions are not merely patterns of bodily behaviour, assignable to the person whose body is involved. In the first place, many different bits of bodily behaviour can constitute one and the same action: nodding, raising a hand, shouting a figure at an auction, posting a sealed bid in Scotland or signing a contract in England, are all ways of buying a house, for in each case the relevant end-result is the same. For this reason too an action can typically be resolved into a complex of sub-actions, and even if we are decided on what action to take there may still be dispute on the particular way it is to be undertaken. If I send a child to the shop to buy eggs, he can go either on one side of the street or on the other; and if I specify which way he is to go, he can start with his right foot or with his left. So too with communal actions. A parish council can be kept in a state of heated ineffectuality wrangling over whether in the new public conveniences the Gentlemen should be to the north and the Ladies to the south, or vice versa. Because of this indeterminacy of the concept of action, we are always having to delegate, and whenever we tell someone to do something we are also authorizing him to make the many sub-decisions incidental to carrying out the commission. To order is also to authorize, and in chapter five we shall see how the need to delegate to others at least the execution of their decisions leads the people inevitably to transfer much of their authority to their civil servants.

Not only can many different bits of bodily behaviour constitute the same action, but one and the same bit of bodily behaviour can be correctly described as doing many different things – he nodded, he fell asleep, he showed what he thought of the leader's argument, he was very rude, he jeopardized his own career. This is because we characterize actions in terms of the purpose or reason for which it was undertaken. If a person is doing something, we can ask him *Why are you doing it?*, and if he cannot give some sort of answer, we no longer say that he was doing anything but regard his bodily movements as a mere reflex or automatism. Actions implement purposes, but a man's motives may be mixed, and so his actions can be characterized in different ways. In particular, significance depends upon context, and the same bodily movement may be read as manifesting different intentions on different occasions as the context is differently construed. A forward movement of the head can signify agreement or be a sign of incipient sleep. To fall asleep if one has been up all the previous night is a venial fault, but in other circumstances indicates either the dullness of the proceedings or insensitivity to the feelings of others. The rules for characterizing actions are complicated, but in ordinary life we have little difficulty in selecting the characterization that is apt for our purpose. When there is a dispute, however, as often in politics, we find it hard to agree what the correct characterization of an action must be.

Because actions are characterized partly in terms of the reasons for which they are done, they are, like reasons, shareable, and not, as bodies are, unshareable. Solomon built the Temple, even though he may not himself have put one stone upon another. Where bodies are concerned we sharply distinguish one man's body from another's, mine from yours, Solomon's from Hiram's;

but where actions are concerned, we do not have to distinguish my actions from yours, but can quite properly use the first person plural, for we can share purposes, and therefore also can share actions, and the fact that a load of cedar was hauled down the slopes of Lebanon by the muscular effort of certain unknown hewers of wood does not prevent its also being the action of Solomon who originated the project and of Hiram who acceded to his request. 'The body politic' is only a metaphor; but communal action is a fundamental fact of social life, and the proper approach to politics is to consider not the metaphysics of corporate bodies but the ways in which we do things together. Not only do we act in common, but individual actions are subject to rules of ownership as complicated as the laws of property. As well as for what I do with my body, I am responsible for what other men do at my request or with my blessing; and my own actions may correspondingly be not only mine but somebody else's too. Things are constantly being done by the Queen or the President of the United States, even though the Queen is at Ascot and the President playing golf. A society will seem to itself to be much more democratic if the actions actually performed by officials are seen as having been done at its instigation and for its sake, and are therefore accepted by the people as being in some extended sense their own. It is largely a matter of social psychology, but is grounded on the peculiar logic of the concept of action, and, as we shall see in chapter seven, has important consequences for the canons of decision-making we should adopt.

Although we often do things, it is difficult to say what it is to do something, and although we often make decisions, it is difficult to give an account of how we reach decisions. For the most part, we decide immediately and almost instinctively as the situation presents itself; the circumstances make it clear what has to be done, and we just do it. Occasionally, however, we are in doubt, and deliberate, seeking counsel or guidance, and arguing over the different possibilities with ourselves and others. We find arguments both for and against each course of action, and ponder them and weigh them, and find it difficult to strike a balance. The two-sidedness of political argument has important consequences. It constitutes one reason for allowing everyone to participate in decision-making: by letting everyone have a say we decrease the chance of any important consideration being overlooked. It shapes our procedures and institutions – prosecution and defence in the law-courts, Government and Opposition in Parliament. Sometimes it is too difficult to strike a balance, and we concentrate on one side of the argument or the other: the defendant can be convicted only if the argument for his having committed the crime is conclusive; a department of state will abandon a proposal it has submitted to a public inquiry only if the objections to it are overwhelming.

Two fundamental points need to be made about decisions: first that they are not arbitrary; and second that in deciding what to do, we are autonomous agents. There is a tension between these two truths, and thinkers have often been so much at pains to emphasize one that they have been led to ignore or even deny the other. Decisions are not arbitrary. Although sometimes it is difficult to tell whether a particular decision is right or wrong, it is always intelligible to ask whether it is right or wrong, and often it is pretty clear what the answer must be. In this, decisions are like the statements of historical fact, and unlike expressions of predilection or taste. We cannot always tell whether a putative statement of historical fact – that the battle of Marathon was fought in 490 B.C. or that Alfred burnt the cakes – is true or false, but it is quite in order for anyone to ask whether such a statement is true or not; and there are many statements – that the Battle of Hastings was fought in 1066 or that Queen Victoria was not amused by Mr Gladstone – about which there is no room for doubt. If I say, however, that strawberries are scrumptious or *crème brûlée* delectable, I am only expressing a personal taste. I speak for myself alone, and if you say that strawberries are nasty or *crème brûlée* sickly, there is no point in saying that one of us is right and the other wrong. Most decisions can be described as being right or wrong, sensible or stupid, wise or foolish. It was a good move on the part of Stephen to put in for a university scholarship, wrong of Robert to try to drive himself home after the party, sensible of Mary to refuse to marry Marmaduke, right of Richard to own up to his escapade last night, and foolish of Gillian to take up smoking. Sometimes we cannot tell – would

Stephen have been wiser to go to Cambridge? Was it stupid of Jane to marry John Plowman instead of Sir James Eligible? – and occasionally, but only occasionally, we doubt if it is worth even asking the question. For the most part, however, decisions are susceptible of evaluation, and we are concerned, when we are deciding, that the decisions we reach should be right rather than wrong, fair rather than unfair, prudent rather than silly, and in general reasonable rather than unreasonable. If this were not so, we should not bother about decision-making. Instead of deliberating, pondering and sometimes agonizing, we should just flip a coin or decide by whim or caprice. The fact that we worry and take trouble over our decisions is evidence that we think of our decisions as being not arbitrary but the sort of thing that can be described as right or wrong, good or bad.

Although we are not arbitrary agents, we are autonomous ones. Each man is free to make up his own mind for himself what he will do. Indeed, this is what it is to be a person, to have a mind of one's own. If someone could not do other than he was told or programmed to do, then we should not regard him as a responsible agent at all. It is because it is up to me whether or not I decide to do something that you can hold me responsible – answerable – for it, and expect me to answer your question *Why did you do it?*; and if I was not free to do or not to do it – if I was hypnotized or drugged or my limbs were forcibly moved by someone else – then I am not responsible and cannot be held to answer for my alleged actions or say why I did them. Because I am free, I always *can* do something other than the normal thing. I can fail to get out of the way of the oncoming car; I can cheek the boss; I can walk out on my wife and family; I can refuse to take my medicine, turn down a good job or a good offer for my car. Often it would be foolhardy, lunatic or plain wrong to do so, and, unless I am an existentialist anxious to assure myself of my own significance by performing some *acte gratuit*, I shall put the matter out of mind without more ado; there are enough problems in life without making mountains out of plain level grass. But although it would be absurd to follow the practical precepts of the existentialists, their logical point is sound. I can decide to act otherwise. And if I so decide, there is no stopping me from reaching that decision, though I may well be prevented from carrying it out. In this, decision-making in life is more open than it often is elsewhere. If I am playing a game, there are rules which constitute that game, and which I must obey on pain of otherwise not playing that game at all. If I refuse to leave the wicket when the umpire says 'Out', I may stay in the middle of a grass field, but am no longer playing cricket. If I refuse to allow that Socrates is mortal having already said that all men are mortal and Socrates is a man, I may not be sent to gaol – after all, it is a free country, and there is no law against one's maintaining the immortality of Socrates – but I shall cease to be speaking intelligible English or to be able to communicate with other English speakers. So too, if I am a mathematician, I must allow that 257 is a prime number; if I am a doctor, I must not commit adultery with a patient; if I am to pass an examination, I must answer four questions. Almost all our activities are undertaken within a framework of rules or aims we take for granted; and while they are granted, many necessities and impossibilities follow from them. But they do not always have to be granted – though life would be impossible if they never were – and we can on any occasion envisage the possibility of acting outside a given framework, and other than in the normal and expected fashion.

The fact that we always can decide differently is of great importance. It explains, as we shall see in chapter four, why the state has to be able to use force in the last resort. It also explains the great difficulty we have in eliciting or imputing agreement about what decisions should be made by, or in the name of, the community as a whole. There is, as Socrates saw, an analogy between being able to decide rightly in public affairs and being able to decide rightly in medical matters or questions of seamanship; but we hesitate to draw the conclusion that we should hand the conduct of public affairs over to political experts, because we feel both uncertain about their expertise and reluctant to deprive the inexpert of all say in what shall happen to them. In other disciplines – medicine, navigation, mathematics and the like – there is a corpus of agreed knowledge which is the basis of the discipline, and if a person chooses to think differently, he thereby shows himself to be an ignoramus. If you claim to be a doctor, there are many views you cannot maintain consistently with that claim; but if you are just deciding what ought to be done, however wrong-headed your views, I cannot rule you out of court. There is no hard framework, as there is with medicine or mathematics or even history; morals and politics are 'soft' subjects, not in the sense that anything goes, but because they lack a rigid and rigorous procedure which will demonstrate the error of at least some erroneous views. If I claim that something is made of silver or iron, you can put the claim to the test, and by a definite procedure either convince yourself that it is true or me that it is false. But if the dispute is about whether a proposed course of action is good or just, then, as Plato observed, we need never agree, and neither can prove the other wrong. Any alleged 'science' of morals or politics is thus suspect, and we can put in question the credentials of those who pretend to be experts without danger of being shown up as pretentious in our turn. From this it is a short step to the egalitarian conclusion that nobody is any better at making decisions than anyone else, and that Jack's view of the matter is as good as his master's. The inference is fallacious, and the conclusion false. There is a great difference between saying that there is no way of proving right decisions right or wrong decisions wrong and saying that there is no difference between a decision's being right and its being wrong. Not only must there be a difference – or we would not try hard to reach right decisions rather than wrong ones – but often we can convince other people of their rightness or wrongness; only, we cannot *always* convince *everybody*, for we have no method or procedure – as we have when the question is whether a specimen is silver or iron, or whether a number is prime or composite – which anybody must accept or else be ruled out of court as an ignoramus. If my existentialist friend decides to leave his wife, throw up his job, put an advertisement in *Figaro* claiming to be the reincarnation of Napoleon Bonaparte and give an interview to *Paris Match* on how he changed his sex, I can be sure that his decision is wrong and unwise, but I cannot prove it to him in the same sure-fire way as I can if he opines that 257 is not a prime number. Nevertheless, his decision still *is* wrong. And, as we shall see in chapter five, although often we are content to let other people decide for themselves wrongly, when decisions matter to us a lot we go to great lengths to find people who will make the right ones for us.

There is no method of always reaching right decisions or avoiding wrong ones, but we can reason about them and check one another's reasoning. If asked *Why did you do that?* we attempt to articulate our reasons as best we can, and in the face of further probing will fill them out more or less adequately. Often we shall succeed in explaining ourselves to the satisfaction of our questioner, even though there always could be another questioner who was not satisfied by the account we gave. In general, however, even the most indulgent critic will find our account somewhat inadequate. Although rational agents, we are inarticulate ones, and find it difficult to formulate our reasons at all fully. Often we act for better reasons than we can say. It is much more important for survival to do the right thing than to say why it is right. Children have an almost instinctive sense of whether a grown-up can be trusted, and often in politics as well as in other walks of life we are guided by hunch or intuition, and sometimes rightly. When pressed to give our reasons we fall back on saying 'I just feel it in my bones', and cannot formulate in any more felicitous phrases what this feeling comes from. It may, of course, be simply prejudice; but we should not jump too readily to the conclusion that it must be. Often it is a leap in the dark, highly fallible but the best that could be done in the circumstances. Deciding is a risky business. Typically we have to make decisions with inadequate information available, so that it will emerge only later whether we decided rightly or not, and provided the decision was justified in the event, it does not matter then how good our reasons were at the time we took it.

Although our reasoning about practical matters is usually inadequate, it is not hopelessly bad, and can be improved by reflection and criticism. A man ponders what to do, and sometimes, as he weighs the pros and cons of each course of action, it becomes evident to him what his best course is. He talks it over with his friends, and as they put forward their proposals and counter-proposals, his own mind becomes clear. Even when, as often, he does not reach complete clarity of purpose, discussion with others can be a help. If their proposals coincide with his, he may be strengthened in his resolution, even though their arguments do not succeed in entirely allaying his doubts. The mere fact that no new objections are put forward is a comfort, for it suggests that there are no hidden snags he has overlooked. In many cases he will adopt their counter-proposals not because he has been completely convinced by their arguments but because he trusts their judgement. Only a fool believes that he always knows best. A wise man knows that there are others wiser than he, and is willing on occasion to be guided by their opinion. It is an obvious point really, but has often been obscured by a misconception of what it is to be an autonomous agent. To be autonomous is to be *able* to decide for oneself differently from everybody else, not actually to do so. If I accept a friend's advice or act on his request, I could have done differently, and am therefore responsible for what I did, even though he also is responsible, having put me up to it. The ideal of the absolutely autonomous agent, in the sense of a person who has made up his mind for himself without relying on what anybody else says, is a figment of the philosopher's imagination. Even the scientist, who traditionally is supposed to think for himself and not rely on authority, has to rely very heavily on the authority of other scientists before he can begin his own investigations. In social matters too, we rely, and, as I shall show in chapter four, necessarily rely, on others not only where questions of fact are concerned, but for guidance about what we should do. In this sense, a certain degree of heteronomy is a necessary condition for us fallible and non-omniscient creatures.

When a decision rests with one man, however difficult it is to say how he should, or does, go about reaching it, there is a certain simplicity and definiteness about the outcome. He must in the end do something, and his decision is implicit in that, even if he reaches it hesitantly, reluctantly, or against his better judgement. Communal decisions are much more difficult. It may be, of course, that we are all of one mind. Such cases are rare in practice, although immensely important in theory. In most cases, however, there will be less than total whole-hearted unanimity, very often much less. All the same, communal action is still possible, and does occur. It is difficult to give an adequate account of the conditions required for an action to be regarded as that of a particular community – were the Germans responsible for what the Nazis did? It is natural to start with very simple cases. Small groups can evolve a common mind about what to do. Committees do. So do gangs. We talk it over, each person putting forward his own suggestions, and saying what he thinks of the suggestions of others, and often a common mind emerges, and we all find ourselves in whole-hearted agreement on what we shall do, which may well be something quite different from what each would have chosen by himself at the outset. But at the end it is what we all collectively and each individually want to do.

We do not always reach whole-hearted agreement; but even when we do not entirely agree, we often, just for the sake of agreement, agree to something that we do not altogether approve. We go along quite gladly, and will defend the decision to others; but it does not depend solely on the cogency of the arguments adduced, and would not have been achieved if there had not been a diffused desire on the part of all of us to maintain the fabric of unity, a general willingness to accept a second best that is acceptable all round, rather than push one's own ideas to the point of divisiveness. The word 'reasonable' in its ordinary use carries the sense of being willing to accept what is generally acceptable, as well as being able to ratiocinate well. It is a term of moral, as well as of intellectual, appraisal. Social life generally, and political argument in particular, is possible only on the basis that many people are reasonable for a lot of the time. It is not just that there is an answer which rational beings can get right. Rather, within a range of actions that are none of them totally unreasonable, a reasonable man will urge what seems to him the best one absolutely, but agree to a less good one which is the best that is generally acceptable. Hence it is that we can commit the taking of a decision to a group of reasonable men – a committee; but their decision will not be sacrosanct. With mathematical calculations it would be absurd to refer them to a committee – anyone can check that the answer is correct, and while we may wish to double check, it would be ridiculous to have seven people conducting the check in common. Equally, but for opposite reasons, it would be absurd to refer questions of taste to a committee. With courses of action, however, we share enough of a common rationality to reckon that another man's judgement will not be hopelessly at variance with ours, but cannot assume that every reasonable man will always reach the same conclusion. We can delegate, and hope that the decisions taken will not be wildly wrong; but they will not automatically be just the same as the ones we would ourselves have taken, and may depend on the exact membership of the committee, the way they go about their business and the terms of reference they are given. A large part of democratic theory arises on account of the gap between whole-hearted and merely working agreement.

There are further degrees of disagreement. As I become more conscious of the gap between what I think we should do and what some other people are prepared to agree to, I shall see our agreement less as a consensus and more as a compromise. Often we have a rational discussion ending in a compromise, some-times we simply bargain. In a compromise the parties agree on a course of action which neither of them thinks entirely desirable but each prefers to the one the other wants. You want to go for a holiday winter-sporting in January, and I want to go sailing in July; so we agree to go to Greece at Easter, where there will be some mountains to climb and snow to feel, but also a good deal of the Aegean to cross in caïques. In reaching a compromise, each party needs to explain what his order of priorities is, and to be prepared to give way on some points in order to win concessions on others. But it is not a simple bargain. It is an endeavour to see things from the other's point of view, to internalize his system of values, and to find a course of action which should rate fairly high whether evaluated by him or by oneself. It is a partial but not a complete sharing of points of view. Each retains his original preference, but recognizes the validity of the other's view and is anxious to meet it, and find a solution acceptable to him as well. A bargain, by contrast, is much more external. I do not try and see your point of view, but merely seek to make a concession sufficient to induce you to give me what I most want. It does not matter to me whether I can find a solution which, I can see, should be fairly acceptable to both of us; so long as you actually will agree to it, I am not concerned at all to evaluate it from your point of view – all I want is to get you to agree to a solution which ranks high on my preference scale. Your agreement is an entirely external constraint upon the solution, not an internalized principle of evaluation.

A bargain is the limiting case of communal agreement in the direction of individual self-consciousness. In the other direction there are many further stages of consent and acquiescence. Often even in small groups there are one or two members with forceful personalities who emerge as natural leaders. One of them sums up the discussion with a 'Let's all go to the Bear', and off they go, dissentients tagging along with the rest of them, not really having agreed to a compromise or made a bargain, but just swept along by the tide of opinion. It would be wrong at this stage to say they had been outvoted. No vote was taken; and if a vote had been taken, the result might well have gone the other way. Rather, it reflects the fact that our minds are often not firmly made up, and that we respond almost instinctively to social pressure. We are imitative by nature, and the mere fact that other people do something makes us do it too, often without realizing it. We very much dislike being out on a limb, and will change our mind, again often without realizing it, rather than feel at odds with everybody else. Even when we are conscious of our disagreement, it often takes great courage to voice it publicly and men will keep their views to themselves rather than stand up for them before the gaze of the indifferent, the contemptuous or the hostile. We keep quiet, we acquiesce; and more generally, and in less extreme cases we are quite ready to have our minds made up for us by those with whom we identify. Nor is this merely a weakness on our part, due to our social nature. Part of our social nature it undoubtedly is. But, as we shall see, in considering the *raison d'être* of the state in chapter four, it is susceptible of a rational justification as well.

3 Votes and Vetoes

Political thinking is dominated by ideals. We embody our values in visions of societies in which they are completely realized without any compromise or qualification whatever. Sometimes such a vision is evidently unrealistic, and we dismiss it as Utopian. More often, it is not Utopian, but could be realized only under very favourable and rather rare conditions. If we lived in very small societies and the issues we had to decide were few and simple, we might be able to reach agreement about what we should do in each case. It is unrealistic, in that our society is very sizeable and highly sophisticated, but it is not so unrealistic that it never could be or never actually is realized in our experience. On the contrary, it is a common experience, especially in late adolescence and early manhood, to be a member of a small group in which everything is decided in common, and universal agreement invariably reached. It is a powerful experience. I feel enlarged, more of a person, capable of doing many things in company I could never have done by myself. I feel important, appreciated, valued and significant, instead of isolated, ignored, frustrated and futile, as when I am all by myself. And therefore I extrapolate from the small gang to the whole nation, and yearn for the day when we can all discover ourselves in one another, and, recognizing that we all belong together, reach decisions about what we are going to do amicably and unanimously. But it is an illusion. The peer group is essentially small, eclectic and transient. Because it is small, everyone can speak, and can take part in every discussion. Because it is eclectic, only those with similar tastes will belong and they will discuss only those questions on which they are likely to agree; and if there is any division of opinion, those differently minded can go their different ways without undue loss. These conditions do not obtain in the state.

Nevertheless, so great is the feeling which peer-group solidarity generates, that we brush aside these objections and continue to insist that somewhere, somehow, the conditions should exist for a perfect democracy, in which each one of us could decide what we were going to do, and feel in consequence completely identified with every decision. We are the better able to do this in that no one of the conditions seems absolutely essential. Large organizations, even nation-states, are sometimes enthused with corporate solidarity, as Britain was in 1940, when everybody felt identified with the country in all its endeavours and all its misfortunes. A committee may contain members of very different outlook, and yet be able to form a common mind on a number of questions. A political party or a trades union may last a long time, and yet go on securing a considerable degree of emotional identification from its members. Thus, although over the years large non-selective societies lose their unity of purpose, it does not seem obvious that they must do so, and we continue to cherish a paradigm of perfect democracy, which alone seems worthy of the name, and alone would constitute a satisfactory form of political organization.

Perfect democracy is possible because of certain facts about group dynamics. We can form a common mind about what to do, because we both want to reach agreement and can do so. Although I have a mind of my own, and always can disagree with you about what should be done, I do not want to be always out on a limb by myself. I identify. I am not only John Lucas, but a Briton, an Englishman, an Oxford man, a Fellow of Merton College. No account of me would be adequate unless it included the fact that I was a member of the Church of England, a member of the Lucas family, a philosopher, a member of the Oxford Consumer Group. In each of these ways my own identity is constituted in part by my belonging to various communities and groups; and my being me depends on my being part of them. Not that I am just the sum of my various memberships and affiliations. As we have seen in chapter two, it is an essential part of my being me that I am more than merely a member of various bodies, and that I am something distinctive, and can be at odds with, and separate myself from, each and all of them. Nevertheless, although I am not just a member of various bodies, my membership of them is an essential part of my being the person that I am. And therefore they are part of me, and I have a deep urge to be in with them. I want to agree. I may also, for different reasons, want to disagree, or I may feel in duty bound to come out into open disagreement; but still, always, I want to agree, and on this fact is based the whole edifice of politics.

Perfect democracy assumes that we always succeed in reaching agreement; ideally whole-hearted agreement, but perhaps only working agreement, or, failing that, a compromise, or at worst a bargain. This rests on a number of assumptions. In addition to the community's being reasonably small, homogeneous, and not required to make very many or diverse decisions, it assumes that everyone agrees about fundamental values, and that everyone is reasonable. These assumptions are not universally true. People can disagree about values, although no community can exist unless some values are cherished in common by its members. Even among those who share values it is not the case that they must agree in every particular case – we may acknowledge the same values but differ in their application in concrete instances. Often people, having once made up their mind, are unwilling to settle for anything other than the best as they conceive it. And so we may fail to reach agreement. If we succeed, well and good – then we know what we should do, and the question *Why should I, individually, do what we, collectively, have decided?* can hardly arise, and needs no answer. If we succeed, we have a complete answer to the great questions of political theory *What shall we do?* and *Why should I obey the law?*, answers so good as to make all others seem shifty and inadequate in comparison. But we may fail, and the most important concession to realism is to consider what our attitude is to be in the event of disagreement.

It may be that a community may not be able to be of one mind about what is to be done, no matter how hard a compromise is sought nor how much bargaining goes on. Suppose five of us want to go to the Bear, but I insist on going to the Eastgate; then we may agree to compromise by all going to the King's Arms, or may agree to go to the Bear tonight and the Eastgate tomorrow night; but if I hold out for the Eastgate, and one of the others is not prepared to give in, we have reached deadlock. And then there are only two possibilities left. Either we say that no decision is possible, or we have some rule or convention whereby we can say what the corporate decision shall be deemed to be, even though not everyone actually agrees with it. Both possibilities have been explored. The former underlies the thinking of the English philosopher John Locke, who wrote at the end of the seventeenth century justifying the Glorious Revolution of 1688, and whose thought has been immensely influential in the United States. The latter underlies the thinking of the Swiss-French *philosophe* Jean-Jacques Rousseau, who wrote in the middle of the eighteenth century, and whose writings continue to fascinate Europeans. Of course, neither writer is as schematic as I shall make out; my account should not be taken as a scholarly or historical exegesis. The real Locke anticipated many of the doctrines I shall attribute to Rousseau, and the real Rousseau was so confused that almost every doctrine and its opposite can be found in his writings. Nevertheless I shall use their names, not as guides to their actual thoughts, but as schematic labels, indicating what others have been able to read into them.

If we stick to the principle of unanimity, we retain the cast-iron answer to the question *Why should I obey the law?*, but lose the ability always to answer the question *What shall we do?* The reason why I must obey the law is that, one way or another, I have agreed to it. I am ultimately my own legislator. The law rests upon my own authority. In most cases I can be presumed still to will that it be the law and be obeyed by me; and if I have changed my mind, I can reasonably be kept to my word. But if a single dissentient voice is enough to prevent a decision being taken, not many decisions will be taken. This does not matter if the decisions are not very urgent or not very important, or if a non-decision is quite acceptable. If all that is at stake is which pub to go to, we can quite well afford not to decide to go to any. Or, in a very different way, if a new law or a new article of the constitution is proposed, it may not matter if it is easy to veto it, because we can probably manage to get along well enough under the old laws or the old constitution. Legislating is a special kind of decision-making, in which the two sides of the question are not on a level: not to enact a law that everyone should do X is not the same as to enact a law that everyone should not do X. But this is not typical of decision-making. We cannot in general not decide what we are going to do. Athens must either decide to keep its treaty with Sparta or break it. *Tertium non datur*. A decision-making body that cannot be relied on to make decisions is not fulfilling its function, and is unlikely to survive long. Normally, only limited classes of decisions are subject to a unanimity rule – the verdicts of a jury for example – and strong pressures are exerted on dissentients to persuade them to come into line. The ancient Parliament of Poland was subject to the only slightly less stringent *nemine contradicente* rule – any single member could veto any decision – and the story is told how in order to prevent one recalcitrant member from exercising his veto, the other members tried to hold a meeting with the doors barred so as to prevent his attending and casting his contrary vote, but he outwitted them by hiding in a stove and emerging only as the vote was being taken, whereupon the other members set upon him and killed him. From which the moral may be drawn: it is better to have only a vote rather than a veto, because it is better to be outvoted than dead; in the rare case where your vote is going to be decisive, there will not be a majority ready to kill you to stop you vetoing their decision.

Even if I am not killed, I may find the possession of a veto an embarrassment rather than a help. For if I am likely to use it, other people are likely to take extreme steps, short of actually killing me, to ensure that I do not use it. In particular, if, as is likely, they possess vetoes too, they are likely to use theirs not in order to protect their interests but in order to damage mine, so as to impress on me the advantages of being amenable to their wishes. Hence, although I might in theory possess a veto, I should not be able to use it for fear of provoking retaliation and having all my own projects vetoed. Even though not in danger of my life, I might find myself worse off with a veto than with merely a vote. It is better to be outvoted sometimes than vetoed always.

We cannot really stick to the unanimity rule if we are serious about decisions being reached as and when required. Locke accommodates this by two manoeuvres. First, where decisions which concern everyone have to be made, they are delegated to rulers by an original contract whereby we all agree to obey the rulers on condition that they rule well and respect our rights. Secondly, wherever possible, we decentralize, and divide up the decision-making into different *provinciae* (in the original Latin sense), vesting the decision in those alone concerned.

Some decisions cannot be decentralized, and must apply to all alike, whether they individually like it or no. Locke has little to say about these. The original contract – the basic constitution, so to speak – lays down how these decisions are to be taken – perhaps by king and parliament, perhaps by president and congress, perhaps by means of some sort of referendum – and the authority of the decision actually taken stems entirely from the original contract. We unanimously agreed that we should all be bound to recognize certain authorities, provided the authorities recognized our rights and the consequent limitations they imposed upon them; and so long as the authorities keep to the conditions originally laid down, we are each individually committed by the original unanimous agreement. Contract theory is only marginally democratic. All that it requires is that somewhere, somewhen, we the people unanimously agreed to obey our rulers on condition they agreed to behave themselves, and have regard to our rights. Once upon a time there was a democratic vote that set up the constitution; but the constitution itself need not be a democratic one. It could perfectly well be a monarchy or aristocracy. All that is essential is that whatever form of government be adopted, it should continue to be a constitutional one, in which those who are entrusted with authority and power exercise it not arbitrarily or for their own good alone, but responsibly and for the benefit of their subjects generally. Locke could be invoked against some forms of totalitarian democracy, and would be perfectly happy with a Whig oligarchy or a Federalist government of the good, the wise and the rich. Locke is not concerned with the questions *Who takes the decisions?*, or *How are the decisions taken?*, but only *In what frame of mind are the decisions taken?* Provided the answer to this question is satisfactory, he is content. It is only when rulers are ceasing to be constitutional and are abusing the power and authority committed to their hands, that Locke raises the question of who ought to rule and whence legitimate authority must ultimately stem. The people are important only as being the people who could repudiate their allegiance to James II, or later, George III. In normal, non-revolutionary, times such an issue is not raised, and we recognize such authorities as there are just simply for the reason that they are there. In a sense – in a somewhat exiguous sense, as we shall see in the next chapter – this is an aspect in which all governments are necessarily democratic, almost according to the unanimity interpretation of Locke. A government cannot be a government unless it is recognized as such by almost everybody. People do not have to like the government or approve of it or agree with it, but must agree that it *is* the government, or it will not be serving its essential functions. The rule of recognition has to be almost universally accepted, or the community will dissolve into warring factions. In a community it is not necessary, as some simple-minded democrats have supposed, for everyone to be agreed about what decisions are to be taken; but it is necessary that almost everyone should be agreed about how decisions are to be taken, that is to say by what decision-procedure disputes are to be settled. And this requirement of near-unanimity is tenuously preserved in the original contract which Locke supposed we all once upon a time entered into.

Locke's second manoeuvre to preserve unanimity is to decentralize. Instead of my having a relatively small say in everybody's affairs, I am to have more or less sole say in my own, and none in anybody else's. I mind my business and you mind yours; and if there is any project which concerns us both, we negotiate an arrangement between us that is satisfactory to us both. By this means Locke preserves the virtue of the veto system – that it allows me to preserve my essential interests and ensures that every decision is at least minimally acceptable – without exposing each person to gratuitous vetoes by offensive busybodies. Each man has his own 'business', his own sphere of influence where nothing can happen unless he agrees to it, and in return each man is required to mind his own business and not trespass on to the preserves of others. It is natural to interpret 'spheres of influence' literally, just as *provincia* in Roman practice came to have a geographical definition. Locke often seems to have in mind a number of separate farmers, each lord of his own domain and only occasionally transacting business with his neighbours. The geographical interpretation, however, is often inapplicable and always misleading. Societies are typically gatherings, not separations. The decentralization posited by Locke is essentially one of function, not of residence. Rather than envisage everyone living on his own estate, we should see each person having at his disposal his own time, talents and money, and entering into bargains with others for their mutual benefit. The market economy of the classical economists is the best model of the decentralized decision-making advocated by Locke.

The market economy has great merits. Although we are schooled to consider its disadvantages, they are arguments against relying exclusively on the market rather than against using it at all. As we shall see, the market does not give a man everything he needs or might reasonably want. Nevertheless, it is right that the chief say in what I do, where I go, how I spend my time, should be mine. Even if I am a wage slave, I am better off than a real slave or a subject of a totalitarian power. I may have to spend my days in boring or degrading work, and feel that I have no alternative but to accept any employment offered, no matter how monotonous or servile. But I have got some alternative that the slave or Eastern European lacks; if I do not do as the employer says, I may go hungry, but I cannot be whipped, as a slave could, or sent to a concentration camp, as happens in totalitarian countries. I have the right to say no. Saying no is always costly, and sometimes very costly. Yet it remains an option we can exercise if we are prepared to pay the price; and even if we decide we cannot in the event afford to say no, the fact that we could remains important to us and to others. The employer never knows but that his unreasonable requests may be refused, and therefore cannot carry on with the assured arrogance of the slave-owner or the commissar. The market economy does not free me from all pressures – how could it? – but it does institutionalize the most valuable aspect of Locke's unanimity rule, namely that in the things most closely concerning himself each man has a veto.

The virtues of the market economy are great, and any society that values the freedom of the individual is bound to incorporate some features of the market, in order that individuals may be able to make some significant choices of their own. But just as freedom is two-faced, so the market economy has its unattractive side. My freedom is your impotence. If I have the sole say on any question, you have no say, and so far as you are concerned the decision is taken impersonally. Similarly, although I can decide how to earn and how to spend my money, the market economy gives me no say in what other people – especially what other businesses – do, even though they may have a pervasive effect on the economic conditions which affect my whole way of life. I feel myself isolated and impotent in the face of vast impersonal forces; I am not allowed to participate in board-room decisions which may spell financial ruin or redundancy for me. Although I am king in my own castle, it is a small and fragile one, which may be overwhelmed by the tide of events over whose course I am debarred, by the same rule as secures my own limited independence, from having control.

Independence and impotence are different sides of the same coin. Underlying the shift in public attention from the one to the other is a growing awareness of our vulnerability under the market economy to the decisions of others. It was all right in a society of independent agriculturists, who traded for mutual benefit but not out of necessity. If a neighbour's terms were too steep, and the bargain seemed unattractive, then the deal could fall through without any cost other than the loss of the projected benefit. Jeffersonian democracy works where everyone who wants to can live off the land, and no one is obliged to sell his labour in order to live. But most countries do not have an available supply of unexploited land, and often there are landless labourers who have nothing to dispose of except their labour, and must sell that or starve. They are vulnerable in a way Locke does not sufficiently appreciate. Other men's vetoes would be fatal for their survival, whereas their own individual vetoes would not cost anyone anything much. Employers are in a stronger bargaining position than individual employees when there is a labour surplus and no fall-back means of subsistence. It may be feasible to redress the balance, by means of collective bargaining on the part of trades unions, or by manipulating the economy to prevent there being a labour surplus, or by providing a fall-back subsistence pay as a part of social security; but in modern industrial societies, most people are employees rather than peasants, and interpret Locke's political philosophy from the standpoint of employees who depend essentially on the market for being able to earn their living rather than that of peasants who do not. We therefore feel much more vulnerable, even if in fact we are not, and do not see in Locke's decentralization the safeguard he sought to provide against the vetoes of others being used to jeopardize our essential interests. Decentralization, although important, cannot be a sufficient safeguard. No man is an island. Not only ought I to be concerned with other men's interests, but what they do must sometimes vitally affect mine, and no complete carve-up of decision-taking can secure to me the sole say in all the things concerning my life and livelihood.

The market economy not only makes us feel impotent and vulnerable, but seems to us immoral. It appears to substitute the profit motive for disinterested concern for others. Although money is a useful vehicle of freedom when we are deciding which pub to go to or which hat to buy, it is a dangerous master when we want to decide what career to follow or what job to take. The doctor, we profoundly believe, should be concerned with making other people healthy, not with making money for himself; and outside the professions too, many men see themselves as rendering services to society, rather than making money out of it. But if we accept the strict logic of market economics we should discount all idealistic motives. I may gratify my moral inclinations, if I like, in the spending of my money, but am being irrational if I am not guided by economic considerations in the earning of it. If stockbrokers earn more than probation officers, and I choose none the less to be a probation officer, I am making a suboptimal use of my time and talents. And this we find quite impossible to believe. We can see that it is good that individuals should be left fairly free to make their own decisions, and we can accept that often they will be guided by considerations of self-interest, and that it is better to recognize it and allow for it, and that the institutionalized selfishness of the market is a lesser evil than the ruthlessness of totalitarian society; but we cannot believe that the whole duty of man as a member of a free society is to drive the hardest bargains he can, and maximize his profits in all his transactions with his fellows. It is a form of self-aggrandizement we may rightly be prepared to tolerate either as the least of available evils or out of set libertarian principle, but not to recommend as the best course of action open to a responsible moral agent.

Underlying our moral dissatisfaction with the market economy is the fact that it is based on a principle of bargaining. Locke's unanimity rule rapidly collapses into an invitation to bargain. If I have a veto, I shall be tempted to use it not only to protect my own vital interests but to extort from others useful concessions in return for my not using it against them. Since it is up to me whether I use my veto or not, and the consequences may evidently be considerable, it will present itself to me as a considerable power vested in me for my benefit, and to be used by me in the most advantageous way possible. The veto makes each person conscious of himself as an individual participant, and therefore a unanimity rule structures the group-dynamics of communal decision-making into a form of game, albeit one played in deadly earnest, between a number of players. On every possible proposal, each player has two alternatives, to agree to it or to veto it. Each player will attach some value to the acceptance or rejection of a proposal. And thus we shall have the formal basis of a 'many-person non-zero-sum game', in which in order not to be left behind in the maximizing race the individual will be impelled to join in a number of coalitions, with complicated trade-off arrangements, in the course of which he will be obliged to mortgage altogether his freedom of action.

One ruthless bargainer rapidly forces everyone else to bargain ruthlessly too, on pain of otherwise losing out. Locke accepts this. He makes bargaining the corner-stone of his theory of the state. The original contract is a bargain, and bargaining plays a prominent role in the adjustment of various interests in the formulation of communal policy. Even to this day, admirers of the United States of America are somewhat embarrassed by the explicitly bargaining approach that legislators bring to bear on the discharge of their official functions. Not that bargaining is altogether bad. Once we allow that members of a community may legitimately have private interests, we shall expect them to resolve their disputes by compromise and bargaining as well as by pure consensual agreement. Indeed, as we have seen, many consensual agreements have an element of compromise about them: in seeing the point of the other man's arguments we may be recognizing his interests, and in moving from our original position to one agreeable to both of us, we may be safeguarding the interests he was most concerned to defend. Once it becomes one of the shared values of our community that its individual members matter as individuals, and that their interests ought to be respected, then it will be a basis of any attempt to reach a consensual agreement that it should be acceptable from each person's individual point of view, and therefore it will have a propensity to compromise built into it. And often we shall prefer an open compromise to a decision we believe to be better but know to be divisive. Much of the work of actual assemblies and parliaments is to arrange compromises rather than discover the general will. Nor is this a bad thing, once we abandon the totalitarian tenet that everyone should be totally identified with the community and should have no interests and cherish no values of his own. Compromises shade into bargains; and bargaining plays a key role in the liberal theory of the state. The great merit of bargaining is that it is external. Bargaining presupposes that the parties are separate beings, each with his own identity and own interests, not absorbed in some Hegelian whole, nor with his actual wishes subordinated to a Rousseau-like general will. It recognizes the individual's right to be himself and make up his own mind about what he wants, in much the same way as the principle of legality enables the individual to maintain his freedom under the law. Much as the law of the land is assimilated to a law of nature, so other people's desires and wants are assimilated to the properties and propensities of natural objects, leaving me free to chart my own course among them as best I can. But the very merits of bargaining are also its demerits. I am not myself in complete independence either of the law of the land or of other people, and it is unrealistic as well as wrong to assimilate them too completely to laws of nature or natural objects. Although it is true, and very importantly true, that I am myself, different from everybody else, and not merely a typical Englishman or a representative specimen of the communal whole, yet it is also true that I am myself only in the company of, and through my relationships with, other persons. The contract theory reduces the state to a glorified mutual protection society, and reduces every community to a joint-stock company, failing to account for the fellow feeling that is a feature of all communal life. If my only relationship with my fellow men is that of a bargainer, I reduce them all to one-dimensional owners of money, and impose on myself the loneliness of the man whose life is made up of £.s.d.

The difficulty about bargaining is that each party is explicitly unconcerned with the other's point of view. If I do a deal with you, I need not be selfish – I might be doing it on behalf of my children, or of my college, or of a charity; but I am not to consider your interests. That is your business. It is for you to decide if the terms I offer suit your book, and for me only to consider them from my side of the table. Business relations are essentially 'non-tuistic'. This makes for ease and efficiency – it is much easier if I am not all the time having to consider your interests and can concentrate on minding my own business – but it is also emotionally unsatisfying and morally unedifying. We want to engage in I–thou relationships not only in our private lives at home but in our effective lives at work; and although we recognize that we cannot be expected to mind other people's business as well as our own, we reckon that we ought not altogether to disregard their interests in deciding our own course of action. Moreover, bargaining is not only non-tuistic and impersonal, but in part positively hostile. The better a bargain I drive with you, the worse it is from your point of view. Although a bargain is essentially a form of mutual cooperation whereby we both may benefit, the division of the benefits as between the two of us is not determined by the nature of the cooperative enterprise, nor by what we each contribute to its success, but simply by the strength of our respective bargaining positions. Aristotle thought that bargaining was a form of justice – 'commutative justice' as it is sometimes called – on the principle that 'Fair exchange is no robbery'. He argued that a man cannot be wronged by anything done with his consent, and therefore not by any contract freely entered into. Hence any bargain freely agreed to must be fair, and Aristotle, believing that fairness, or justice, was a sort of equality, endeavoured to prove that in every exchange each side benefits equally. It is an impossible task. Bargains may be accepted, but they can be hard; and although it can be argued that every bargain must be advantageous to both parties, or they would not both agree to it, no argument can show that it is equally advantageous to them both. In so far as we can measure individuals' advantage, it is perfectly possible for one party to take advantage of the other's need and charge an extortionate price for his services. Political economy has never developed a theory of fair exchange or the just price, but only of free exchange. And this, though it ministers to our individualist ideals and our need for freedom, fails to satisfy our equally strong collectivist concerns and our aspirations for justice.

The principle of unanimity has two disadvantages. Unanimous agreement does not always naturally emerge, and if we insist upon it, we introduce pressures which distort the dynamics of the group, and by conferring on each man a veto, replace the natural flow of argument by a restricted bargaining procedure. Although we pay great respect to each man's opinion, if a man insists on being the odd man out, we do not see why we should allow him to dictate to us. And, anyhow, there may be more than one awkward customer, in which case deadlock could ensue, and no decision be possible. But if a community is to survive it must be able to produce answers to questions on time. We can hope that a general will may emerge, but we cannot rely on its always doing so, and therefore we have to have a decision-*procedure* which will be sure to produce a definite result. There has to be a procedure which every member of the community can recognize as being *the* decision-procedure, and which will reach results that are unambiguous to everyone. It may be casting lots or seeking auspices, it may be by plebiscite or referendum, it may be by authoritative utterance of monarch or pope; but it must be some formal procedure, carried out in due form, producing a result which is *deemed* to be the decision of the community.

Since every corporate decision-procedure rests upon some

convention, no such decision-procedure has to have the exact form it has. There is always an element of artificiality about any decision-procedure, and we always could consider having another which was better. Rousseau makes use of this point to claim that

the moment the people is legitimately assembled as a sovereign body, the jurisdiction of the government wholly lapses, the executive power is suspended, and the person of the meanest citizen is as sacred and inviolable as that of the first magistrate; for in the presence of the person represented, representatives no longer exist.*

But the conclusion does not follow; the general will and a decision-procedure are incomparable, and the one cannot replace the other. It may be the general will that a particular decision-procedure is not satisfactory, and ought to be replaced by some other decision-procedure. But even so, some procedure, some convention, is required to elicit the general will that such a decision should be taken. Rousseau's own example witnesses against him: 'The consuls, at such times, were no more than the presidents of the people': if an assembly is not to degenerate into a babel, there have to be some rules of order, a president or a chairman to apply them and to call speakers in due order. We may believe that the *Comitia Tributa* or the *Comitia Centuriata* was a better means of eliciting the will of the *Populus Romanus* than the Senate or *Comitia Curiata*; but only in as much as they are themselves orderly procedures. Rousseau himself restricts the frequency of meetings of the people, and remarks that the Roman *Comitia* should be called only on certain days, by a proper authority, and provided the omens were favourable,† and maintains that any assembly of the people not called in due form 'must be regarded as having no legal sanction. Any business transacted at them must be held to be null and void, since even the order to assemble must proceed from the law.'‡ Without these safeguards it would be possible to call a meeting at short notice, without giving adequate warning of the matters to be discussed, with the result that many people might not be present, and many would not have had

* Rousseau, *The Socal Contract*, book 3, chapter 14.
† Op cit., book 4, chapter 4.
‡ Op. cit., book 3, chapter 13.

time to think over the proposals being made, and would not be able to put forward effective counter-arguments against them. Such meetings are sometimes emotionally satisfying and are often the means whereby the unscrupulous manipulate public opinion for their own ends; but they have only a rather tenuous connection with any useful concept of the general will.

Every decision-procedure has some element of artifice in it, and each has its merits and demerits. If we are concerned that the procedure should not only be impartial but be indubitably so, there is much to be said for tossing a coin or drawing lots. But most communal decisions are similar to individual decisions and are taken in somewhat similar circumstances, and therefore are taken in a similar fashion with a period of deliberation being followed by one or more particular individuals making his own decision. If there is only one man in whose mouth lies the final decision, no further problem arises; and it is one of the traditional arguments for monarchy that it avoids the elaborate artifice of taking and assessing votes. Nevertheless, although the theory of voting is a good deal more complicated than commonly supposed, it is possible both to have a coherent theory and to work it in practice.

A vote is a stylized voice. Each man is asked the same simple question – either *Shall we, or shall we not, do X?* or *Whom shall we appoint to this post?* – to which only one-word answers can be given. Each man's say, therefore, is standardized, and can be compared and collated with another man's say. The questions admit of only a finite number of possible answers, and the number of people giving each of the possible answers can be added up. Thus we can tabulate everyone's opinion in succinct form. The interpretation then to be given to the results admits of dispute. We need some formula, some convention, some rule of procedure, by means of which we may translate the voting figures into a communal decision. We might have a near-unanimity rule, whereby two, or six, electors were enough to defeat a motion; or we may require a three quarters or two thirds majority; but often a bare majority (or in the case of elections a bare plurality) of votes is deemed sufficient. One advantage of the simple majority rule is that it is symmetrical. It does not matter whether the question is put in the positive or the negative form, the outcome will be the same. If we have the two thirds rule, there is an incentive to try and twist the terms of the motion, in order to have the advantage of the rule; there will therefore be terminological and procedural disputes, which will require some further decision-procedure to settle. For some sorts of legislation this may not matter, especially constitutional legislation or the alteration of entrenched clauses; but in those questions of policy which must come to the supreme authority, where the two alternatives are logically symmetrical, a simple majority rule is the rational one to adopt.

Taking a vote is a decision-procedure. It contains an element of artifice, but it is not totally arbitrary or irrational. The formula we adopt for translating the voting figures into a definite decision is a convention, and like any convention requires above everything else that it be itself well-nigh universally agreed. To a very large extent it does not matter what procedure we have – whether a simple majority or a two thirds vote, or summing up by a chairman, or casting lots, so long as we all agree that this is our procedure and we will be bound by it. Indeed, once any such procedure is established, it is, as we shall see later, self-justifying. Hence any voting procedure can be argued to be authoritative merely by reason of its having previously been accepted. The rules of the political game are what they are. Provided they exist, it is in large measure pointless to argue whether they are the right ones or not; sufficient that they are generally recognized for what they are, namely the decision-procedure we happen to have for the resolution of disputes. But it is not quite pointless. Although voting is in one way on a par with casting lots or taking auspices, and enjoys the automatic assumption of authority that any established decision-procedure attracts to itself, it has also an independent rationality of its own. For a vote, unlike any other procedure, has some necessary connection with what people want. If we decide which pub to go to by tossing a coin, we may find that the coin comes down tails, which means the Eastgate, whereas everyone really wanted to go to the Bear. Similarly, if we have a chairman or a king or a pope, there may well be a question on which he has strong views, and in spite of all the contrary considerations urged by everybody else, he may persist in enunciating as the sense of the meeting a proposition clean contrary to what everyone but he wants. With votes this cannot happen. If there is a majority for a proposal, more especially if it is a two thirds or three quarters majority, but even if it is a bare majority, it cannot be the case that what everyone individually wants is clean opposite to what we all are deemed to want collectively. Any voting procedure, from the requirement of a simple majority upwards, has the merit that, in those cases where there is genuine agreement about what shall be done, the decision elicited by the voting system is bound to be the same as the general consensus. If we are all in agreement, then the vote will not distort the fact; and, *per contra*, if according to the vote we have decided to act in a certain way, then it cannot be the case that it is what none of us want to do. As between different requirements for different sorts of majority, we cannot lay down any absolute preference. We can, however, pick out the requirement of there being merely a simple majority as being the least stringent requirement that will satisfy these conditions, as well as being the only one that satisfies also the symmetry condition.

Rousseau is confused about the relationship between individual votes and the general will, and seems to say that if I am outvoted, I realize that my vote was cast mistakenly, and that I had been under a misapprehension about what the general will was, and now that it has been correctly revealed to me, I shall acknowledge that this is what I really wanted all along. We can alleviate the absurdity of his argument by recognizing that often there is a band-wagon effect whereby if I know what is generally felt on some question I shall come to have similar feelings myself, and more importantly by insisting that the frame of mind in which each man casts his vote should be a responsible and representative one, not a selfish and individual one. When voting, I should not properly ask myself the question *What do I want?*, but rather *What do I think that we should do?* Even with these allowances, however, it is clear that often I shall be outvoted, and shall continue to think that the decision deemed to have been taken by the community is, from the community's own point of view, the wrong one. The problem of political obligation is going to be

much more difficult for Rousseau than for Locke. Locke, in virtue of his unanimity principle, can always answer the question
Why should I obey the law? but often is embarrassingly unable
to answer the question *What shall we do?* Rousseau with his
simple majority rule can be unfailingly relied on to produce
answers to the latter question, but cannot evade, as Locke can,
the full force of the former.

There are many arguments why I should obey the law, and
many that do not depend upon the general will. All these are
available, even if I am outvoted. I still can see that I should obey
the law in order not to suffer penalties, in order that society may
not break down, because the law is right, because I promised to,
because I was consulted, because a large part of me is constituted
by my being a full member of the community in good standing,
that is, a law-abiding one. These arguments all remain valid. In
addition there may be arguments which apply to members of
communities that take their decisions by means of a vote. The
mere fact of having been able to exercise a vote may go far to
assuage hard feelings. It shows that the community accorded
full respect to one's person, even if on the actual occasion they
disagree with one's views. More important is the fact that the
taking of a vote is, properly speaking, not an isolated incident,
but part of a much larger process. It is the penultimate stage of
the decision-procedure, and is to be understood in the context
of all the argument and discussion that has preceded it. Hence,
if the voter has discharged his duty responsibly, he will have
attempted to understand the arguments on either side of the
question, and therefore, even if the decision goes against him, will
still appreciate the reasoning behind it. Instead of merely being
told what he has got to do, he may see why he is being asked to do
it. And this may be an advantage. For since political reasoning
is dialectical, it is characteristic of political decision that it is
decided by the balance of argument. In my opinion the balance
may go one way, and in yours it may go the other; but we each
are capable of appreciating the force of the arguments the other
way, if they are put to us. If I have actually engaged in argument
with you, I may see the force of the considerations which lead
you to disagree with me, even though I assess their force not quite

as highly as you do. We disagree on what should be done; but we agree on there being quite strong arguments for doing the thing that I want done, and quite strong arguments for doing the thing that you want done. The disagreement between our conclusions is much greater than that between our reasoning, and if we are in on the reasoning we are much more likely to accept the other's conclusion, should the reasoning go against us, than if all we are told is that 'they' have decided in a way we believe to be wrong. The administrators of provincial and American universities are not bad men; but they are commonly supposed to be bad by their academic employees, who are told what they must do, but have no opportunity of discovering the real reasons, and therefore impute bad ones gratuitously. Those few academics who are in on the decision-making have a quite different opinion of the vice-chancellor, the registrar or the president, regarding him as a fallible mortal indeed, who may well be wrong on the issue in question, but not wrong-headed, not an inhuman monster out only to satiate his power-lust and make life difficult for dons. It is not, as the lecturers say, that the professors have been corrupted by power; but merely that being involved in decision-making, they understand the difficulties that have had to be faced, and the reasons for the actual decision adopted.

These considerations often weigh with the defeated minority. But they may not. It is no comfort knowing the reasons behind a decision, if they were in fact thoroughly bad ones. If it was the outcome of a factional dispute or personal *animus*, I shall be less inclined to accept it and make it my own, knowing that it is, than if I do not know and can charitably suppose that there were sound reasons for it. Again, involvement may make me *parti pris*. I may not have had any strong reasons at the outset, but may have been caught up in the debate, and discovered all sorts of points of principle at stake which I would never have thought of, if I had not had occasion to take sides. Up to a point this latter argument can be countered: we need all the objections to a course of action to be canvassed in advance in order to avoid embarking on it unadvisedly. A certain divisiveness in the decision-procedure is therefore an advantage, in as much as it results in proposals being properly criticized. It saves us having to detail a particular person to be a devil's advocate. But although the devil's advocate is sometimes unsuccessful and loses his case, his disappointment is a price worth paying as an insurance premium against making costly mistakes. So too a certain degree of disgruntlement on the part of the minority is acceptable, because it is only if proposals are opposed that the unwise ones will be rejected.

Where we do not find ourselves able to enter into the reasoning of the majority but have no grounds for impugning their integrity and sincerity, we can regard their decision only in the same light as that of the arbitration of one man who has found against us. Men, although not perfectly rational, are to some extent rational, and are more likely to reach reasonable and right conclusions than are purely random processes. Therefore, even if I am in a minority on this particular occasion on this particular issue, I shall in general do better to submit to decisions arrived at by a vote after the arguments have been put, than to depend on the toss of a coin. Even if I lose the vote, I have had a hearing, and, though I have lost out on the particular issue, it is a good general policy to be able to have a hearing: the general advantage outweighs the particular setback.

This argument does not apply if I am in a permanent minority, nor if the majority is continually biased, unfair or oppressive. The very merit of human judgement over random arbitrariness – that it is goal-directed – becomes a demerit if the goal is one of oppressing some part of the populace. We take great care that judges are not biased, corrupt, prejudiced, or liable to 'pick on' anyone; the same care must be taken to prevent majorities from abusing their power. We cannot, normally, have the safeguards we have with judges – careful selection, limited discretion, answerability, appeal; our chief safeguards are first a sense of fairness on the part of the majority, and secondly the fact that different questions will result in different and randomly distributed divisions between majority and minority. Provided this happens, although a man who finds himself in the minority may think the majority wrong, or even biased, he will not think that they are picking on him, and can reasonably expect that on other questions he will find his views espoused by the majority, and therefore carrying the day. So long as these conditions obtain, it is reasonable for a man, finding himself in a minority, to be willing to be overruled on the general principle of taking the rough with the smooth.

It follows that having a vote is valuable, and is an additional argument for political obligation, provided that three conditions are satisfied: first, that it is part of a decision-procedure in which real discussion and debate is possible; second, that the majority have not reached their decision in a grossly factional spirit; and third, that the division between majority and minority is a fluctuating one, and is not a permanent one, leaving the same people always in a minority and always outvoted. These conditions are very far from being always satisfied; but it is only when they are satisfied that a voting system with a majority rule can claim a 'general will' answer to the problem of political obligation.

Locke was forced to decentralize because his unanimity rule was so cumbersome that the only way to get business done was to exclude everyone not immediately concerned with the matter in hand from having any say in it at all. Rousseau is not under similar pressure. In the ideal case, where numbers are small, the community is fairly homogeneous, and not very many or very difficult decisions have to be taken, there is no reason why every decision about everything should not be taken by everyone. Indeed, democrats are apt to be jealous for the sovereignty of the people, and to be quick to resent any *lèse-majesté* on the part of individuals claiming to order their own affairs without reference to the organs of popular authority. Rousseau is a totalitarian. Not only is the democratic vote a reliable way of securing decisions on any and every question, but it is the only reputable way, and ought to be employed on any and every occasion. But this denies all freedom and privacy to the individual. He can never take any decisions for himself, or arrange his own affairs without a blaze of publicity. He can never be himself, but must always be just another member of the body politic in which he has only one vote, while other people muster between them many more. The difficulty with Locke's democracy was that the individual felt impotent because he could never mind other people's business; the difficulty with Rousseau's is that he cannot even mind his own. Locke gave him a very large say in very little, and over the years it has been realized that the little is too little to secure to the individual a reasonable livelihood; Rousseau gives him a very little say in everything at large, most of which is of no great concern to him, but a few things of which matter very much. Under Rousseau's regime he has no special rights or authority over the things that he is most concerned about – what to do with himself, how to earn his living, where to reside, whom to marry – and in exchange for not having effective control over his own life is given a very small finger in a very large pie.

The impotence engendered by Rousseau's polity is different from that engendered by Locke's. Locke's individual is isolated and futile. Rousseau's frustrated and pushed around. Locke's has too little he can call his own, Rousseau's nothing about which he can be sure his voice will be effective, nowhere he can manifest his individuality, no means whereby he can take the initiative. For a vote is a poor substitute for a voice. It is too stylized to express personality or to ventilate individual views adequately. Useful though voting is in enabling a community to reach a decision when it has to, it does not and cannot capture the movement of minds in the process of arguing with one another and reaching agreement. It is not enough to be able occasionally to answer questions when we are asked them; we want sometimes to be able to pose questions, put forward proposals. What is important is not only the possession of the vote but the opportunity of taking the initiative. Modern democratic theory, which on the whole has followed Rousseau rather than Locke, has been peculiarly blind in this respect, and people have been surprised and pained by the violence of recent movements of protest. But violence has been largely generated by frustration, and has been sustained by its being the only effective means of making the community take notice and even consider questions that agitate the protesters. If my only constitutional rights take the form of a very small finger in a very large pie, I shall find the sheer inertia of the pie a complete clog on all my efforts to remedy things that seem to me evidently wrong. I want to do something about the Third World, or the homeless, or pornography, or the maintenance of educational standards. But most people are not interested.

If I try to get a discussion or debate, it gets squeezed out by next business, and when it comes to voting there is no way I can really express my convictions, and anyhow my one vote is swamped by the many *don't cares*. In the end I vent my frustrated fury by breaking things up, and find that this does make people realize the intensity of my feelings. Demonstrations have come in because ballot boxes have been too insensitive to register the strength of individual feeling and have had the effect of stifling initiative. Largely, of course, this has been the effect not so much of Rousseau's ideal of democracy as of the size and complexity of modern society; and, importantly, our actual political system is not organized entirely on Rousseau's tenets, and contains many features that enable initiatives to be taken and mitigate the dilution of my vote by everybody else's. Nevertheless, many of the distempers of today stem from the logic of Rousseau's interpretation of democracy, and especially from excessive concern with votes to the exclusion of all the other parts of the decision-procedure which alone make voting meaningful. Much as Locke's veto gradually degenerates into a selfish (or at least, non-tuistic) bargaining procedure, so Rousseau's votes come to be construed in overtly economic terms. The politician sees himself as dealing in votes just as the oil man deals in oil, and voters approach elections in a spirit of political consumerism. We begin to feel a certain revulsion at the sterility of pressure politics, much as we did at the vanity of economic aggrandizement. Our humanity seems in the end to be denied as much by Rousseau as it was by Locke. Locke made out that the worth of man was to be measured only in money; Rousseau sees his significance only in the exercise of his vote, and the value of a proposal only in terms of the votes it will attract. And once again we complain that this gives us, although in a new guise, what is essentially a one-dimensional doctrine of man.

It is easy to criticize. Locke and Rousseau have been set up as extreme versions. In real life their adherents benefit from compromise and common sense. But even in extreme form they have something to teach us. For each is founded on an intuition about human beings, and both of them are true. Locke and the tradition of liberal democracy is an attempt to work out the understanding

4 Authority and the State

Actual societies are very different from the ideal societies of the democrat's dream. Men are less reasonable, less agreed about fundamental values and less anxious to reach agreement than democrats like to think. Our communities are also much larger and more heterogeneous than ideal ones are supposed to be, and have to deal with a great pressure of business. They are therefore much more impersonal, much less consensual, and far more professional than Rousseau would care to contemplate. Although the models proposed by Locke and Rousseau are valuable as models, because by idealizing some features, they enable us to follow out the interrelationship of others, they are models only, and cannot be carried over to actual societies or regarded as blue-prints to which we should attempt to make actual societies approximate. Rather, we should see what form the government of actual societies must take, and then consider how far and in what way different people should participate in it. As a society gets larger, more heterogeneous and more sophisticated, the simple question of whether it is a democracy or not, in the original, Greek sense of the word, becomes less and less meaningful, and should be replaced in part by questions about how far the canons of justice and freedom are observed and in the main about the degree to which people can and do participate in the processes of government.

Our primary experience of the state is of an *authority* we are *obliged* to obey. This is true both as a matter of personal biography and national history and logic. Long before I was old enough to vote, join in political discussions or otherwise partici-pate in the processes of government, I was told I must go to school, must not drive a car until I was seventeen, and must not help myself to sweets in the village shop; and if I asked *Why?*, I was told that there was a law against it. Equally in the history of nations, parliamentary democracy is a late comer. Long before there were parliaments or elections there were kings and nobles, and even where there are the outward forms of democracy, men are more conscious of the law as an external restraint on their freedom of action than as a manifestation of their own autonomous choice. We are subjects long before we are citizens. Nor could it be otherwise. Being the sort of agents that we are, imperfectly informed, not entirely rational, nor altogether altruistic, we need the existence of some authority far more insistently than we want ourselves to constitute it. Any authority, provided that it exists, will therefore be largely self-justifying. And our problem is not, as most thinkers have supposed, to establish or justify authority, but to tame it.

Authority is a concept which has its place in the context of justification and argument. A justification is in terms of authority if it rests upon somebody's word, either an actual utterance by a particular person on a particular occasion or something written in a particular place. 'Why do you think Peter will turn down the vice-chancellorship?' 'His wife told me so.' 'Why do you hold Alcibiades responsible for the Sicilian expedition?' 'My authority is Thucydides.' So too when we justify not beliefs but actions. 'Why are you knocking down that wall?' 'My boss told me to.' 'Why are you dipping your sheep in disinfectant?' 'The law says I must.' 'Why don't you have an affair with Mollie?' 'It says in the Bible that adultery is wrong.' In each case, instead of offering a complete justification of our own, we refer our questioner to something said or written, and cite that as our reason. If I am driving in a built-up area, I might reduce my speed to 30 m.p.h., and explain that I did so in order to diminish the risk of running someone down; but I might instead explain simply that the law said I must. In the one case my justification rests upon features of the situation from which I infer what I ought to do, and you may question my 'facts' – 'there won't be anybody about at 4 a.m. on a Sunday morning' – or claim that the facts do not support the conclusion – 'if you were going at 40 m.p.h. you would still have plenty of time to stop' – and I may counter your objections and we may continue to argue for a long time; in the other justification, however, the possibilities of endless discussion are cut short, the whole case rests upon somebody else's word – if you don't believe me, go and ask him, or look it up for yourself. Often, of course, our justification involves a bit of both. Some arguments can be adduced, but they are not conclusive, and we supplement them by an appeal to authority, being the more willing to accept what the authority says because it seems reasonable in any case. This mixed mode is of great importance in politics, but first we need to consider the rationale of those justifications which are simple appeals to authority. In these, so far as I am concerned, there is no room for further argument. Authority has spoken, and that is enough for me.

But, of course, it may not be enough for my questioner. It is always possible to question further. But although it is always possible, we could not always do so, or we would never get anywhere. We must begin somewhere, even though there is no one starting place from which we must all begin. The concept of authority is thus difficult to handle. It is inherently questionable, yet not actually questioned. It may seem irrational, but is not. On the contrary, it is both natural and deeply rational for human beings to be guided by authority. Men, being social animals, are imitative by nature and have a strong herd-instinct. But this apart, it would be irrational to reject all authority out of hand. I am not omniscient. I am not infallible. I am not self-sufficient. If I am to act in a state of imperfect information, I must be prepared to accept guidance from others, or else condemn myself to acting more uninformedly than I need; if I want to play in an orchestra, I do not know – I cannot know – when all the other performers will be minded to make their notes, and the only rational course is to be guided, like them, by the conductor's beat. I do not have a monopoly of good ideas, and sometimes I should do well to follow the lead of others who have a vision that has not been vouchsafed to me. Again, once I recognize that I may be mistaken, it becomes irrational to insist on always getting my own way, expecting everybody else to fall in line with my own plans. I may be wrong. I know this, as does everybody else. So I cannot expect them all always to follow my suit. Even if I were omniscient and infallible, I ought still to be guided by the ex-

pressed wishes of others if I cared for them at all or had any regard for their status as independent centres of value. We know
more than our children, and are more rational, but still let their
letters to Father Christmas guide our Yuletide actions. These
considerations combine to make it rational to accept authority.
The first is of particular interest because it admits of a games-
theoretical treatment and of particular importance because it
shows how authority can be self-authenticating. There are many
non-zero-sum games where two or more parties will do best if
they concert their strategies. If they are unable to communicate,
success will depend on each guessing what the others will do, and
acting accordingly. Consider two people, say husband and wife,
who have lost each other in New York. Each has to decide where
the other will look, and look there too. Apparently, most Americans would expect their spouses to look for them in New York
Central Station.* If this is so, and once it is known to be so, life
becomes much easier for visitors to New York. Merely by making
a public choice of a rendezvous, a person could enable us all to
know what to expect of others, and so to coordinate our actions
the better. And this sort of situation occurs again and again. As
motorists, as property-owners, as companions-in-arms, we are
constantly needing all to be following the same pattern without
there being any internal reason for following, or for others to be
following, one pattern rather than another. Therefore, if anyone
gives a lead we shall do well to follow it. If a man steps into the
road at a busy junction or when a lorry is backing into the
highway, and starts directing the traffic, he will be obeyed. For it
is in every driver's interest that all should cooperate to avoid
collisions. So, too, when a man takes command in a theatre that
is on fire, and orders each row to file out in turn.† We obey, not
because the man has been granted legitimate authority to give us
orders, but because he is there. And so it is also with the established authorities of the state. We obey, first and foremost, not
because the authority is legitimate, but because it exists. Once

* T. C. Schelling, *The Strategy of Conflict*, Harvard University Press,
1966, page 55n.

† S. I. Benn and R. S. Peters, *Social Principles and the Democratic
State*, London, 1959, page 21.

established, it is self-authenticating. We need authority, in all sorts of social situations and for all sorts of purposes, and any one who can supply that need is in a fair way to be rewarded with our obedience. This argument is particularly important because it does not depend on either the governors or the governed having any special virtue, and argues from the fact that we are none of us possessed of perfect information to the conclusion that we all have reason to be loyalists. Any authority, once established, has a claim on our allegiance, which will continue, in the absence of powerful considerations to the contrary, for no other reason than that it is established. Hence the deep conservatism of politics. Authority is not only self-sustaining, but self-justifying, and we are impelled to accept any authority there is because it is the only way of regulating our behaviour so as to avoid collisions.

Of course, it may do more. Consider the account of Philip Augustus, King of France:

King Philip was staying at Paris and one day he was walking up and down the royal chamber thinking about the affairs of the realm. He went to the window and looked out on the Seine, it being his habit to refresh his mind in this way. There he noticed the intolerable stench made by carts passing through the city churning up the mud, and he found it insupportable. There and then he resolved on a great and necessary work which none of his predecessors had dared to undertake for its great expense and difficulty. Calling together the burgesses and the bailiffs of the city he gave orders that all the streets of the whole city of Paris should be covered with hard strong stones.*

The King achieved a public good not merely by providing the means whereby separate individuals could concert their efforts, but also by his vision, his initiative, his drive. It is typical of governments. They not only maintain law and order, but discern new needs and devise new ways of satisfying them. We look to our leaders to lead, and like to be led by them, for they often have the imagination, the inspiration and the pertinacity that we lack, and can enable us to achieve collectively what we could never have achieved by our own individual, uninspired and uncoordinated efforts. We are not merely individuals playing a game

* Rigord, *Gesta Philippi Augusti*, quoted in R. W. Southern, *Mediaeval Humanism and Other Studies*, Oxford, 1970, page 179.

together under conditions of imperfect information, but are conscious of ourselves as members of a community with many shared values and shared assumptions. It is perfectly possible, therefore, for someone other than myself to know my own individual good better than I do myself, and my good is constituted not only by an individual good but by the common good of the communities of which I am a member. Anybody who is able to articulate the values of a community and give a lead towards our being able to achieve them deserves to be followed, and if his authority is already recognized he will be, and his authority will be further enhanced by its exercise to good purpose.

To accept authority is not only rational, but, as we saw in chapter two, reasonable in a somewhat wider sense. I show that I do not regard myself as the only pebble on the beach. Not only do I allow that I, the great and wonderful I, may conceivably be mistaken, but I acknowledge that you, he, she and they have a value of your and their own. Contrary to what some philosophers have said and many young rebels believe, doing what other people say is often a virtue. It is good to be loyal to friends, and to be loyal means being prepared to subordinate one's own will to theirs, and on occasions to act even against one's own better judgement because this is what they want. Sometimes, of course, it may be one's duty to refuse to follow their line, if it is manifestly wrong, and to remonstrate with them instead; but such cases are rare, and in general loyalty is shown in not insisting on one's own view of what is best but being ready to go along with them and helping them achieve their own sub-optimal purposes.

Authority seems to be very much a one-way relationship, but it is not. It seems as if it is just me telling you what to do. But you do not have to do it. You are a free agent. There are no coercive, although there may well be sensible, arguments why an autonomous being should act in a particular way. If you do what I say, you are accepting my authority, and it is only because it is accepted that it exists. Thus it is a mistake to think of government as being only about what the rulers decide. Their decisions are important only because those who are ruled are prepared to be ruled by them. It is always possible for authority not to be accepted, and occasionally this happens, as Richard II in England, James II in Britain, George III in the American Colonies, Louis XVI in France and Tsar Nicholas II in Russia discovered to their cost. It is only in extreme circumstances that a regime breaks down and loses its authority, but the fact that this can occur makes it clear that authority is authority only in so far as it is accepted as such, and that while authority is an attribute of the governors, acceptance is an attribute of the governed. Important consequences flow from this. In the first place, it provides a point of entry for arguments in favour of participation. Rulers too readily reckon that the exercise of authority is not anybody's business but their own; and the fact that authority is correlative with acceptance shows that government is not simply something that rulers do, but is, rather, a function of the whole community, and thus constitutes a cogent argument against the governed being altogether disfranchised from the business of government. Some thinkers go much further and maintain that the need for authority to be accepted establishes the essentially democratic nature of all government, but it is a very exiguous form of democracy. Acceptance, in the sense in which it is correlative with authority, is something very much less than approval or even consent, and comprises every shade of acquiescence and apathy, and even quite vigorous disapproval and dissent. The Norman kings were able to impose their rule on a large number of unwilling subjects. It is not enough simply to reject authority, for authority is natural and inevitable, and if we want to reject the authority of one regime we can do so only by replacing it with an alternative. Richard II would never have lost his throne had not Henry Bolingbroke raised his standard against him, nor James II without William of Orange being ready to be a rival focus of loyalty and source of leadership. We can never just decide, but must always decide *between* alternative courses of action, and similarly cannot decide against a government but only decide between one government and another. It is a merit of the system of elective autocracy, which we shall discuss in chapter ten, that it institutionalizes such a choice, and makes moderately effective this otherwise exiguously democratic aspect of government. But it does not have to happen like this, and entirely undemocratic forms of government are perfectly possible. All we can say is that since some measure of acquiescence on the part of the governed is essential, it follows that government is of its nature a function of the governed as well as of the governors, and that therefore it would be desirable to arrange for it to have not only their bare acquiescence but some more active form of consent.

Authority always needs to be accepted, but always may be rejected. It is always possible to question what has hitherto been unquestioned. If I justify a belief or action by reference to Thucydides or the Bible, or the law or my boss, you may ask why anyone should accept the authority of my boss or the statute book, or the Bible or Thucydides. Such questions can be asked, and, within a particular context, answered. But the questioner can always question further, and I can never hope to prove conclusively to the determined sceptic that his doubts are untenable; only, after showing each one of them to be groundless, I may perhaps persuade him that they are all futile. Political philosophy has often taken the sceptic too seriously, and has attempted to adduce logically compelling arguments why he ought to obey the law; and in seeking to furnish arguments of a greater degree of cogency than the subject matter will admit, has put forward specious, deductive arguments which turn out to be broken-backed, instead of humbler ones which, although not conclusive, are nevertheless sound so far as they go. We do not need to maintain the divine right of kings or believe that a long time ago our forefathers entered into a social contract which established the rights and duties of the ruled. Rather, authority exists *de facto*; and because it exists *de facto*, it acquires a *de jure* legitimacy. We start from the fact that there is an authority and I obey it, and from this incline towards the conclusion that I not only do obey it, but should. But it is not an inescapable conclusion. There is no chain of deductive logic which forces us to admit that whatever is, is right. The right of the establishment is presumptive, not divine. I cannot prove that Elizabeth Windsor, either by divine inheritance from Adam or by right of conquest in 1066 or by an agreement made in 1688, is entitled to my obedience in all things. What I can argue is that I ought to obey some authority, and that since Elizabeth II is our acknowledged Queen, hers are the commands I ought to obey. A critic is perfectly entitled to question my conclusion, but if he does, he must indicate which part of my argument he is rejecting, and why. He may be denying that I am under any obligation to obey anybody at all – perhaps because he has been reading Kant, and believes heteronomy to be bad. If so, I shall need to listen to his arguments and point out their invalidity, but shall not need to defend the Queen's claim against the pretensions of the Jacobites. My arguments will have to be very different if the critic has no doubts about political obligation in general, but is a republican and believes that the only people who are worthy of our obedience are Presidents like M. Pompidou or Mr Nixon; or, again, if he is a Marxist, and maintains that only commissars can be the legitimate holders of authority. In none of these cases would it be necessary to counter the sceptical positions about political obligation generally. It would not even be necessary to show – though Britons are too ready to assume it – that the British Constitution is better than all others; all that is required, once the general obligation to obey laws has been admitted, is to show that the existing authorities are defensible, that is, to rebut claims that they are so bad that even the politically obedient ought not to obey them.

Although the question *Why should I obey the law?* or *Why should I obey the civil authorities?* is, happily for us, not normally a serious question, it is an important one. We are fortunate. Our government has seldom been so bad that we have had to rebel. But we should not assume that there could never be circumstances in which it would be right to rebel; and it is only by pondering the question *Why should I obey the Law?* that we can be in a position to decide what are the limits of lawful authority and what are the circumstances in which we are no longer obliged to obey. But we should be very, very cautious. In the afterglow of the Glorious Revolution of 1688 it seemed quite reasonable to regard revolution as the remedy for bad government, but we, who are familiar with revolutions of the French or Russian variety, are uncomfortably aware that it is not enough to reckon that a regime is intolerable; it is also necessary to consider whether the alternative may not be worse. Revolutions have a nasty habit not only of leading to purges and reigns of terror, but of not remedying the original wrongs. Napoleon was more absolute than Louis XVI, Stalin more Tsarist than the Tsars, and many East Africans must now feel that it was no good booting out Obote in order to admit Amin. Revolutions are all right only if they can be relied on not to go too far and to observe the rules of civilized behaviour. It is another of the merits of the modern Anglo-American practice of elective autocracy that it provides the possibility of an institutionalized revolution every four or five years, usually long before things have got to so bad a pass that passions are deeply aroused or blood is likely to be shed.

Autonomy means not only that we collectively may refuse to accept the authority of the state, but that each of us individually can. Hence the need for coercion. Because, as we saw in chapter two, there are no coercive arguments available in politics, the state has to be able to fall back on physical coercion in order to ensure that its decisions are, and are known to be, effective. If anybody not only could decide to act contrary to the law, but could actually carry his decision out, then some people would. For the state, unlike a voluntary association, is unselective. We have some degree of choice whether we join a political party, a trades union, an evening class or a university, and the decisions of such bodies are not likely to be totally unacceptable to any of their members. But we have no choice about what country we are born in, and few people are effectively able to emigrate; and therefore some of us sometimes will not only be tempted to disobey the law but will actually try to do so. Unless such people can be prevented from doing so or made to realize that it does not pay, the law will break down. This for two reasons. The sort of authority that will satisfy the need each of us has for guidance, in view of our imperfect information, must be unique and exclusive of all others. We cannot in an orchestra have two conductors; and however bored you may be at having to beat the drum only when you are told to and not when you feel like it, it is inherent in the whole exercise that you should conform and should refrain from giving an alternative lead. There is no value in having a rival rendezvous in New York. If political authority is to be effective in coordinating our efforts and regulating our behaviour, everyone must know at any time and in any situation where he stands and to whom to look for guidance. Political authority must not only be generally accepted, but accepted by everyone to the exclusion of all competitors. Not only can no man serve two masters, but each needs all his fellow citizens to serve the same master, if he is to be able to rely on their being in step with him and not likely to tread on his toes or be in the way of his own footwork.

The second reason for the state's needing to have coercive powers at its disposal is much more traditional. Often it would be to my advantage, but very much to someone else's disadvantage, for me to break the law; and similarly to his advantage, and very much to my disadvantage for him to do so. If I can do you down, I shall do better than if I could not, but you will do much worse; and vice versa. Therefore, argued Plato, we all enter into an agreement with one another whereby we each forgo the liberty of doing others down in return for their likewise conferring on us the much greater benefit of never being done down by any of them. It is the generalized case of what is now known in the theory of games as 'the prisoners' dilemma'. It arises whenever two or more people are free to choose independently courses of action which affect one another, and affect others more adversely than they benefit the chooser. In such a situation each will have a reason for choosing one way, but if everybody does so, all will suffer. All would be better off if none of them attempted to maximize his own benefit, but at every stage each will be better off, whatever the others do, if he chooses what is most advantageous to himself. In some situations we may all be sufficiently enlightened and altruistic to act so as to maximize the common good, but the state, because it is unselective, is bound to contain some inadequately altruistic and enlightened members, and sooner or later someone will attempt to get away with breaking the law, hoping to obtain for himself both the benefits of other people keeping the law and the advantage of himself being unconstrained by it. If he does get away with it, then others will follow suit. For we are all tempted. If we all were utterly selfish, as Thomas Hobbes, the seventeenth-century English philosopher, supposed, then the only way of preventing each man from making the attempt would be to give the state sufficient power to inflict such penalties that in each and every case crime did not pay. We are not all as utterly selfish as that. We are sometimes prepared to be quite altruistic, and for the most part are prepared to be guided by enlightened self-interest and forgo the gains of law-breaking provided others forbear too. But we need to be reasonably sure that others actually will forbear. If we cannot count on others obeying the law we shall soon stop obeying it ourselves. The state must be able to coerce the minority of actual law-breakers, so as to assure the law-abiding majority that they are not being mugs. The law must be enforced, or it will cease to be in force. Only if the state can show its law-abiding subjects that those who obey its commands can rely on everyone else doing so too, will its authority continue to be credible. And since not all members of an unselective community will do so willingly, there must be means of ensuring that they will do so willy-nilly. And this means that the state must exercise not only power, but coercive power, and be able to use force.

Authority needs to be distinguished on the one hand from advice and on the other from power and from force. In each case something is being said to someone, often in the imperative mood; the test is to consider what happens if the imperative is not complied with. If I give advice, and it is not accepted, there is no conflict. For when I give advice, it is only my reasons, and not the fact that it is I who articulate them, that should weigh with my hearer. I am helping him to make up his own mind, not making it up for him; and often the best service I can render is to enable him to discover his own views by expressing ones he comes finally to reject. But in so far as he regards me as an authority, he will be guided by me without having been persuaded by my arguments, even though he may believe me to be wrong. It is not a relevant rejoinder where appeals to authority are being made to say 'But I am not convinced' or 'I do not agree.' But of course he may reject my authority – that is, he may not regard the fact that I tell him to as being a reason why he ought to do what I tell him say 'But I am not convinced' or 'I do not agree'. But of course he may account the answer sufficiently undesirable for him to reckon that his best course is to obey. If this is so, then so far as he is concerned, what I say goes, and we say that in this matter I have power over him. If I have power over many people in many matters, we say simply that I have power. But this elliptical way of speaking can cause confusion, since whether what I say goes depends a lot on what I say and to whom I say it. A rich man in a department store can have all his orders fulfilled; but he cannot buy your house if you choose not to sell it to him, nor may he buy justice or votes. Even those possessed of political power are often very much circumscribed in the choices they can effectively make. Mr Wilson and Mrs Castle were unable to carry their Industrial Relations Bill, the President of the United States was unable to achieve what he wanted in Vietnam; but in both cases they were properly said to have power, because in a large number of matters, although not in those ones, the things which they said were to be done were in fact done, and any adequate account of the course of events would have to refer to what they said in order to explain why things happened as they did.

The limitations of power are often overlooked, because supreme power is invariably coercive power, that is to say it is power backed up by the control of force. Force, like power, addresses itself to the man who is not necessarily convinced that he should obey; but whereas power is evidenced if there is any consequence of non-compliance which is sufficiently undesirable to move the man to comply, force is more peremptory in tone, and answers the question *What happens if I don't?* with a brusque 'You shall, willy-nilly.' Power is resistible, although not – or at least not usually – resisted, but force cannot be effectively resisted. I may refuse to vote the way the Whips tell me, if I am prepared to lose my seat at the next election, but a condemned criminal cannot effectively say 'no' to the judge's order that he go to prison. Since bad men exist, who are entirely deaf to the voice of reason, it is necessary, if laws are to be effective at all, that they should be enforced. We therefore endow the civil authority with an apparatus for law-enforcement which involves the potential deployment of force, and this has given rise to the twin beliefs that the power of the state is irresistible and that it only exists as a consequence of human sin. But the power of the state is very different from the force under its control, and typically the most powerful states are those which have few, because they need few, forces to maintain law and order. Force is required only against the recalcitrant, whereas power derives as much from unforced support as from forced obedience. Force can be seen as a remedy for, and in that sense a consequence of, sin, but power cannot. For wherever an authority is generally accepted, and people regard it as incumbent on them to do what it enjoins, it will for that very reason have power. Authority, and therefore power, is engendered by the existence of any sort of community, and not all communities are founded on the fact of sin. But such power and such authority is not in any way absolute, as force is, at least so far as the individual is concerned.

Although they can be distinguished, power and authority go naturally together. Samson was judge in Israel because his were the decisions nobody dared gainsay. The very fact of possessing power often confers authority and a person whose authority is accepted is thereby possessed of power. Many thinkers, recognizing the concomitance of authority and power, have sought to eliminate the former and explain the whole of politics in terms of the latter. But this is a mistake. Not only does might differ from right in our thinking, but cannot subsist in practice without some support from it. Although an unselective community must be capable of dealing with recalcitrant people who are, emotionally speaking, outlaws, and therefore must maintain an apparatus of coercion, yet it cannot coerce everybody. Indeed, it cannot most of the time coerce most people. Not only must it rely on the willing support of some people whose cooperation is required to man the vital positions in the apparatus of state – even a dictator must rely on the loyalty of his henchmen not to murder him in his sleep – but it also relies in a weaker way on the acquiescence of all those whose information is required if the state is to be able to take cognizance of the many matters it needs to attend to if it is to be a state at all. The Irish Republicans have sought the allegiance of the Roman Catholics in Ulster, and in so far as they have obtained it, Roman Catholics have ceased to give information to the British authorities, and in particular have referred their own disputes to Irish Republican leaders for arbitration, whose decisions they respect and will, when they are flouted, enforce. To this extent there is a breakdown of the British administration, and if it became complete, the Queen's writ would no longer run in some parts of Northern Ireland, which would be then more like a territory occupied by an invading army than an integral part of the realm. From this abnormal case we can see what the normal one is. Some degree of acceptance is required. The degree required varies. A government with a strong apparatus of coercion can manage with a minimal degree of acceptance by the rest of the people, and *per contra*, a government which enjoys not merely the acquiescence but the positive consent, or better still the enthusiastic support, of the people can manage with a minimal apparatus of coercion. To borrow an alien terminology, the more a government can rely on the masses, the less it need rely on the party, and vice versa. The Anglo-American tradition has been to have the apparatus of state as weak as is consonant with its essential functions being adequately performed and to rely on a high degree of cooperation with the people. It is one of the sad features of our present time that this tradition has been eroded. The fault lies on both sides. Governments have been increasingly impatient with the slow pace of consultative procedures. They want results quickly, before the next election. They have tended, therefore, to set up their own agencies, staffed by civil servants, to hustle things along. Equally, we have become much more bolshie. We think of the government as an alien power, to be obstructed by strikes, demonstrations and even violence. And therefore the government in its turn comes more and more to rely on a narrower and narrower base of paid civil servants who can be relied upon to do what they are told without question or argument. This untoward development has come about largely as a result of modern theories of democracy; and it is one of the main political problems of our age to reverse it, and to secure that the most essentially democratic aspect of every government – that its authority should be widely acceptable – shall be restored.

If we think of the state as the body that exercises coercive power, then the distinction between ruler and ruled will seem fairly sharp. It is pretty clear who is wielding the truncheon and who is being hit by it. But the distinction becomes blurred as we broaden our view and consider not just coercive power but power generally. Into which class does a doctor fall? He is indispensable for some purposes of state, and has a special position, laid down by law – only he can sign death-certificates, sick-notes and pre-scriptions; but he does not make laws or lead armies or control the police. The government cannot manage without doctors. It needs their cooperation in running the Health Service, in formu-lating laws about hygiene, and in generally ministering to the nation's health. But it would seem absurd to make out that doc-tors were just government officials in the way that civil servants are. So too with teachers, clergymen, lawyers, and even journa-lists, businessmen and trades-union leaders. The multifarious purposes of government cannot be achieved by the government's resources alone. If it is to achieve them, it must be able to secure the cooperation – best the willing positive support – of many other people who in other respects would naturally be accounted as subjects rather than governors. To this extent the logic of government acts as a taming influence on Leviathan. If a ruler wants to be successful and effective, he must win the loyalty of his subjects by good government and responsiveness to their needs. Barbaric governments have, for that reason, been in-effective and backward. Even Stalin and his successors, in order to keep up with the Americans, have had to heed the advice and the aspirations of their scientists and technologists. From this general feature of government rather cosy consequences have often been inferred. No government can be that bad, it would seem, and our own government must be really quite good. The government of Britain is open to argument, and does take advice from many non-politicians, and therefore seems to itself and to them to be a model of responsiveness, and no further theory of democracy or practice of participation is called for. There is much truth in this conservative theory of government, but not so much truth as to exclude all ground of criticism. What is true is that the government does need and obtain the cooperation of some of its subjects, and there is no sharp divide between ruler and ruled. But it does not follow that everyone who should be is consulted by the government, or that it is as responsive as it ought to be to pleas or proposals from its subjects. The fact that of necessity some doctors have some say in how a hospital is run constitutes an important counter-example to the thesis that we can sharply distinguish the rulers from the ruled, but does not of itself secure either that any doctor has any say in foreign policy or that any patient has any say in how a hospital is run. Neither of these happens in the natural course of events, but must be fostered by special institutions, and must be argued for not on the basis of the nature of the state but from explicit principle.

5 Platonic Professionalism

Journalists sometimes succeed in taking photographs of the Queen yawning or looking bored. They picture truer than they know. We accept that those who are in power are beset with cares – uneasy lies the head that wears a crown – but forget the drudgery and tedium that fills their daytime hours. Private individuals are a happier case. Often they need not bother with things that bore them. But the state, just because it is the state, must be ready to decide any dispute which is brought to its attention, not necessarily in the terms in which it was originally posed, but sufficiently definitely and decisively to keep the peace. The public authorities do not have to decide whether my views on free will are true or not, but must either uphold my right to maintain them in a particular place at a particular time in a particular manner or else hold that I was wrong to do so – e.g. if I were to interrupt a church service or the proceedings of a court, or alternatively if what I said was libellous. They cannot completely disengage themselves from the question, and care for none of these things saying, dismissively, 'It is none of our business', because then they would be abdicating from their role as keepers of the peace. If the state is to maintain peace within its borders, it must be prepared to intervene in any dispute which cannot be otherwise resolved, in order that people shall not resort to fisticuffs. Of course, this does not mean that the state should always be interfering. If the guide-lines are laid down clearly, most people will be able to settle disputes without resort to the civil authorities; and where there is resort to them, often they need not enter into the merits of the question at issue, but merely lay down who, in the given circumstances, is entitled to have the decisive say. Nevertheless, there remains a sense in which the state must be prepared to give some sort of answer to any question that is addressed to it, and hence attend to a residual stream of questions that cannot be otherwise resolved. Few people read *Hansard* for fun. Its columns are filled with uninspiring speeches about uninspiring topics, and most of the debates in the House of Commons are as desperately dull to listen to as they are to read afterwards. We are deceived by the panoply of power – the gold and glitter of the Crown jewels, the red dispatch boxes and television cameras on great state occasions. We forget the continuing care that must be exercised all the time on all sorts of matters, most of them of no great moment. High office is sometimes nerve-racking, and that certainly has its effect on those who hold it, but far more influential is not so much the difficulty of sleeping well at nights as that of staying awake during the day on account of the desperate dullness, as it would seem to most of us, of the innumerable issues which arise and have to be decided; and that has deep consequences for any democratic theory of the state.

The argument from the need for continual attentiveness is the most fundamental one for setting the rulers apart from the ruled. It is reinforced by three others, the argument from coordination, the argument from time, and the argument from competence, which together constitute a powerful case against having important decision-procedures at all democratic.

The argument from coordination arises from the fact that large corporate bodies are liable to lack sufficient singleness of purpose to decide sensibly or to carry their decisions through. Decisions are not taken in a vacuum, but each is taken in a situation largely constituted by the other decisions that have already been taken. If we have decided to grant independence to a former colony, we can no longer decide to station one of our armies there; it is no good deciding to build a large waterworks, if we do not also ensure that there is enough electricity available to work the machinery when it is installed. In reaching each particular decision, we need to bear in mind what we have already decided and done, and what we are planning to do. Else we render ourselves ineffectual. Whether our aim is some simple goal, like victory in war, or some continuing condition, like the maintenance of law and order, it will be achieved only if we make a number of subsidiary decisions, appropriate in the light of circumstances, to maintain the desired direction in the flow of affairs. Otherwise, adverse winds or unforeseen fluctuations in the tide of events will take us off course, and our original decisions will never come into effect. Large bodies are always in danger of deciding each question separately, 'on its merits', and not in the context of the original decisions and the subsequent ones already taken. For even if the original decision is generally accepted and there has been a majority in favour of each particular subsequent decision, the number of those who have voted in favour of all the decisions may well be small; and only those who have actually been in favour of the action taken at every stage are going to find themselves feeling naturally the context in which the present decision needs to be considered. The others, who at some stage or other have been against the action taken, are going to be much less committed, both emotionally and intellectually, to the actual context of decision, and are correspondingly less alive to the logic of the situation. Their sense of corporate identity will be dimmed by actual dissents: instead of addressing themselves whole-heartedly to the question of what subsidiary action should be undertaken now in order to implement the original decision in the light of those other subsequent actions already decided upon, they are likely to be continuing earlier debates, and arguing how much better it would have been if their advice had been heeded at an earlier stage, and how, if so, we now would have been in a more advantageous position to undertake the action proposed. It is only human to want to say 'I told you so', but the inevitably hypothetical nature of such reproaches blurs the harsh actuality of the situation in which further action is being called for. Hence the different members of a corporate body are in danger of addressing themselves to the wrong question when called upon to consider what action is to be done next, and of basing their decision unconsciously on false premisses. Only where there is a strong sense of corporate identity, and many opportunities for reminding each member what the situation actually is, as opposed to what it would have been had his view prevailed all the time, can a series of decisions be expected to constitute a coherent whole. Such special conditions apart, some of the decisions made are likely to render nugatory others already taken and to make the original decision fail in its purpose. The whole sequence will appear inconsistent and ineffective and such that no single man in his right mind could have undertaken them all.

Two remedies for the incoherence of corporate decision-taking have been evolved. The corporate body may polarize or it may delegate. It may polarize, like the House of Commons, into a relatively stable majority and minority, the majority being large enough to carry the day on each separate question, and its leadership small enough and sufficiently homogeneous to ensure that all the decisions fit together into one integrated and effective programme. Or it may delegate. Like a County Council, it may take the main decisions, and leave it to officials or sub-committees to carry them out; more often, the officials or sub-committees will not merely execute a policy already decided upon, but make their own proposals about policies to be adopted. In either case we vest most of the decision-making in the hands of relatively few people, because only those who are charged with responsibility for the conduct of affairs will in fact give their minds sufficiently to the task to bear in mind what they have previously decided and what they subsequently intend to do.

The argument from time is less fundamental than those from coordination and from the continual need for attention, but much more often urged. Deciding takes time. It takes time to apprise oneself of the relevant facts, to consider the different courses of action that are open, and to weigh the various arguments in favour of and against them. Snap decisions are bad decisions. If we are to have good decisions, we must spend a considerable amount of time on each decision. Since there are a large number of decisions to be taken, it follows that the people as a whole cannot take them all. Not only would it be impracticable, but often it would be wrong. It would be wrong to substitute for the courts of justice trial by public opinion poll, because most people will not have given enough attention to the facts of the case to be able to reach a fair decision. It is better to delegate. A few people are authorized to decide the particular question at issue, and charged with the responsibility of giving enough time and attention to reach a good decision. Such delegation is possible, because men are more or less rational, and on some questions at least are likely mostly to reach the same conclusion; and such delegation is necessary, because men are limited and can ratiocinate about only a limited number of questions within a given compass of time.

Deciding things takes not only time but information and thought. And we are, most of us, not very well-informed nor very good at thinking. It would be no use the government designating New York Central Station as the rendezvous for New York if it had in the meanwhile been demolished prior to redevelopment. Only those who have the relevant information can take useful decisions, and even if many people could acquire the relevant information, only a few in practice do so. Much more contentiously, a certain amount of intellectual ability seems to be required. Although some questions are so simple that almost anyone can decide them adequately, others are complicated and may require both clarity of thought and generosity of feeling if they are to be answered really well. Most people are not competent to decide issues of state, and if we attach importance to those decisions being good decisions, we shall have to reserve them for the select few. Plato thought that only his Guardians, after a lengthy education in mathematics and philosophy, should be allowed any say in the running of the ideal society; and we, in Britain, entrust almost all the effective power to a Civil Service, similarly selected and similarly dedicated to the public interest. But we shy away from admitting it. The argument from ability is telling, and we often act on it, but seldom say so, for fear of seeming undemocratic if we suggest that some people are less good than others at knowing what to do. It seems to derogate from autonomy and clearly runs counter to any doctrine of equality to claim that the decisions made by one man are worse than those made by another. If we believe in autonomy then the important thing, it seems, is not to criticize and lay down what decision a man ought to have taken, but simply to accept that he has decided, and recognize his decision as an authentic expression of his autonomous will. As liberals and democrats, we should be anxious to cherish each man's right to make his own decisions, and hesitate to characterize a decision as bad, unless it can be proved to be bad beyond reasonable doubt – and in our present sceptical age nothing is beyond reasonable doubt. Democracy, it is said, does not make for deference. We cannot expect other people to defer to our opinion that they are wrong. Indeed, even to entertain that opinion smacks of authoritarianism, unless we can prove that they are wrong by appeal to some decision-procedure rather than expecting our opinion to be accepted merely on the basis of our simple say-so. We cannot any longer reckon that other people will or should accept our authority – nowadays only an appeal to reason can be countenanced; but since no amount of reasoning can prove to a person that a moral or political decision of his was indubitably wrong, it seems to follow that we should drop the habit of criticizing or evaluating other people's decisions, and refuse either to judge or let ourselves be judged. Equality, too, says that any one man is as good as any other, and so denies that we are entitled to discriminate between one man's decisions and another's. Once we allow that decisions can be evaluated, we shall be led to say of some men that their decisions are characteristically better than others', and soon we shall be distinguishing an élite of Aristotle's sensible men from a lumpenproletariat who ought not to have any say in great matters because they are too stupid to decide them well.

These arguments are very strongly felt, but mistaken none the less. No argument from freedom or reason or scepticism or equality can yield the conclusion that we ought not to evaluate decisions, because any decision to act on such a conclusion would itself run counter to that conclusion. It is not enough for me simply to say that you have a right to make your own decisions for yourself and leave it at that, because if you were to decide not to tolerate some third person's behaviour, I should be compelled, by my own principle of freedom, to stigmatize at least that decision of yours as a bad one, however indubitably it was yours. So, too, I cannot decide on the basis of reason that no decision can be adequately based on reason. If I am a sceptic, I may doubt whether I can ever dub your decisions wrong, but must equally doubt the assertion that I never can. Egalitarians may begin by reckoning one man's opinion as good as another's, but, like the liberal, must at least make an exception against the man who denies this fundamental premiss of theirs. The arguments from equality to non-discrimination, from freedom to indifference and from scepticism to tolerance, although pervasive and persuasive, are fundamentally incoherent. They also run counter to the facts. It is difficult in practice to believe that one man's decision is as good as another's. Nobody believes it where any technical matter is in dispute, and few act on it where non-technical questions are at stake. Doctors can be wrong, but we do not reckon that journalists are more likely to give us good medical advice. And equally, when it comes to difficult decisions in our own personal lives, we think that some people are wiser than others, and more likely to give us sound advice. In public affairs, we tend to think that some men are great leaders, in war or peace, and better able to guide our affairs than others. We would not have exchanged Marlborough or Wolfe or Wellington or Montgomery for a chance-chosen private on the grounds that he was bound to have a baton in his knapsack. In matters of life and death, whether in politics or morals, our real beliefs show themselves – and are that some people have much more of a flair than others for doing the right thing.

The argument from competence, together with the arguments from coordination, time and the need for continual attentiveness, constitutes a powerful case against democracy, at least as an answer to the question *Who shall take the decisions?* Most decisions should not – cannot – be taken by everybody. The effective choice must be vested in the hands of a few, and everybody else must have only a limited, usually a very limited, say. We are bound to delegate. It does not follow, however, that the delegation must be, as Plato supposed, complete, nor that it must always be to the same people, nor that the decision-making should not be democratic in other senses of the word. But it has often been thought to follow. Many thinkers outline some ideal democracy after the manner of Rousseau, extol its merits, note that it is impracticable for one or more of the reasons given, and without more ado commit all the effective power to the party or the committee of public safety. What we need to do, instead, is to unpick the arguments separately, and consider how we can meet the valid points they make without being pushed into a wholesale abdication of power by the people in favour of the professionals.

Let us begin with the most powerful argument for professionalism, Plato's argument from competence. Once we allow that the decisions of one man may more often be right than those of another, and attach importance to the right decisions being made, then surely we should get our decisions from those most likely to give us good ones. And so indeed we should – but subject to several qualifications about the nature of political argument which greatly alter the spirit in which we confer authority or allow our Guardians to give us guidance. Plato assumes that knowledge of what is good to do is like knowledge of mathematical or scientific truth, and is fond of drawing an analogy between the opinions of the ignorant multitude about matters of morals or politics and about medicine or navigation. But although the multitude is often wrong, even the experts are fallible. Some men may be more rational than others, but still are only imperfectly so. Not even Solomon was wise enough always to decide well. Indeed, it is not clear that to *every* question in politics there is, as Plato assumed, a unique right answer which a sufficiently rational man would reach. All we have shown is that *some* practical questions admit of answers that are right or wrong, and that some men may be better at deciding them than others are, not that the former are infallible nor the latter always wrong. Political theorists are prone to the vanity of the first person plural. We find it natural, you and I together as we set the world to rights in the bar or over a cup of cocoa before we go off to bed, to agree about what ought to be done, and what we should do if only we were in power, without ever a thought that we might be wrong. We happily assume our own infallibility when we are holding forth, but should remember that actual decisions are likely to be taken by Them rather than by us, and that even the most admirable administrator can make mistakes. Nor should we rule the opinions of the inexpert out of court. There is a difference between morality and medicine and between politics and navigation which Plato overlooked. Men without medical or navigational qualifications are not qualified to hold an opinion on medical or navigational matters at all, and if they presume to give us their opinion on these matters, they can be told to shut up. Medical and navigational questions are ones on which only experts can pronounce. But there is no similarly exclusive expertise of morality and politics. The Athenians were right, in spite of Socrates' complaint to Protagoras, to be willing to listen to anyone when the question turned on an issue of justice or the public interest, although they were quick to silence the inexpert when any technical matter was under discussion. Right to listen, not right always to follow. Some men's advice may be bad, and we may well be wise to reject it, in part because advice previously tendered was bad; but we cannot reject it out of hand, in the way that we can reject out of hand the advice of non-mathematicians about mathematics or non-scientists about science. If the physicists are agreed about relativity theory and tell me that nothing can go faster than light or that mass and energy are equivalent, I may not think that it makes sense, but I am not in a position to gainsay them. The consensus of expert opinion is conclusive. The consensus of informed opinion on moral or political matters, however, is not conclusive. The Archbishop of Canterbury may be right when he tells me I ought not to trade in my wife for a trendier model; Plato's Guardians may be right when they tell me I ought to spend the best years of my life researching into the foundations of mathematics; the economic experts in Whitehall may be right when they tell me I ought to buy a second colour TV. They may be right, but they are not necessarily right. Their say-so does not finish the matter. I can still wonder whether they are really right. I may be wrong, but I am not necessarily wrong-headed, if I think differently. Whereas it would be absurd to ask non-medical men to diagnose diseases, we are not similarly impelled to disfranchise laymen from moral and political debates. It may be that they are usually wrong, but it cannot be assumed *a priori* that they always must be. I may, if I am wise, be very ready to be guided by the Archbishop of Canterbury in moral matters, but it is not part of the nature of morality that I have to take it from him; and similarly in politics it often is the case, and if I am wise I shall acknowledge it, that the civil servants know best. But it does not have to be the case, and sometimes indeed is not the case, and needs to be argued for in individual instances and not taken for granted wholesale.

Indeed, not only can the ordinary non-professional man be right but sometimes he will be. This follows from the nature of the state. The state is an unselective community, and is not defined by an enumeration of its goals, which might then define an expertise which some professionals were expert at. In this it differs from institutions which exist for specific purposes, such as hospitals, schools, universities and churches. Doctors, not hospital porters, should do most of the deciding in hospitals; dons, not janitors or students, should do most of the deciding in universities. For, granted the rationale of these institutions, the best decisions will be taken if they are taken by professionals. The state, however, cannot be similarly circumscribed in the values it espouses. Although, as we shall argue in chapter seven, it necessarily has some values, there are many others it might have. Whether or not it espouses them depends ultimately on the values its citizens are prepared to avow, which cannot be known altogether *a priori*, but only by actually asking them. Each man is, necessarily, *the* authority on what he himself thinks and wants. And if, as we shall argue in chapter six, the public interest is in part constituted by individuals being able to realize their objectives, it follows that no professional administrators, however well-qualified and however well-intentioned, can be left to take all the decisions for us. We cannot have a monolithic system of government on Plato's model, because we do not have the monolithic system of values which it presupposes.

The argument for total delegation also misconstrues the nature of communal action. Fundamentally, communal action is a form of cooperation. Usually, as we saw in chapter four, some are giving a lead and others are being led, but even then it is a two-way process, and those who are led are contributing something and not just receiving instructions. Our attitudes in time of war or great national danger, like our attitudes when beset by serious disease or in jeopardy at sea, are untypical. These cases establish what they were intended to establish: that some guides are better than others; but the element of cooperation is minimal, and we are almost entirely followers and hardly fellow-workers at all. It is a mistake to regard them as the norm, or to construe government exclusively from the consumer's point of view. Not that the consumer approach is entirely wrong. In politics, more often than we like to suppose, we are consumers, and it is illuminating to apply consumer standards to the government 'product' not only with regard to the provision of electricity supplies and postal services, but even in respect of the maintenance of law and order, and the more obviously political activities of the state. Often our problem is one of quality control, and, as we shall see more fully in chapters ten and thirteen, we are concerned not so much to achieve the best as to avoid the worst. We pursue what is known in the theory of games as a 'minimax' strategy. What the minimum acceptable standard is, depends on the issues involved. Nothing very much will go wrong if a parish council is incompetent. We are prepared to sacrifice some good decisions for the sake of other ideals we value, such as that of allowing other people to have some say in the taking of decisions. But only to a limited extent. We can put up with decisions on some matters being less excellent than they might have been, but, where important issues are involved, will not long accept their being decided by incompetents. The Athenians thought it more democratic to select their leaders, including their war-leader, the Polemarch, by lot; but then the effective control of affairs fell into the hands of the generals, the Strategoi, who were still elected, and so could be chosen for their competence. Recently in Britain we have very much widened the range of people from whom juries may be selected, but have at the same time been having more and more cases tried by a judge alone, because juries are not really competent to understand the cases or reach a right decision. Although we do not think adjudicating is as difficult as winning a war or guiding the nation's destiny, and do not attach such overriding importance to getting the best man for the job, we set great store by the courts handing down decisions that are just, and regard this as a difficult job, for which we demand a high minimum standard of competence. The consumer attitude has been well exemplified in the recent reorganization of local government. The Maud report favoured larger units, because it felt, although it could not prove it, that they would be more 'efficient'. If we are merely consumers of education, housing and welfare services, then there is a case for large units (though often in practice large units prove less efficient than small ones), with most of the decisions being taken by appointed competents, not by elected incompetents. But although efficiency *is* important, political consumerism is an inadequate account of government, and we may well come to regret the transfer of power from local representatives whom we can know to distant officials who may be more efficient but will never happen to meet us in the pub or at the races.

For we are consumers, but not merely consumers. Most of us most of the time are moderately well content to leave the decision-making to professionals, and provided they do the job properly we do not complain. But we are not prepared to go the whole hog, and abdicate all power to the government. Even from a consumer's point of view it would be unwise – Plato put great trust in the rule of serious-minded intelligent men, but he was well aware of the corrupting tendencies of power; and history has shown that even meritorious meritocrats may over the generations come to be more alive to their own interests than the interests of those they nominally serve. Not only would it be unwise, but, again from a consumer's point of view, it would be incoherent: full consumer satisfaction can only be achieved if there is some sort of market research. The government cannot do its job properly unless it finds out what the governed actually want, and this involves asking them, and, as we shall argue in chapters ten and twelve, taking some notice of their answers. Representative institutions are not merely a form of public opinion poll on the popularity of governmental policies although they fulfil something of that function. We do not see ourselves simply as consumers; although the processes of government are very largely, for most of us, a fairly external matter, what government is essentially about is not providing us with certain services but enabling us to cooperate with one another in order to achieve goals and values held in common. We are agents who cooperate, not recipients who consume. And if we are to cooperate we cannot be excluded altogether from decision-making procedures. Often we are content to be told what to do, but not always. Sometimes we want to know why. We want to be given reasons, persuaded not ordered. And giving reasons involves listening to objections and meeting them, not just adducing arguments of one's own. Therefore even if we grant that professional administrators are much better at administering public affairs than the rest of us are, we still shall not accept Plato's conclusion in its entirety. Somehow, somewhere, sometimes, the non-professionals need to be brought into the picture and allowed to have their say. For, after all, it is they, as well as the professionals, who are expected to obey the law, and whose cooperation is required if communal purposes are to be achieved.

Plato's argument from competence is telling, but not conclusive. We may well need the aid of professional administrators to run the government, but should not delegate all the decision-making to them or hand ourselves over absolutely into their power on the grounds that they are wiser than we are. They are not that wise, nor we utterly unwise; and anyhow, government is not a machine to be run but a joint enterprise in which we are all to some extent involved.

The other arguments for delegation still remain, and we find ourselves pushed to Plato's practical conclusion by the exigencies of the case. The argument from time is the one that impresses itself on us most. We cannot all be full-time functionaries of state. But from this it does not follow that there should be a few permanent full-time functionaries, and that the rest of us should have no public function at all. It is at least formally possible that we should all take it in turns to discharge full-time functions on a temporary basis, and other functions permanently but part-time. The Middle Ages made much use of temporary full-time officials. Aristotle regards it as characteristic of democracy that all citizens take it in turns to rule and be ruled. It is clear that this meets the requirements urged by the first and third arguments: the argument from continual attentiveness and the argument from time. Most of us, necessarily, cannot give all our time to public affairs, and therefore in particular cannot be available all the time to deal with emergencies. But we could give some of our time, and be continually available for a season. One could serve on the council for one year, and for one month of that spend every day in continuous session of the standing committee. Mayors and sheriffs hold office on this principle, and although many people are unwilling or unable to hold such offices, more people can be mayors than can be M.P.s.

Although those who undertake the general oversight of public affairs have to be continuously available, most problems emerge only slowly and can be decided at our convenience. They still take time. But they do not have to be decided by full-time decision-makers, and therefore can be delegated to different people according to the different questions at issue, especially where the decisions are relatively independent of each other, as in issues of justice. I may occasionally be called on to act as a juror; I have to give a lot of time and thought to one case, but I do not become a permanent public servant. Having given our verdict on the one case for which we were empanelled, my fellow-jurors and I are discharged, and return to our private affairs. And the same can hold good in many other fields. I can be interested in one or two aspects of public life – consumer affairs, education or the environment – without being deeply involved with every other aspect. So far as the argument from time goes, it is perfectly feasible to delegate different questions to different people. If decisions are to be taken properly, some people have got to give a lot of time and thought to them. But they need not be always the same people – and, indeed, other things being equal, it is desirable that as many different people as possible should be involved in having a very full say in some aspect of public business.

Although the pure argument from time can thus be side-stepped, it merges into others that are more difficult to escape. In local government, mayors and sheriffs have become more and more figureheads, with the real power oozing into the hands of the town clerks and clerks to the County Council because the temporary incumbents are never in the job long enough to get all the facts at their fingertips or understand all the issues and how they bear on one another. We could surmount the former difficulty by adjusting the term of office. The argument from coordination, however, cannot be altogether avoided, but does not prove absolutely the need for total centralized control by coordinators. A large body cannot without guidance take a large number of decisions, or it will decide ineffectively. But it can take some, and these can be the important ones. And having taken some important ones, it can delegate their further implementation to different bodies. Although we must decide how much to spend on education and how much on health, there is no reason why we should not leave the relevant committee to manage within its budget, or, better still, devolve most of the decisions to the managers of the various schools and the boards of the various hospitals. Coordination between different departments can be achieved quite largely by discussion between them, and only occasionally is there required some sort of arbitration by a higher authority. For the most part, the need for coordination arises within particular policies, and it is relatively seldom that foreign policy and education policy constitute a seamless web in which no aspect of the one can be altered without unravelling all the other. Governments like to make out that their policies all hang together because then they are in a stronger position to fob off critics of any one policy by reference to some other one which the critics are not in a position to understand. Different policies sometimes have some bearing on one another but seldom a very intimate one. We need to pay respect to those professionals who have given their minds to public affairs and are in a position to coordinate our policies, but should not assume that different policies form such a tightly integrated whole that it is impossible to alter any without upsetting the rest, or that we must therefore hand over to them all effective say in how different policies are to be adjusted to fit in with one another.

We need not delegate absolutely, but it is difficult not to. Even to give instructions is, as we saw in chapter two, to authorize, and delegation generally involves a substantial transfer of power, which easily acquires a momentum of its own and goes on until it is complete. We authorize the official or committee to exercise discretion, within limits usually somewhat indefinite, over the means to be employed. True, the official or committee is accountable for its actions to the main body, and may be asked *Why did you do it?* by some member of the main body, and be obliged to give an answer, justifying the action in terms of its general commission. But it is clear that an official or committee cannot be called to account for most of its actions, because of the shortage of time. Moreover, the main body has neither the information nor the understanding for effective control. Even when a justification is demanded, a very exacting standard of justification cannot be required, because of coherence of purpose: the main body cannot expect that the decision should be shown to their satisfaction to be the best possible one, but only a reasonable one; for it was because there were many such, and the task of making a coherent choice from among them was one the main body was ill-suited to perform, that it was delegated to the official or committee, and therefore no criticism of its choice on this score can be entertained. In normal circumstances what the official says goes. Even on major questions falling within his province, even on questions determining what his commission is, it needs a bold – or a foolish – man to bid the experts nay. Even on matters the main body can and should decide, the recognized inadequacies of corporate decision-making inhibit it from exercising its authority, and thus encourage a continuing transfer of authority to its officials or committees, and an even more persistent transfer of power.

Delegation need not, however, be always a derogation of authority and power. We too readily assume that authority and power are like money, and can be conferred on one man only at the expense of someone else. But since they arise in the context of telling people to do things, they, like action itself, have the peculiar property of being shareable. Just as under certain conditions my action may be also your action, so, under conditions yet to be elucidated, my exercise of authority or power may be yours too. So it often is with delegation. We delegate to one man decisions which we do not need the help of all to reach, and where any one man's decision is more or less as good as anybody else's. In so far as decision-making is a rational process, the question *Who takes it?* should not have any bearing on the decision itself, and one man's decision should be as good as another's. It will not worry me much that I did not choose which books were bought for the library or which paint was used in the hospital if I reckon that had I had the choice I would have made the same decision or, if different, different only on matters themselves indifferent. Your having drawn up the library list does not diminish me unless it was done wrong, or as an assertion of your own ego, or against my wishes or advice; and if, on the contrary, it was done well, in accordance with values we both share, and in a reasonable and unassertive way, I shall see your deciding not as a diminution but as an implementation of the authority and power we jointly possess. The question of who takes the decisions thus gives way to questions about the identity, or, rather, the 'identifiability-with', of decisions. What is it that makes a decision taken by an official or a committee one which I would, or conceivably could, have taken myself had I been charged with taking it? What are the essential requisites for me to be able to identify myself with it, and what differences will I be ready to disregard as unimportant? It is largely a question of the values the decision manifests. In simple cases if you carry out your commission, I have no grounds of complaint. The commission defines the relevant goal, and everything else, within wide limits, is a matter of indifference. But even in the simplest case there are some limits. If I send a child to the shop, I may leave it to him which way he is to go, and the order in which he moves his feet, but if he went by a very circuitous route or if he moved his feet exceedingly slowly, the fact that he had been to the shop as requested would not free him from reproach. It is never enough merely to have carried out a commission; always there are some implicit understandings as to the manner in which it was to be carried out. And as the cases become more complicated, we begin to be more explicit about the standards of reasonableness required. We begin to specify the frame of mind in which the decision should be reached, and, in difficult cases, also the steps by which it should be reached. At the very least we require that the decision be considered from the point of view of the community as a whole, and not exclusively from some individual or sectional standpoint.

Plato required his Guardians to satisfy this condition. They were to pursue the good of the whole city, as they saw it, and to be ready to sacrifice their own individual or corporate happiness to that of the ideal society. Exactly the same can be said of our civil servants. They serve, and they serve well. The decisions they reach, although not to everybody's liking, are reached conscientiously, and are intended to promote the public good. This is a necessary condition, but clearly not sufficient. We try and achieve a sufficient condition in the administration of the law, where we delegate vitally important decisions absolutely, but attempt to ensure that the decisions finally reached should not depend in any way on who was charged with making them. Since men may differ about the rights and wrongs of a case, we fill out our untutored intimations of justice with the more fully formulated rules of law, and require judges to be guided by precedent and jurors to decide only questions of fact, and feel it is a serious criticism if it can be shown that one judge is likely to decide differently from another, or that the composition of a jury affects its verdict. There are other, less stringent, conditions which in many cases may be sufficient, in particular a certain regard for the ideals of freedom and justice, which we shall elucidate further in chapter seven.

The administration of the law is a special, although important and illuminating, case. In most other cases we do not give nearly such precise instructions as we do, in effect, give the courts, and therefore are less willing to give them, within the limits of their commission, a free hand. Some further communication between the main body and the official or sub-committee is provided for. It can take many forms. The initiative may come from either, and may come before or after the dubious or difficult decision. In the speech from the throne the government takes the initiative and seeks in advance approval for the decisions it proposes to take. In the Middle Ages many magistrates gave an account of their stewardship at the end of their term of office. Parliamentary questions are asked by non-official members of the main body usually after the event, and opposition motions seek to influence the decisions the government is going to make. In these and other ways, some sort of communication is possible about the sorts of decision which are, and more importantly, which are not, acceptable. It is characteristic of democratic government not only that the rulers should try to pursue the good of the community as a whole, but that they should be ready generally to share their reasoning with the community as a whole. They should not only be benevolent, but responsible. They should be generally ready to answer the question *Why are you doing that?* both in order that we may identify with the decision and as a safeguard against tyranny, corruption and the grosser forms of incompetence. But accountability costs something. We often reason better than we can say, and will produce better results if we are free to be guided by hunch than if we have to justify every step. The more strictly we hold them accountable, the more the administrators are obliged to make not the best, but the safest, decisions. Civil servants cannot afford to be imaginative or enterprising, because they must always be prepared for a parliamentary question on any decision they make, and are therefore encouraged to be cautious and hide-bound. Accountability is a form of quality control. We avoid the really bad, but have to forgo the really good. It is a price well worth paying to avoid the great evil of misgovernment, but always there will be some question whether we are not fettering discretion too much, and insuring too heavily, at the cost of making it impossible for the decision-makers ever to discharge their commission, against dangers that can be adequately guarded against in other ways. Where it is very difficult to decide rightly, and much depends on it, we minimize accountability in order to maximize discretion, like the ancient Romans, who appointed a dictator in times of national emergency. In less hazardous situations we cut fewer corners in order to have more adequate safeguards all along the line, but there will always be pressure from the administrators to be given a freer hand, and to have to give their account only seldom and in general terms. We have to strike a balance, and, what is more difficult, devise institutions which will prevent the balance being shifted in the course of time, and will enable the administrators to get on with their job without effectively emancipating them from control by those they are supposed to serve.

This tension between the need to delegate authority and the desire not to abdicate it altogether can resolve itself into a number of different compromises. Two paradigm cases deserve notice. In the first we have the principle of the dormant veto. The official or committee formulates fairly detailed proposals which the main body can either accept or reject. Normally it accepts – and often complains that it is merely a 'rubber-stamp' – but it can reject, and occasionally does, and thus acts both as an occasional safety-valve and as a continual warning to anybody tempted to abuse the authority entrusted to him. In ancient Sparta the Apella – composed of all citizens – could only approve or refuse to approve proposals put before it; in twentieth-century Britain, Parliament can only acquiesce in delegated legislation or negative it. The question put demands a Yes or No answer, with the Yes being highly specific and the No correspondingly vague. A succession of Noes is too vague to give any guidance to government, and indeed, whenever the answer is No the proponents will complain that it is an unconstructive answer, and that the main body is merely wrecking their work; the logic of the question is against the answer often being No, and some pressure will be generated against its ever being so.

The second paradigm case is that of the outline alternatives. The choice may be either of persons – to be officials or members of a committee – or of programmes. In either case the future course of decision-taking is left fairly vague. The voter does not know in any detail what he is letting himself in for, but he has a correspondingly freer choice between the options available. It would be irresponsible always to vote No: no logical opprobrium attaches to voting for one person or one programme rather than another, even though to vote for one is to vote against the other. The alternatives are not exhaustive, and may not be exclusive, but there is almost inevitably some real difference between the candidates or programmes on which he does have a real say. And, as we shall see in chapter ten, there are pressures making the decision reserved for the voters the most important decision of the day.

Delegation generates a sort of aristocracy. The officials and members of select committees are bound to be better informed than most of the members of the main body, if only because they spend more time on their particular job and having fed upon the royal jelly of power have acquired some regal divinity. It is easy to assume – because it is largely true – that the conduct of affairs depends on a relatively small number of reasonable and responsible men, and that they alone have anything of value to contribute to the public decision-making process. But this practical conclusion is no more inescapable than Plato's theoretical one was. True, we must delegate: but we need not always delegate to the same people. True, we cannot impose strict accountability all along the line; but we can take steps to reserve some important decisions to a wider number of people, and to ensure that at least some delegated decisions are effectively scrutinized. Nevertheless, the distinction between the rulers – characteristically well-informed, often competent, sometimes full-time, sometimes permanent, usually both – and the ruled remains. There is a continually recurring tension between the people at large who have of necessity at best only a part-time interest in public affairs, and the professionals who are always available to attend to any public business that needs attention. The people at large will tend to be interested only in rather large questions of general significance which they can reasonably comprehend and on which they can come to some rational conclusion; the professionals will tend to be absorbed in minor matters of detail, and obsessed with facts and practicalities, and there will be a constant tendency for each to misunderstand – and often to despise – the other. Tension will arise between those who occasionally and unpredictably intervene with strongly held opinions on large matters and those who are continually concerned with day-to-day business, who are familiar with all the facts and all the difficulties, but who both are insensitive to how the matter strikes those who are at the receiving end of government, and are not happy discussing major issues of principle. Writers have traditionally distinguished the executive from the legislative and judicial branches of government, and would construe the arguments here adduced as establishing the need for the executive, and to a lesser extent the judicial, branches as opposed to the legislative branch. The traditional distinctions are not all that helpful; but some of the traditional problems of the relationship between the executive and the legislature can usefully be seen as variations on the interplay between the full-time professional ruler and the part-time would-be participator.

6 Interests

Men have interests. Often it is assumed that this is a regrettable, or even an avoidable, fact, and that in the ideal society decisions would be taken without regard to any particular interests that any particular men might have. That is a mistake. Not only is it a fact, but, as we shall shortly see, it is a necessary fact, that different men have different interests which greatly influence the decisions they make. Any theory of the state must recognize the realities of human nature. That we have interests which often conflict is a typical, and sometimes indeed desirable, feature of human life. Rather than avert our eyes from the interested nature of many of our actions, we should attempt to understand what interests are, and the part they should play in political thinking.

Interests are values, but not all values are interests. I can cite somebody's interests as a reason for doing something, just as I can justify doing it for the sake of justice or of truth. Unlike other values, however, interests are assignable. If I talk about interests, it always makes sense to ask *Whose interests?*, and I must be able to answer that question, or confess that I do not know what I am talking about. Usually I will specify a person, but I may specify a group or community – the interests of the dockers, or of the National Association for Mental Health – and in particular I may specify the interests of the whole community, and talk of the public interest. But I must be able to assign an interest to someone or somebody; whereas if I do something for the sake of justice or of truth, it makes no sense to ask *Whose justice?*, or to say that it is done for the sake of my or your truth.

Interests are not only assignable, but imputable. I can, to a greater or less extent, and subject to some qualifications yet to be stated, say what your interests are without your telling me. Hence their importance in political thinking, where we often have to deal third-personally with what various people may in their own first persons want or desire, without being able actually to ask them. Instead of consulting them, we consult their interests. Interests are what a man may look after on another's behalf. They may be conveniently classified under three heads. In the first place each person is presumed to have an interest in preserving his own life, health and freedom. Secondly, each person can be said to have an interest in securing conditions which, whatever he decides to do, will enable him the better to do it. Money is the paradigm example. It is clearly in my interest to have money, because it will provide the means wherewith I may secure whatever ends I may adopt. A similar argument is often given for educating children against their wishes. It is tempting to stop there, and claim as many philosophers do, that all other concerns a man may have are not interests but ideals. Certainly we often pursue ideals which cannot be described as interests. But it is difficult to maintain a sharp distinction between the two. Often our assessment of what would be most in a person's interests will depend on idealistic values – as when we argue that it is in a child's interest to be brought up a Christian or to be given moral education. Often also our view of our interest overruns any definitional limitation. I make plans not only for myself and my old age, but for my children and my heirs, and extend my self-concern to my estate. So, too, I identify with my college, my university, my country and my church, and see their good as my good, and pursue it with the same tenacity as I cherish my bodily health and financial well-being. Although from the point of view of metaphysics there is a sharp distinction between me and everybody else, that distinction is, fortunately, not nearly so sharp from a moral point of view. Not only can I be altruistic – concerned with other men's concerns as being other men's – but I can take them to my own heart, and make them altogether my own. The proof that this can happen is that sometimes we see it as a vice, which altruism never is. We sometimes blame a man for nepotism or jingoism, seeing these as a form of selfishness, extended and rarefied no doubt, but betraying a sort of self-love all the same, which, if pursued to the exclusion of other considerations, can be an occasion of blame. I can extend myself not only to embrace other people, but also to espouse impersonal ideals. I am not wrapped up with every ideal I avow, but I am with some. With some values I may have only a dispassionate desire that they should prevail, but with others I have in addition a passionate commitment, and am as absorbed in them as I am in my college or my country. They help to constitute my identity, and I am so much identified with them that my interests consist as much in the realization of these values as in the maintenance of my bodily health and liberty. These idealistic interests are of importance in politics. Many 'interest groups' exist in order to further them – The Society for the Protection of Unborn Children, The Howard League for Penal Law Reform, The Royal Society for the Prevention of Cruelty to Animals; and although these interests are in some important ways unlike the individual's paradigm interests of life, health and freedom, they are not completely distinct, but are, rather, linked by means of a continuous range of intervening instances.

We can now see why different interests are all regarded as interests, and why we inevitably have interests, each man's potentially conflicting with other men's. My interests stand to me in the same way as your interests stand to you. Our concerns vary in part systematically. *I* am hurt by a thorn in *my* foot just as *you* are hurt by a thorn in *your* foot. *I* hasten to get to the pub before closing time in order to pour beer down *my* throat, just as *you* hasten to slake *your* thirst. I pay money into my banking account, hope that I shall obtain a good degree, and fear that Amaryllis will spurn my suit, just as you pay money into your account, fear that you will get a bad degree, and reckon that Chloe is bound to look on you with favour. There are considerable similarities between my concern and yours, and we can formalize them in the general pattern x . . . x - - - where x can be replaced by I/me/my or by you/you/your. Nor is it just a contingent similarity. If there are any values and any agents aspiring to realize any of them, then there must be some values assignable to each agent himself, varying from one to another in a systematic fashion. For to be an autonomous agent is to have a mind of one's own, which one makes up for oneself, and then oneself implements in action. I am myself because I can decide what I am going to do and then do it. And so I must attach peculiar importance to my being *able* to carry out whatever it is I have seen fit to do. I am necessarily concerned with my own freedom of action, and hence with my own life, health and liberty, just as you are necessarily concerned with your freedom of action, that is your life, health and liberty, and everyone else with his life, health and liberty. Of course, I may also care for your freedom and effectiveness, and you for mine; but that is only contingently the case – and, alas, sometimes not the case – whereas my concern for my own freedom and effectiveness is more than merely contingent, and can be presumed on no other evidence than that I am an autonomous agent. Every community is based on its members having certain values in common, but there will be others that vary systematically from person to person, just because each separate agent is another self, so that his concerns are peculiarly his own, and must to some extent be different from those of everybody else.

But we have to be careful how we describe these concerns, or they will not vary systematically from person to person. You could not care less if Amaryllis thought ill of you, and I should be greatly alarmed if I found Chloe looking on me with favouring eyes. Only under the special description of 'one's girl-friend' can our fears and hopes of Amaryllis and Chloe respectively be compared; and the whole point of our loving them is that they are not just girls like any other girls, but each a unique individual, essentially different from everybody else. In describing them in general terms, we miss the main point. The main point is essentially non-vicarious, that someone says in the first person 'I love Amaryllis' or 'I am rather keen on Chloe'. Similarly with hobbies, opinions, enthusiasms and political causes. It is true that these are typical concerns of human beings, and therefore should be characterized and cherished as human interests; but it is a passion for bird-watching or Bach, and not just for my hobby, that really animates me, and I justify my opinions and my political causes as being true and right, and not just as being mine. Under these, more revealing descriptions, interests may not be necessarily exclusive. Each man has his own hobby, but many of us share an enthusiasm for Bach. Conversely, I share an interest in girls with many members of my own sex, but not, I hope, an interest in Amaryllis. When we are dealing with interests, quite a lot will turn on how they are characterized, and in particular whether they are necessarily exclusive – my life is mine, and nobody else's – or potentially shareable – my unenthusiasm for the Common Market may be felt by many. Often in using the language of interests, we are in danger of mis-describing them and introducing a subtle distortion into our account of human affairs. For, although some values vary systematically from person to person, not all do. We are not selfish agents operating within the same general scheme of values, with each merely wanting as much as possible of the good things that are going; we sometimes share the same values and sometimes are in disagreement about what constitutes the good. Amaryllis is different from Chloe, walking from playing squash, philosophy from economic history. There is a certain deadness in describing these all as interests, some happening to be espoused by me, others by you. Nevertheless, we often have occasion to. For we often want to consider affairs on behalf of another person, and put ourselves in his shoes, and then it is his interests we say we are considering. We cannot fully enter into his concerns without identifying ourselves very much with him, but we need not dissociate ourselves entirely from him, and the concept of interest arises from our partial concern with his concerns. It follows that it is fuzzy-edged and dependent on context. The more closely a person identifies with a man and understands him, the more interests of his he is able to recognize and protect. The consul in a foreign country can hope only to secure a fair trial for his compatriot and release from arbitrary custody; a solicitor can look after his client's finances, but not his love affairs. A friend, who is, according to Aristotle, 'another self', can further the interests of the heart as well as of the pocket: you may tell Amaryllis nice things about me, and urge her not to be put off by my oaf-like behaviour and assure her that underneath I have a heart of gold, and I may bully you of an evening to settle down to some revision, and keep telling you that Chloe is much more likely to respect you if you have got a second rather than a plough. Even intellectual interests can be protected. If I hear my friend's views attacked, I may well in his absence defend them although I do not share them, putting forward to the best of my ability the arguments he uses, and seeking to counter objections which in my own opinion are unanswerable. I cannot pretend that his views are my own, but I can stand up for them on my friend's behalf and undertake myself the steps that he would have taken had he been there. In intellectual, as in practical matters, we can often understand the decisions of others even when we do not agree with them, and therefore can ascribe an interest to another even though it is not one we have ourselves. But the extent to which we actually ascribe interests will depend in part on how close we are in sympathy and understanding, in part on the conventions of the social context within which we operate, and sometimes on the values that the man actually avows.

Because we use the same word, 'interest', in each case, we are tempted to assume that the interests of an individual are all homogeneous, and measurable on a one-dimensional scale. Interests become for the politician what utilities are for the economist, a sort of shadow money, measurable, summable, and even inter-personally comparable. The mistake is most commonly made with regard to the public interest, but with private interests also we need to point out that they are not one-dimensional; more technically, they are 'non-Archimedean'. Although we can put interests in some sort of order of importance – regarding some, like life, liberty and health as central interests, and others, like being in a locality with good TV reception, as fairly peripheral – we do not put them into a strict order, nor are we always ready to regard interests of different types as being commensurable. Rather, different sorts of interests arise in different contexts. Those interests that can be ascribed to a man by almost anyone else have a very intense bearing on the questions that they are relevant to, but the range of such questions is not itself very extensive. Everybody knows my concern in staying alive, and if it is a question of life or death, my concern for life will weigh very heavily indeed. Doctors' orders are highly mandatory but seldom given. Again, if I am in danger of imprisonment, everyone will expect me to be anxious to retain my liberty, and I shall forgo almost everything else to do so. But the consul's advice –

not kissing in public in Spain, nor bathing naked in Greece, nor reading the Bible in buses in Russia – although to be acted on, is strictly limited in its scope. It will keep me out of prison, but cannot tell me how to make the most of my trip abroad. I cannot rely on my solicitor, any more than on my doctor, to give me general guidance on how to live my life, nor again on my bank manager. Each can advise me on the one sort of interest, and where their advice conflicts we are inclined to follow the doctor rather than the lawyer, and either rather than the bank manager. But there are far more decisions in which money is importantly involved than ones concerning major problems of health or matters of law. And for the most part, money too is a limiting rather than crucial consideration. The actual pattern of my choices, although within a framework determined by my interests in life, health, liberty and wealth, is itself the result of my pursuing much more personal and pervasive interests, which could not be ascribed to me by remote third persons, but only on the basis of some closer understanding. People need to know me fairly well to understand what makes me tick. They will recognize many pervasive interests of mine which constantly influence my decisions, but seldom override the interests which could be imputed to me by a wider range of people. My interest in philosophy is continually affecting the decisions I make, and tells you far more about me than my interest in staying alive, but I am unlikely to have myself brought from the hospital, against the firm instructions of my doctor, in order to attend a meeting of a philosophical society. Although I invariably would rather philosophize than complete my income tax return, on occasions I do the latter in order to avoid trouble with the law. I leave the company of friends in order to go to committee meetings, and put off family plans in order to attend to business. A person who inferred that I rated committee work more worth while than friendship, or that I was more interested in business than in my family, would be in error. What he should infer, rather, is that individual interests cannot be given an Archimedean ordering or arranged on a simple one-dimensional scale; and that often those interests most readily overridden in particular cases are the ones with the greatest bearing on the general run of decisions taken.

The concept of interest is under strain, reflecting the tension that underlies the two fundamental insights of Rousseau and Locke, that *Men are all equal* and that *Men are all different*. Because men are all equal, we reckon that all have some concerns the same; life, health, wealth, freedom are good for everyone equally, and if we care for people at all, we shall care for these interests of theirs, without having to ask them, sometimes even despite their specific disavowals. We are, in this sense, all potential paternalists. We can know what another man's interests are, without his telling us, and sometimes even better than he does, just simply by virtue of his being a man, and this knowledge permeates the whole of our political thinking and underlies many of our public institutions. But although the concept of interests provides the logical basis of paternalism, it provides the logical basis for liberalism too. For the essential similarity between all men is that they all have minds of their own, and so each can make up his mind for himself, and be different. It is built into our idea of an autonomous agent, not only that he must value his freedom and his general ability to realize his aspirations, but that he will espouse values, not necessarily the same as those of other people, and will be especially concerned about just these. In the same way as it is part of our common humanity to have and to cherish houses, friends, girl-friends, families, although we do not all have the same house, the same friends, the same girl-friend, the same family, so also it is characteristic of being a man to have his own opinions, his own ideas, and ideals of his own affirming. What these are we cannot say for him. All we can say from a third-person standpoint is that he is a person, able and entitled to speak in the first person, and that we must let him speak for himself and hear what he has to say.

The public interest is often referred to in political argument. We appeal to the public interest when we are justifying decisions or arguing about what ought to be done. It is invoked to justify quarantine regulations, licensing laws, conscription, and many forms of taxation which would be indefensible on grounds of justice or freedom alone. It covers a wide – and, as we shall see, dangerously indeterminate – range of considerations which bear on decision-making and could be both adduced by, and addressed to, anyone. Without such a concept, political debate would be seriously handicapped. Democrats in particular need it, because it seems to provide an adequate answer to the third question we ask of decisions – *In what frame of mind are they taken?* Democracy is government *for* the people. Decision-makers should be guided not by their own personal or class interests, nor by party prejudice, nor factional feeling, but by the interest of the people as a whole, that is to say the public interest. And so far as it goes, it is a good answer. But by itself it does not characterize democracy to the exclusion of other forms of government. Democrats are not alone in seeking to serve the public interest. Medieval monarchs, like Plato's meritocrats, were enjoined to, and enlightened despots and hereditary aristocracies have sought to do the best, as they saw it, for their country, often at great cost to themselves, even (in the case of the Japanese nobility) to the extent of voluntarily abdicating their own power. Although some rulers have been self-consciously selfish, and others may have been unconsciously biased in their assessment of where the public interest lay, the blanket imputation of self-interest as the guiding principle of all rulers is unwarranted. It is a generally-received maxim, and quite largely acted-on, of all forms of government, democratic and non-democratic alike, that decisions should be taken, not in the private or corporate interests of the decision-makers, but in those of the community as a whole. In view of the natural temptations to selfishness, it is a maxim that needs constant repetition in every age. But by itself it is not enough to make a government democratic.

Indeed, too much emphasis on the public interest is dangerous for democracy. It naturally engenders a paternalistic form of government, run by Platonic professionals. Since interests are typically third-personal, they are what other people can know best about and look after. If our criterion of policy is what the public wants or what the public thinks, then we must consult members of the public and let them say for themselves what they want or what they think, but in so far as our criterion is the public interest, consultation seems unnecessary. If I am to know what the governed want or think, I must ask them, because it is part of the logic of the concept of wanting and thinking that each man is the authority on what he wants or thinks. But since arguments about the public interest can be adduced by anyone, my view is as good as theirs – indeed, quite likely better, if I am in the government and have given the matter a lot of thought. The public may well not realize where their interest lies: they may think that red is a better colour than brown to indicate the dangerous live wire in an electric cable, or that there is little benefit in abolishing shillings and dividing the pound into 200 half ps instead of 240 d; but they are wrong, and provided they are not allowed to obstruct the path of progress, may even come to recognize in retrospect that the gentlemen in Whitehall did know best. If public interest is to be our guide, it is likely to be better appreciated by the intelligent and dedicated men who gave their lives to the public service than by the untutored minds of the general public or the prejudiced minds of those with some special axe to grind. Sometimes, of course, the fact that the public, along with their representatives in Parliament, are misguided, may impose a restraint on the timing of measures. Some may have to be deferred because public opinion is not yet ripe for them; or it may be wise to wait for a Parliament of suitable party complexion before pushing through the necessary legislation. But these are constraints on the means available for carrying out the proper policies, not criteria for choosing them. Opposition, whether on the part of private individuals, interest groups, or Members of Parliament, is something to be neutralized or circumvented. Minor concessions may be made to disarm it, but it is not to be taken seriously as constitutive of public policy, and should not be allowed to impede the government in its pursuit of what the public interest really requires. If we make concern with the public interest the sole test of good government, and if the public interest is a single determinate concept whose application to particular cases can be calculated by intelligent men, we make every other democratic aspect of the decision-making process dispensable, and are laying the conceptual foundations for centralized government on paternalist principles, highly inimical to all claims for participation.

The monolithic view of the public interest not only precludes participation but can lead to arrogance on the part of the rulers.

Rulers, naturally and properly, see themselves as the guardians of the public interest, and so, naturally but improperly, come to regard those who oppose them as motivated by sectional or private interests inimical to the public interest. And it may be so. But the public interest is not sufficiently clear-cut to sustain accusations of selfishness against those who reject one particular interpretation of it. Every interpretation of it is open to dispute – I once defined the public interest as 'that about which reasonable men may reasonably disagree' – and the ruler's interpretation may be as partial as those who oppose him. For to decide on one course of action rather than another as being in the public interest is none the less to favour one set of actions, exemplifying one set of values, and having certain consequences, rather than another set of actions, exemplifying another set of values, and having certain other consequences; and it is in the nature of the case that some members of the community will be gratified or benefited by the course of action adopted and others will not. The ruler, if he uses the language of public interest, may see his course of action as being conducive to the public interest, and his opponents as being motivated by selfish unconcern for the public interest, but that is not how they will see it. They will see the ruler as being in the pocket of one sectional interest which is pursuing its advantage at the expense of theirs. Richard II was fond of claiming that only the monarch should decide policy, because only he was activated by a disinterested zeal for the public interest. But to his subjects his understanding of the public interest seemed to be dictated by a small coterie of favourites, and to be more for the favourites' advantage than for the benefit of the country as a whole, and in the end they deposed him. Modern cabinet ministers pride themselves on being 'tough', and see it as a virtue to have ignored entreaties and to have ridden roughshod over all opposition, and often they are motivated by a general concern for the public interest as they see it. But those who oppose them may have been animated also by an altruistic vision of the public interest, and will find the rulers' imputation of selfishness on their part abrasive. Controversy is embittered by the assumption that what is at issue is something so simple that only the wrong-headed could be wrong.

The public interest is not a simple, positive one-dimensional concept. Often it is a negative one. It is used to exclude some other reason for acting. A treasury official, because he is representing the public interest, may argue against a pay claim put forward on behalf of civil servants, although it is in his own personal interest that the claim should succeed. A man may report an erring motorist to the police not out of spite, but in the public interest. The populace may want to go to war, but be restrained by a statesman who knows that the public interest is in the maintaining of peace. It may be in the public interest that a notorious criminal be locked up out of harm's way, and yet we hesitate to incarcerate him because to imprison anyone without due trial is repugnant to our ideals of justice and freedom. In each of these cases the term obtains its force from what it is understood to exclude, and it would be a mistake to assume that it had one single sense throughout. A cabinet minister is supposed to be guided by the public interest and not to allow his decisions to be influenced by any concern for his own pecuniary profit, but it is not supposed that he should be equally careful not to consider the interests of his own political party. A civil servant, however, should be as uninfluenced by party interests as by his own financial ones. Both seek the public interest, but it means different things to them on account of the different institutional context in which they operate.

The public interest is not entirely a negative concept, but has some positive content. Three separate strands can be distinguished in the meaning of interest when transferred from individuals to the body politic. One is a basic reflexive sense founded on a straightforward analogy between states and individual persons. Each state has an interest in its own continuance, in being able to maintain itself against aggression and internal subversion, and in having a secure supply of essential materials, in much the same way as individuals have an interest in their life, health and liberty. The defence of the realm and the maintenance of law and order are two reasons of state which are customarily acknowledged as having great cogency when they are adduced to justify public policies. But they are not the only ones. States do not exist merely in order to continue to exist, but rather, like all communities, are founded on various values held in common, and these in turn give rise to other public interests. In addition to their necessary commitment to justice and freedom, many states are welfare states, and are as such explicitly concerned with the well-being of their members. Other goals have been pursued, from world conquest to making the world safe for democracy, and from being an education to Hellas to maintaining intact the Roman Catholic way of life; and each of these has its bearing on the public decision-making and will find expression in an appropriately different understanding of the public interest. Disagreements about such values are reflected in disputes about what constitutes the public interest. If the quality of life or the abolition of poverty are the values we cherish in common, we shall regard measures to prevent overpopulation as being in the public interest; whereas if we are set on the pursuit of military glory or national aggrandizement, we shall give bonuses to those mothers who serve the public interest by giving birth to, say, ten or more future warriors or members of the *Herrenvolk*. Such interests might better be characterized as collective or common interests, and interests of the first kind as national interests, but in recent years the word 'public' has been increasingly used to include both of these, as well as interests of the third kind, where the word 'public' is used to indicate that the interest is not assigned to this or that man but is assignable indifferently to *any* member of the state. The provision of postal services and public transport is in the public interest because they are available not only for those who actually use them but for any who might like to. The state provides many facilities of this sort, and if a facility is to be made available to members of the community at large, the state is the natural organization to provide it. It is in the interests of road-users generally, and hence in the public interest, that dangerous drivers be banned. But whereas it is very much in the dangerous driver's interest to defend himself vigorously against accusations, it is usually not particularly important to me personally to bring another motorist to book, and, rather than put myself to the trouble of prosecuting him, I will let the matter drop. Unless the state takes up cudgels on behalf of the public interest by appointing public prosecutors to press home charges, most crime would go unprosecuted; and so, more generally, the state seems to have a special duty to cherish public interests of this third kind.

Even in its positive significations, therefore, the public interest is highly heterogeneous. Moreover, conflicts between one aspect of the public interest and another are endemic. The clearest example comes from the administration of the law. It is in the public interest that crime should be suppressed, for that is one of the reasons why we have the state; but it is also in the public interest that the liberty of the individual be secured and that justice be not only done but seen to be done. And this creates a conflict. We could suppress crime far more effectively by giving the police more power – power to detain suspects and to punish people they were sure had done wrong. But to confer such powers would conflict both with the individual's liberty, which requires that a man can rely on not being detained or punished provided he has not been formally accused and formally proved guilty of having definitely broken the law, and also with the requirements of justice, which lay stringent conditions on the way in which a man may be tried and the grounds on which he may be convicted. Again, it is in the public interest that there should be well-maintained roads, and some authorities have resorted to conscription to secure labour for the upkeep of roads, and many at present expropriate any land they think they need for road-building; but this aspect of the public interest comes into collision with another which sees in conscription and compulsory purchase a derogation of the values of liberty and justice that are, even more than ease of transport, fundamental to the existence of the state. The public interest thus has many faces. It is in the public interest that there should be policemen and public prosecutors, but it is in the public interest also that there should be legal aid for the accused, and that no man be convicted unless proved guilty in due form of law and beyond all reasonable doubt. The state not only is founded on many values, but necessarily so. Whatever other values it espouses, the state must cherish the maintenance of law and order, and must also as we shall argue in the next chapter, cherish liberty and justice. And these can often conflict.

Even though the public interest turns out to comprise a highly heterogeneous collection of considerations, it might still be possible to evaluate them all on a single quantitative scale, and perform a cost-benefit analysis of each proposed course of action. The utilitarian philosophy of the last century encouraged men to assume that they could operate a calculus of utilities, whereby they could work out which policy was likely to prove most advantageous. Perhaps their techniques were not yet quite refined enough to give wholly adequate answers, but they could in principle give decision-makers definitive guidance on what ought to be done. The Gross National Product could be precisely calculated, and it was the business of government to maximize that. How it was to be accomplished was a question of extreme difficulty about which even the experts might be uncertain, but, according to this view, the disagreement was solely about means, and we were all agreed about the ends we should be endeavouring to achieve.

Supporters of the cost-benefit approach can muster some arguments on their side. In the first place decision-makers do make decisions and thereby show what their order of priorities really is. They talk of weighing arguments, and it seems only reasonable therefore to generalize the weights which different considerations have in particular cases to constitute a single universally-applicable measure. In its original utilitarian form at least, there is the further merit of construing benefits imputed to the public in terms of those actually enjoyed by individuals. If the greatest happiness of the greatest number be our guide, at least we shall not embark on a policy that makes everyone miserable for the sake of some megalomaniac goal which is deemed to be in the public interest. Furthermore, we are given a method of balancing public against private interests: in spite of the fact that a benefit available to anyone is, usually, only marginally important to each single person, we can, by multiplying the benefit to each by the number of those by whom it is enjoyed, assign sufficient weight to the public interest to enable it to outweigh individual private ones.

The first of these arguments may be countered by the observation that evaluative arguments do not generalize nearly as readily as is assumed. Each decision is a particular decision in a particular case. Although in one case we may give greater weight to considerations of justice than to those of freedom, and in another to those of freedom than to those of the suppression of crime, it does not follow that we generally prefer justice to the suppression of crime. The cases are different, and it depends very much on the circumstances of each particular case how the arguments of justice, freedom and crime-prevention bear on the question at issue. Even where many of the circumstances are similar, we cannot exclude the possibility of there being some further circumstance in the one case but not the other that will make all the difference to how we ultimately decide the case. We therefore cannot count on being able to generalize. The metaphor of weighing arguments is only a metaphor, and cannot carry a whole general theory of how a definite measure may be assigned to every consideration in every case. Although utilitarianism defines the public interest in terms of individual happiness, it has, paradoxically, proved paternalistic rather than libertarian in its applications, and 'happiness' has become what is ascribed to individuals by civil servants on the basis of treasury statistics rather than anything they are given any say about. Moreover, and much more seriously, with any quantitative measure of individual and public interests it is always possible that the interests of a single individual, no matter how central or how precious, may be outweighed by the purely peripheral interests of a sufficiently large number of other individuals. There always will be some calculations of interests which will show it to be expedient that one man should die for the people, if expediency is simply a matter of totting up totals and there are enough people. We are on the horns of a dilemma. We must either say that an assessment of the public interest is not conclusive as to what policy should be undertaken, or acknowledge that considerations of the public interest cannot be measured on a simple one-dimensional scale. On the first alternative, we can carry through a cost-benefit analysis, as we do with purely economic issues, but in the end it would still be an open question whether we ought to act so as to maximize such aspects of the public interest as had been implicitly defined by our calculations. It might turn out that, by a quirk of biochemistry, one man's kidneys had concentrated in them an immensely valuable chemical substance, and that we should be far better off if we liquidated him now instead of enjoying the benefits of his labour for the next few decades. But although clearly in the public interest as thus understood, we might still regard it as wrong that this one man should die for the sake of the G.N.P. Alternatively, we might try and set a value on human life. After all we sometimes have to make life-and-death decisions in times of war, in shipwrecks and in medical emergencies; often we make some such calculation in debating the pros and cons of capital punishment. In such a case we might include all considerations of justice and right, and regard the assessment of public interest as an over-all assessment, constituting a direct recommendation for public action. But then, if our scale of values reflected what we really believe, we should find that it was non-Archimedean, that is to say, no matter how many people share a marginal benefit, there are some central interests that are incommensurable with it, and cannot be outweighed by any multiple of it.

In fact we should do both. We should ascribe a non-Archimedean metric to public interests in so far as we attempt to measure them at all, and we should also insist that considerations of the public interest, no matter how cogent, may yet be over-ridden by considerations of justice, of freedom, or of other ideals, which cannot be conveniently accommodated within the terminology of interest at all. We should say, first, that public interests are too heterogeneous to be measured on a simple quantitative scale, just as private interests are. Some interests of the state are central, and have priority over most other considerations. For the sake of national defence conscription is justified, but it would be entirely unjustified for Britain to resort to conscription in order to secure greater industrial production than Japan. That is to say, I can be required to forgo my liberty and jeopardize my life for the sake of national survival, which we regard as a central public interest, but not for the sake of added national prosperity, which is much less central. Arguments of public security are very compelling when they arise, but they do not often arise. It is a point which governments like to fudge. Sometimes secrecy is essential for national security. We must prevent foreign powers from finding out how our defences are disposed, and need an Official Secrets Act to protect ourselves against espionage, and can rightly deprive spies and informers of their liberty in order to maintain the safety of the state. It may also be true, as bureaucrats are fond of arguing, that the public interest requires that the cloak of confidentiality should cover all the deliberations of the executive, and, more generally still, that we should refrain from divisive criticism of the government. The British government has long used the Official Secrets Act to protect not only national security but departmental secretiveness, and the White House in 1973 argued that the President could not be required to come clean about any of his doings, and that since the public interest had clearly suffered from the Watergate revelations, no further investigations should be made. We reject these blanket invocations of the public interest, applying with overriding cogency in all sorts of cases, and insist on distinguishing some cases, fairly limited in extent, in which the public interest in secrecy is paramount, from others, arising much more often, where although there may be a public interest in confidentiality or in not voicing divisive criticism, it is only one among a number of considerations, and may well be outweighed by some private interests or some other aspect of the public interest. If an enterprising journalist gets hold of plans in the Department of the Environment for running down the railways, it may be against the public interest that they should be published, in as much as they may strengthen the suspicion that the Department is in the pocket of the road lobby; but that does not override certain ideals we have of freedom, nor would it justify the journalist's being prosecuted, although the different public interest in executive confidentiality would justify the sacking and perhaps the prosecution of the civil servant who broke trust and disclosed the document. As with private interests, the less mandatory a public interest is, the wider its range of application. Far more files are protected by the requirement of confidentiality than by that of the security of the realm, although it is far less important that they should be. Even so, the requirement of confidentiality still gives relatively little guidance to decision-makers, who take it for granted and are much more concerned with a different aspect of the public interest, namely that the government should be, and should be thought to be, doing a good job. Many decisions are taken with this end in view, and it is a pervasive guide to decision-making, but one readily overridden. Although criticism of what the government is doing is unwelcome and against this aspect of the public interest, and governments do what they decently can to prevent criticism, not all means are acceptable. Journalists who damage the government's image cannot be sent to prison, but may be no longer invited to press conferences. Members of Parliament who are insufficiently enthusiastic for their own party's policies are not refused re-adoption, but are unlikely to be given office. A general sense of euphoria and satisfaction with the government is in the public interest, and is an aspect that constantly bears on decision-making, but is not allowed to override other public and private interests that are more central and mandatory.

Our thinking about the right to strike reveals a similar complexity. Striking is against the public interest. The country would be a better place if we could all work together amicably. In order to avoid strikes much legislation has been passed and many conciliation procedures have been established, and the need to avoid industrial unrest is, or should be, constantly present to the minds of those who have charge of the nation's economy. But we do not in general prohibit strikes. Only if I enlist in the armed forces or join the police am I absolutely forbidden to strike, because strikes in those limited but crucial organizations would imperil the defence of the realm and the maintenance of law and order, which are central interests of the state. In other essential services the right to strike is somewhat abridged, again for obvious reasons. The maintenance of electricity supplies is a fairly central interest in modern conditions, and it is reasonable that the relatively few people who choose to take jobs in that industry should forgo their freedom to withhold their labour as and when they please. But although wild-cat strikes are highly damaging to the motor industry, we cannot pretend that the manufacture of motor cars is as essential to our well-being as the supply of electricity, and we therefore regard the public interest involved as less mandatory and more easily overridden by other considerations.

Even though we refrain from imposing an Archimedean ordering on interests, we still should not think that all political argument can be carried on in terms of interests, or that something's being in the public interest is a conclusive argument that it ought to be done. Interests are important, but not all important. We should beware of trying to expound political argument and political practice entirely in terms of interests. The concept obtains some of its force by contrast, and the public interest often is understood to exclude various ideals. To maintain the army and the police is beyond dispute an action in the public interest, but to spend money on research or overseas aid, although it may fulfil a public ideal, is not what we should normally describe as being in the public interest. There is a danger, if we talk too much of the public interest, that we shall engender a 'public utilities' view of the state. We need to leave ourselves room to recognize shared ideals, and should not be ashamed to talk of the common good. Moreover, although the terminology of interests is useful in political discourse because it enables us to consider people without consulting them, which often, especially in large societies, we cannot do, it is for that very reason dangerous. It seems to make consultation otiose. Often it induces arrogance on the part of rulers. It suggests a too limited view of the nature and aims of government, and readily leads to neglect of individual rights. Interests, because they are substitutes for consultations, are a second-rate currency. To the extent that they can be ascribed vicariously, they lack the authenticity and precision of first-person avowals. We are dealing with values and aspirations at second hand, and are likely therefore to handle them crudely and fumblingly, and can only deal with them at all because there are some people who embrace them in their own persons at first hand. Although there is all the difference between being devoted to your interests and being disloyal, your interests, without qualifications, do not provide a rule whereby I, or anyone but you, can always decide what actually to do. If you are ill I can look after your interests for you, or if you are abroad, or if you are a minor, because these contexts define the sort of considerations by which I should be guided; but I cannot look after all your interests all the time in all respects, without sometimes asking you what you think, and referring to you for decisions on various questions where one interest of yours conflicts with another. The concept of the public interest is similarly dependent on first-personal espousal. Although I can adduce arguments based on the public interest without actually asking the public their views, I cannot operate the concept in a complete vacuum, but must on some occasions by some means communicate with people, and discover from their first-hand avowals what their views and values actually are.

Different communities may exist to realize different values, and states too may be based on a variety of values. But states are necessarily concerned with justice and freedom, and to that extent are restricted in the decisions they may take. In ancient Athens there was a proposal to put to death the generals who, after winning the battle of Arginusae, failed to rescue the shipwrecked survivors. It so happened that Socrates was in the chair on the day of the debate, and he refused to put the proposal to the vote as being unlawful: a man could be condemned only after proper judicial trial. Whereupon there was a great uproar, and it was said to be a terrible thing if anyone prevented the people from doing whatever they wanted. But Socrates was right. There are things that the people·should be prevented from doing. Our most fundamental objection to Rousseau's democracy is that it is totalitarian, whereas we are constitutionalists and believe that not everything the state decides is right. If, for example, the government pushed a bill through the Houses of Parliament for the summary execution of all women whose names began with Mac and then forced the Queen to give it the royal assent, there is no doubt that it would be valid statute law, but none the less wrong for that. The voice of the people is not the voice of God.

Although we can thus contrast the ideals of justice and freedom with that of democracy, from another perspective they are complementary, and indeed almost constitutive of it. Decisions may be taken democratically not only in virtue of who takes them but of how they are taken and in what frame of mind. A democratic decision is one taken after full and fair discussion in which all sides of the question are examined and everyone with anything to contribute has been allowed to have his say. And again, a decision is arrived at democratically if those taking it have taken into account what has been said and are trying to reach a reasonable consensus with which everyone can agree. Socrates was not only right to insist on the proper procedure, but thereby showed himself to be a truer democrat than the mob orators opposing him. And in our large communities in which it can hardly ever be strictly said of any decision that it was taken *by* the people, we are inclined to apply the word 'democratic' on account of the way decisions are reached and the temper of those who take them. Even in the original sense of the word, where it is always possible that the people will decide to act contrary to the canons of justice and freedom, there is none the less a natural congruity. For, as we saw in chapters two and five, actions are not necessarily *performed* by persons but often merely *owned*. And, in particular, people will acknowledge as their action not only what they actually did but what they approved of or would have approved of had they thought about it. In the nature of the case very few decisions could really be taken by more or less everybody, but many can be regarded as being more or less everybody's because they flow from decisions that have been so taken, or because they have been taken in everybody's name, or at least because more or less everybody sustains them with general support and approbation. For this to happen the decisions must be taken in such a manner and spirit that nobody need disown them. Without going into the rights and wrongs of the case, we are prepared to accept responsibility for decisions that have been taken after proper discussion and with due consideration for the interests involved and opinions expressed, and reckon that they are fair enough and acknowledge them as ours. But we rapidly repudiate decisions that are illiberal or unfair, not only when we are at the receiving end but quite generally, and regard them not as our decisions but 'Theirs'. The ideals of justice and freedom are thus not only inherent in the concept of the state but also crucial to our being able generally to identify with the decisions taken by the state. We can scarcely be said to participate in decisions merely on the grounds that they have been reached in conformity to the canons of justice and freedom, but we are willing to acknowledge them as ours on these grounds alone. Only thus in a large modern state can the bulk of the decisions be deemed democratic in the original sense of the

word. And the more the decision-procedures conform to the requirements of justice and freedom, the more there will be opportunities for participation, in a substantial sense, by the people
concerned.

Justice and freedom are both concerned with the individual, but
in different ways. Freedom addresses itself to the question *Who
shall take the decisions?* and answers 'The person most concerned',
whereas considerations of justice apply not to the question of *who*
should take the decisions but to *how* they should be taken and *in
what frame of mind*. The definitions of justice given by Justinian
and Aquinas – a long-term steady determination to give each man
his due – attempt to characterize the frame of mind; the practice
of lawyers has been more concerned with the procedure: they
insist that both sides of the case be heard, and that decisions
against anybody's central interests – deprivation of life, liberty or
property by way of punishment – be reached only in virtue of
some definite laws being clearly applicable by reason of indubitable proof from firm evidence. In reaching decisions there should
be a certain dispassionate tenderness towards individuals. Decisions contrary to the interests of members of the community shall
not be taken unless ... How we fill out the 'unless ...' depends
on the sort of decision being taken and the sort of objection being
made. For an issue of justice to arise, the objection to the decision
has to be based on its adversely affecting some interest, of a more
or less exclusive kind, of some assignable individual or corporate
body.

We can see why we need justice. Each of us has interests of
great concern to himself, but not normally or naturally of great
concern to other people. A few may sympathize if they hear that
my life or my job is in jeopardy, but they will not bestir themselves very much. And therefore, in the absence of special pro-
visions to the contrary, interests of exclusive or primary concern
only to isolated individuals, however much they mean to the
persons concerned, will be swamped by public indifference. But,
since we all are vulnerable, we all understand the danger. Since
each man's interests are important, some vitally important, to
him, and since interests are what each man can assume other men
to have, we have good grounds for a rational sympathetic concern

with the interests of each. It is useful once again to think in terms of the theory of games – although this should be seen not as an account of how we actually reason, but rather as a rational reconstruction which will illuminate some features of our thought – and to see our concern with justice as a 'coalition' formed by every player to preserve his own private interests against the casual unconcern of others. Unless we all set great store by justice the time may come when one of my important interests is damaged or endangered, and everyone else will pass by on the other side. Just because you are not by nature sufficiently interested in my life or liberty for it to be safe for me to leave it to you to make sure I am not deprived of either by inadvertence or malice on the part of the authorities, I feel I must exert myself to make sure that they are safe. And because I care much more about my life and liberty than about almost anything else, and you about yours similarly, I make an alliance, so to speak, with you and with everybody else, whereby I forgo the convenience of not having to bother if you or anybody else are unjustly imprisoned or unjustly done to death, in return for everyone's being equally eager on my behalf. A coalition is the means whereby a number of interests, each of passionate concern to only a minority, can prevail over a majority hostile or indifferent to each. In our present culture we almost instinctively coalesce to ensure that the life and liberty of each of us is given the protection of judicial process. We identify with other men, which is easy to do since we all have an idea of what life or liberty means to a man, and we are wise in so doing, because we all are better off if nobody is unjustly treated, even though it may cost us a certain amount in blood-pressure or effort in making other men's interests a matter of common concern.

The argument from the theory of games constitutes a cogent, but not the only cogent, argument why we must be concerned with justice. It underlies one version of the contract theory of the state, in which each individual makes a bargain with every other individual to make common cause in securing just treatment for everyone. In another version the contract is not between each individual and every other individual but between each individual and the state. The metaphor of a contract is not very helpful here, but expresses an underlying concern which is important and shows why the state itself must have a special concern for justice. The state has power. It could utterly destroy me, and ride rough-shod over all my interests without a moment's compunction. If I thought that this might happen, I could not identify with it. I might fear it. I might manipulate it. But I could not accept it, or internalize its authority as binding on me. If I am not to regard the state as utterly alien, I must have some security, some reason to believe that my affairs are of concern to those who wield its power, and that they will not treat me with malice or indifference. Justice makes power tolerable to me, and to each one of us indi-vidually, and therefore to us all. But it is also of concern to us not only individually on prudential grounds but collectively out of the respect we all feel we owe to a fellow human being. I am concerned that he shall be justly treated not merely because I fear that it may be my turn next – do I seriously believe that I might wake up tomorrow with a black skin living under South African pass-laws? – but because I have some idea, at least with regard to the more obvious human concerns, of what it must be like to be him. He did not ask to come under the rule of the state any more than I did. He just found himself obliged to acknowledge its authority, exactly as I did, and the fact that he is willy-nilly a member of an unselective community does not mean that he has consented to being merely its plaything. I do not know much about him, but if I recognize him as a human being at all, I must assume that he has certain interests, and if I am to admit him to any sort of fellowship or community, I must insist that we show some reluctance to flout his interests, and if I am to acknowledge him as a member of the same unselective community as I am myself, I must want the community to show him the maximum consideration that is consistent with our potentially having to override his interests, should circumstances warrant it.

Justice does not require that we never harm another man's interests. That would be impossible. Interests conflict, and we have to decide between them. We do not expect the decisions of justice not to be painful. Statues of Justice show her carrying a sword. Contrary to the ideal of Locke, we do not give a man a veto over all decisions affecting him; we do not even give him a vote, only a right to be heard. These two principles of natural justice, that no man should be judge in his own cause and that each party should have a hearing, both stem from our recognizing that men have interests, and our tenderness towards them. Men are partial towards themselves. We know it, and therefore debar a man from decision-making when his own interests are involved; we respect it, and therefore give him every opportunity of showing the decision-makers that right is on his side. Only if, having had the opportunity, he fails to adduce adequate arguments, and, on the contrary, the decision-makers find compelling arguments for overriding his interests, do we think a man is justly deprived of them. Even though, in a world of imperfectly rational men, we cannot rely on an individual's actually agreeing to a decision against his interests, we set ourselves the ideal of showing such great consideration for him that we will take only those decisions that he rationally should accept even if in fact he does not.

We think of justice as being rational, and so it is, but only imperfectly. It needs to be rational, because only so are we justified in harming another man's interests, and only so can we hope to reconcile him to our adverse decision. But often, as elsewhere in practical reasoning, there are weighty arguments on either side, and it is a difficult matter to decide where the balance lies, or to pick on any one as sufficiently compelling to justify deciding against an individual. But we must decide one way or the other. If we are to be able always to reach a decision, and will decide only for cogent reasons, then we must enhance the cogency of some arguments by enshrining them and attributing to them peculiar strength. We therefore use legality – respect for conventions properly promulgated – to eke out justice, remedy its unclarities and ambiguities, and enable it to serve its social purpose of always yielding definitive decisions in disputes. Although we may differ, and there may be no way of resolving our differences, so long as we are considering only the merits of the two sides of the particular case in isolation from everything else, we do not consider only them. Life is not lived in a vacuum, and although it is a requirement of justice that cases should be decided on their merits and not for some extraneous reason, yet the cases are, and

must be, construed in context, and given specific content in the
light of current assumptions and previous decisions. The rule of
precedents, that like cases should be decided alike, not only is a
formal requirement of rationality, but also constitutes a material
supplementation for the decision of individual cases. Having
decided in one case how far different rights extend, we use this as
a yardstick for subsequent cases. Once it is known that we have
struck the balance between one man's right and another's in a
particular way, it defines the right and gives it more specific content for the future. Rights need to be *specified*. We have to specify
how far they extend in the face of conflicting claims by others,
and lay down, in many cases where there is right on both sides,
which shall prevail. People then know where they stand. Within
wide limits any arrangement is just, provided it is clearly understood and freely accepted. Within the range of different arguments from justice, we may agree to give priority to one, and
override others. And this agreement or convention not only
acquires a certain utility but, because it is independent of the
parties to a particular dispute and is publicly ascertainable, has
some of the marks of justice too. Convention, either evolved in
the course of deciding particular cases or explicitly adopted by
legislative process, can specify, and even sometimes constitute,
justice. Many modern thinkers have gone much further and
made out that justice is nothing but convention. That cannot be
true. Some decisions can be seen to be flagrantly unjust without
any appeal to other cases or special enactments. Laws themselves
can be criticized as unjust. And, in deciding how laws, themselves generally unobjectionable, should apply to particular cases,
we are constantly appealing to general considerations of justice.
We should not see legality as supplanting justice, but as supple-
menting it. We need conventions, in questions of justice as well
as elsewhere, because we are imperfectly rational agents operating in conditions of imperfect information. Laws give us the
guidance we need. But not any laws. Some laws could be down
right unjust, and many are less apt than they need be for the job
of specifying how justice is to be achieved. Much as authority
generally is valuable because it gives definition to political action,
but does not itself constitute the political good, and can be

criticized, or even in extreme cases rejected, if it fails to serve the welfare of the community, so legality is valuable as giving practical definition to our ideal of justice, without thereby replacing it. It imports a certain rigidity into the law, and can lead to harshness or unfairness. But the general principle of specifying justice in the form of specific rights is fair enough, and is the only way in which those ideals can be realized in a world of finite and fallible human beings.

Justice at present has been specified too tightly. Our legal system gives great consideration to rather few interests. A man's central interests – his life, liberty and, in previous ages, his property – are chartered, and can be overridden only for very good reasons indeed, established beyond reasonable doubt after stringent trial in which he has had every opportunity of faulting them. Lawyers have laid it down in black and white exactly what are and what are not adequately compelling reasons for harming a man's chartered interests. And for the sake of greater definiteness, the rules of procedure have been stylized, and the slightest defect in procedure is liable to vitiate the decision altogether. Such rigid restrictions are in place when the chartered interests of the individual are in jeopardy, but not when less central interests are involved. The pity of it is that, through their insistence on strict legality, lawyers have been led to confine their attention to an unnecessarily limited range of interests, and to regard all the others, since they could not be strictly defined or defended, as not being justiciable at all. It is good that central interests should be given very full protection. The ordinary citizen goes about his daily business with no apprehension that he might be killed or injured by anybody; nor need he fear that he might be imprisoned by a commissar, or 'invited to make a contribution to party funds'. At one time in Britain and America property was regarded as sacrosanct along with life and liberty. Such a concern with property can properly be criticized as being too restrictive – it is a central interest of landlords and *rentiers*, but not of the landless labourers who depend for their livelihood not on rents or dividends but employment; but the result of contemporary criticism has been to make our concern with other men's interests more restrictive still, and we are now too happily unconcerned with the subject's defence against expropriation by the state. The most spectacular cases are where the state, following the example of Ahab, covets not merely Naboth's vineyard but his house also as a suitable site for an airport or a road, and believes that nothing should stand in the way of its imperious will. Other cases abound. Few taxpayers realize that if the Inland Revenue make a mistake and say that the taxpayer has not paid his taxes when he has, they are entitled to seize his goods, and auction them, and the fact that he has already paid gives him no redress whatever. So far as the law is concerned, we hold our homes and goods at the pleasure of the Department of the Environment and the Inland Revenue, and it would be a bold man who believed that neither of these institutions ever made a mistake. Nor are our contacts with the state limited to money matters. Most people at one time or another are ill, and need to make use of the National Health Service. Most people were young once, and needed to be educated. Most people will be old sooner or later, and will need some sort of care. In these and many other ways we have interests with regard to the state, and to other institutions and other people; but we have not given these interests any adequate protection. A man may be refused a passport, a driving licence, a telephone, a supply of electricity, or, until recently, deprived of a job at the whim of his employer without any redress. Clearly, to lose one's job is not as bad as to lose one's head – one can always hope to get another job – and people in Britain are in a much better position now than they were in the reign of King Henry VIII or than they are in many places abroad today. Nevertheless, the current orthodoxy which distinguishes a few chartered interests, which are defended by law, from all the rest which must be defended, if at all, by individual enterprise or political activity, gives rise both to a lot of injustice and to a diffused sense of impotence and of being of no importance to the powers-that-be.

Rather than define justice, as the lawyers do, in terms of procedures, we need to go back to the more fundamental insights of Justinian and Aquinas, and speak of justice as being a frame of mind. In reaching decisions we should be generally reluctant to harm the interests of others. Generally, but not always. Sometimes the structure of the situation precludes the consideration of certain interests. If I am competing against you in a game or for a prize or a job, my only duty is to play fair, and the fact that my success can only be at the cost of your failure is no reason for me to hold back. Or again, if I am going on holiday or choosing a tie, I am under no obligation to consider the interests of hotel-keepers in different resorts or of the different manufacturers of different sorts of tie. Other interests are too peripheral or too remotely affected to warrant serious consideration. But such special cases apart, I am under some obligation to think twice before hurting anyone's interests. This obligation is often speci-fied as a duty of giving anyone whose interests are in jeopardy a right of making representations on his own behalf before an adverse decision is reached. But in some cases my duty is to con-sider, rather than to hear, him. In appointing to a job or award-ing a prize, I do not have to invite the candidates to argue their candidature, but I should be unjust if I did not give some thought myself to their merits. That consideration, rather than any pro-cedural principle, is the underlying requirement, was shown by our sense of affront when the Minister of Town and Country Planning once at Stevenage told objectors to his proposals that they could say what they liked at the public inquiry, but his mind was already made up. He was flouting this, most fundamental principle of justice. The right to be heard carries with it some right to be heeded. Procedures are valuable in as much as they guide decision-makers' thinking, and prevent the official mind from setting hard until it has considered all the relevant factors; but they are vain unless some notice is taken of the points made. How much notice should be taken depends on the interest in jeopardy, the other considerations bearing on the question, and the structure of the case. In addition to his life, liberty and prop-erty, a man has an interest in his livelihood, his prospects, his pension, his reputation, his neighbourhood, his environment, in having a licence to drive, a passport to go abroad, in having a telephone, a supply of electricity and gas, in being able to ob-tain credit, help and advice, and in innumerable other ways. These interests do not all need the elaborate safeguards that pro-tect life and liberty. When it is only an electricity supply that is in jeopardy, we do not need to treble check and require that all evidence be given on oath and subjected to cross-examination; but still we should take care, and not lightly disconnect a man, claiming that we are entitled to whenever we feel like it. We should not only give notice, but if he claims that he has paid the bill and we think he has not, find out the truth before going further. We need less evidence and less indubitable proofs than in criminal cases, but that is not to say we do not need any at all. Before cutting a man off, we need, if not to treble check, at least to double check. We need to make sure that there are no mistakes on our part, and that his interests are not being needlessly sacrificed to our convenience or incompetence. It is the double check, the thinking twice, that distinguishes the judicial frame of mind from that of other decision-makers. They also think before acting, and if they reach a decision – to disconnect a supply or refuse a licence – on false assumptions, they are guilty of maladministration. If, however, they are to decide judicially, they must do more than avoid maladministration. They must have paused before reaching a decision adverse to anyone's interest, and considered whether they had to reach that decision, or whether there was any alternative open to them. They must be reluctant to reach an adverse decision, and decline to do so if the facts are not adequately established or could be differently construed; and many reasons which would weigh with others, and would certainly suffice to ward off any charge of maladministration, will still not weigh enough with them to override important interests of the citizen. Not that these interests can never be overridden. Other considerations may be important. In keeping a man in a job, one must have regard not to his interests only, but to the needs of the job and the interests of his fellow-workers and of consumers. We must not seek to impose on decision-makers in the name of justice too great a tenderness towards men's interests, or we shall once again encourage them to make out that their decisions do not involve issues of justice at all. For a long time contracts of employment were such as to exclude them, and government officials still argue that their decisions are administrative, and hence, they allege, not judicial at all. It is a false antithesis. A decision may be both, and most government decisions ought to be both. Governments, because they have greater power than any other bodies, ought to show greater tenderness towards individual interests. They must not merely express regret when public expediency demands that somebody's interests be sacrificed – that will seem to the victim mere crocodile tears – but must make manifest a settled determination to give full and effective consideration to the interests of individuals, and to shape their policies in conformity with the canons of justice.

Justice engenders one form of participation. Although, as we have seen, it is not always specified in the procedural principle that those whose interests may be affected have a right to be heard, it commonly is. Only by giving a chap the chance to challenge the case against him do we manifest a real reluctance actually to decide against him. Hence, as we shall see in the next chapter, it is on justice that one of the best and most insistent arguments for participation is based. Often, in practice, these arguments shade into ones based on an appeal to freedom. This is because many of the more peripheral interests of an individual are difficult to identify or characterize under an exclusive description. Even at the extreme, however, where a man is simply interested in politics, and has some opinions of his own on public affairs, issues of justice arise, which have a bearing on how decisions should be reached and in what frame of mind we should take them. We owe it to each man as an individual to respect his right to think for himself. We should be doing him an injustice, as well as denying him political liberty, if we forbade him to ventilate any views on politics, or systematically and invariably shut our ears to them. Our concern for the rights of minorities is founded partly on the principle of justice, and we import this concern into our understanding of the word 'democratic', which requires not only that the people shall decide, but that they shall do so only subject to certain procedural safeguards and only in a certain frame of mind. We do not regard it as democratic if a proposal is put forward and carried at once without an adequate opportunity of opposing it or a fair hearing being given to the arguments against it: that is to say, we attach greater importance to the proceedings being parliamentary than to there being an impressive majority revealed in the poll. If it were just simply a matter of voting, there would be no need to safeguard the rights of minorities: the decision would be everything, and if the majority wanted something then they should not be obliged to hear tedious speeches urging the opposite. But we think we owe it to our fellow members to listen to their views even if we do not ultimately agree with them. If I am never allowed to voice my preference for the Eastgate, but am simply told that the vote is for the Bear, then I am not a full member of the group, but only a satellite, who is allowed to tag along if he likes, but is not given any real say in what is going to be done. The difference between being in a minority and being merely a satellite is that a serious attempt has been made to be of one mind with a minority, whereas a satellite is an outsider all along. The attempt to reach agreement is serious in as much as in argument there is a real give and take, and we really attempt to persuade potential dissentients of the wisdom of our proposals, and really lay ourselves open to be persuaded by them of the cogency of their objections. In as much as the attempt to reach agreement was serious, the underlying unity of purpose and sentiment will be greater than any division of opinion revealed in a vote. And where, as often, many members approach a question not with an open mind but with prejudices, they still manifest respect for the opposition point of view by allowing it to be put, and listening to it with such patience as they can muster. Communal decision-making is not like choosing a new hat. We are not just concerned with discovering what we happen to fancy, but are under a duty to act responsibly; and in particular, to give to the decision-makers our real reasons for putting forward proposals, and to provide proper opportunity for opponents to declare their opposition, and in due course to adduce their arguments. Unless we do this, we are failing in responsibility and in responsiveness. We are failing in responsibility because we are presuming to decide without letting our case run the gauntlet of argument, and it is in the nature of argument about action that it does not in general admit of clear-cut decision-procedures, and that we cannot be sure in advance that we have sewn up the argument so completely that there is no possibility of second thoughts being required. We are also failing in responsiveness, because we are acting as though our fellow members did not have minds of their own, and their opinions were of no value and had no chance of being right. And not to give each man due attention is not to give him his due.

In the Middle Ages justice was the great political virtue, and it was held that if only monarchs would be just, all would be well with their realms. Now, however, we not only attach an independent value to freedom, but realize that not all decision-making can be guided by the canons of justice alone, because not all practical questions admit of answers that are definitely right or definitely wrong. In order to make questions justiciable, we have to structure them rather carefully. We have to specify and define rights and duties, and supplement the intimations of natural reason by custom and convention, precedent and enactment. Many political questions, therefore, cannot be settled without artifice by appeal to justice alone. However fully we specify justice, we cannot charter all interests or identify all those men who may feel themselves affected and ought to have some opportunity of expressing an opinion. A man may be interested in gaining promotion, but equally he may not; whereas he must be interested in preserving his life or health. A man may have a dislike of the Common Market, but it does not stand to reason that he should; whereas it does stand to reason that he should have a dislike of imprisonement. We cannot know whether a man is deeply concerned, or indeed whether he is concerned at all, except by asking him, and more weight therefore has to be given to the fact that he expresses an interest, and correspondingly less to argument about the merits of the case. Justice is no respecter of persons, but freedom is. Justice requires us to be impersonally tender towards all parties alike, reaching an adverse decision only for good reason based upon the relevant circumstances of the situation, and the fact that somebody wants to have the decision go one way rather than another is not a relevant fact for justice, whereas for freedom it is.

There is some opposition between the ideals of justice and freedom, but not an absolute one. It is not an absolute one, because freedom is more about who shall take decisions while justice is about how, and in what frame of mind, they should be taken. Freedom and justice can be combined, if the decisions are made by those immediately concerned, as required by freedom, and if they make the decisions in the right manner and in the right frame of mind, as required by justice. If I make my will, it is an exercise of freedom, because under English law it is I who am entitled to dispose of my worldly goods on my death; but it may be an exercise of justice too, if I give careful consideration to the claims of my relatives, my friends and my good causes, and attempt to assign to each what seems right in view of his relationship to me, his likely needs, my debts of gratitude, and the good use to which the money would be put. Nevertheless, there is some opposition. The emphasis of freedom is on my un-fettered choice, whereas justice is concerned to lay down guide-lines, which often must seem to be fetters on free choice. In so far as men are rational agents, we may hope that each individual, when entrusted with making a decision, will do so in the right manner and in the right frame of mind. We may hope, but can-not count on it. And when, as often, men fail freely to decide in accordance with the canons of justice, then if our concern is for freedom, we shall allow the unjust decisions to stand, whereas if it is for justice, we shall be willing to abridge the freedom of the decision-maker in order that the right decision may be made. If Chloe unjustly rejects your suit, and refuses to come to a Com-men with you after having said she would, you have no remedy. Fancy is often unfair, but must be free. So too, if I choose to spend my pocket money on fish-hooks instead of aniseed balls, or choose to go to a theatre instead of a concert, or buy a hat rather than a dress. Considerations of justice barely arise, because we think it important that people please themselves, since it is only by often so doing that they can discover themselves and learn what it is to be authentic. Justice, although important, is not enough. It manifests concern for the individual, but is too im-personal to give scope for the full development of the personality. If individuals are to fulfil themselves as individuals, they need freedom. And freedom, as much as justice, is an ideal to which the state is necessarily to some extent committed.

Freedom is a great ideal, but an elusive one. It is of central importance because we are autonomous agents, who have values we want to translate into action, both individual and corporate.

Freedom is a necessary condition of moral activity, and indeed of being a rational agent. Only if the state has some concern for the freedom of its subjects can they be expected to identify with the state or feel beholden to obey its edicts; and we impute to the state an obligation to cherish freedom on the same basis as we impute to subjects an obligation to obey the law. We therefore believe that only a free society is a good society, and that it is the function of law and political activity generally to enable people to be as free as possible. But, while we are very sure that freedom is a good thing, especially when we do not have it, we find it very difficult to say exactly what it is, or to give positive examples of when we really feel that we are free. Some thinkers respond to this by concluding that freedom is altogether illusory, others by defining freedom in a certain way and standing pat on that definition. Freedom is defined as the absence of legal restraint, or the absence of arbitrary coercion, and these are maintained as good things which no society ought to be without. Such an approach has the merit of focusing attention on a few fundamental freedoms, and making sure that, whatever else we say, we never fail to emphasize the pre-eminent importance of these fundamental forms of freedom. But it has the corresponding demerit of imposing a definitional stop where further discussion is needed, and failing to elucidate all the uses of the word, and therefore failing to accommodate all the aspirations which men may legitimately have. There is a danger that the old-time liberal, just because he fails to see what is worrying the modern radical, will fail to communicate with him at all, and so leave him insensitive to the importance of the civil liberties that it was the liberal's glory chiefly to espouse. Civil liberty is an important form of freedom, perhaps the most important one, but not the only one; and if we are to understand freedom fully, we must consider it in all its forms.

Freedom is not a simple quality. When I say that somebody is free, it is not like saying that he is white, or healthy, or weighs fifteen stone. The statement needs to be filled out, indicating either *what* he is free *to do* or *what* he is free *from*. These two basic senses, *freedom to* and *freedom from*, are interrelated; and in particular, if we can elucidate the different meanings of *free-*

dom to, we shall have no difficulty in understanding the different sorts of *freedom from*. *Freedom to* needs to be filled out by a verb of doing. And often it will depend upon the particular action or activity in question, what sort of freedom is being looked for. My freedom to come to tea with you today is a very different sort of freedom from my freedom to stand for Parliament, my freedom to marry whom I please, my freedom to lead a moral life, or my freedom to achieve some state of final felicity. But although these freedoms are very different, they are not totally different. What is common to each case is that the question of freedom is antecedent to the question of choice. If I am not free to do something, then there is no point in asking me to do it, or adducing reasons why I should. If I have told you that I am not free to come to tea this afternoon, then there is no point in your inviting me; and if I am not free to make up my mind about what I ought to do, then there is no point in your giving me advice or moral exhortation. Being free to do something is thus somewhat like being able to do it, but with a greater emphasis on the first-personal point of view. If I am free to do something, then I can consider whether or not to do it, and it is up to me whether I actually do or not; and if I am not free to do something, then further discussion is pointless, and deliberation is ruled out from the start. Different proposed courses of action can be ruled out for different reasons. My reasons for not coming to tea with you this afternoon may be very different from my reasons for not burning smoky fuel, or from my reasons for not insulting the American flag, or from my reasons for not joining the Congregational Church. But in each case, if there are reasons which, in my view, are quite conclusive, then the question of whether or not to undertake the action is ruled out of court, and I report the fact that it is not a serious option open to me by saying simply that I am not free to do it. If I am not free to do something, then you can ask me why, and I must give some conclusive reasons, which will not need further discussion; if I am free, then I must be prepared to consider it, and it is reasonable for you to argue or plead with me to do it.

Freedom is often confused with ability. Particularly when economic freedom is under discussion, people are liable to feel them-

selves unfree if they are not able to have everything they want.
But even though I were legally or economically free to be a
Member of Parliament or marry the girl of my choice, I might
be unable to, because no party would adopt me or because the
girl would not have me. In such a case we should say that I
could not get into Parliament, or could not win the girl's heart,
not that I was not free to. Freedom is concerned with internalized
reasons against doing something, not external obstacles to success.
If I am not free to do something, then I am not saying that if I
tried I should not succeed, but that it is in some sense out of the
question for me even to try.

Freedom to can thus be elucidated in terms of conclusive
reasons against. Such overwhelming reasons have a modal logic.
They indicate what I *must not* do, what it is *necessary* for me *not*
to do, or what it is, within the context of discourse, *impossible*
for me to do. We are familiar with the idea of there being different sorts of necessity, possibility and impossibility. We distinguish logical necessity from physical necessity, and both from
social necessity and moral necessity. We say that the concepts of
necessity, possibility and impossibility are systematically ambiguous, and that the same internal logic between the three
modalities of necessity, possibility and impossibility holds in a
number of different universes of discourse, where different
sorts of modality, logical, physical, social, or moral, are being
discussed. The same holds good for freedom. Freedom is systematically ambiguous, because there are different sorts of reason,
and therefore different sorts of conclusive reason, against undertaking different actions. I am legally and socially free to come
to tea with you this afternoon, because there is no law against it
nor any sense of social impropriety, but I am not morally free
because I had already promised to go to tea with Matilda in
L.M.H., and I ought not to let her down. Or alternatively, I may
be morally free, in the sense that I have no moral obligation not
to, but I still am not free to accept your invitation, because I
want to get on with some work; I want to spend the whole afternoon in the Bodleian, and not break off in the middle to make my
way to Worcester.

Freedom to needs to be filled out by some definite verb before it becomes definite itself. Whether or not I am free to do something depends on what the something is, so that we know what could constitute conclusive reasons against doing it. *Freedom from*, by contrast, is less specific. We know what it is to be free from pain, free from financial worry, free from committee work, for these are things which will stop a man from being able to decide to do anything. They are very generalized reasons against doing most of the things a man might want to do, largely because a man will devote most of his efforts to warding off or alleviating these evils, and so will be precluded from embarking on any other enterprises. Only if I am free from certain ills am I free to undertake any of a wide range of activities. This is why we use the same word. The common strand of meaning is the absence of conclusive reasons against; in the one case, reasons against that are specific to the action in question, in the other, reasons of a general sort that would rule out not just one proposal but almost any.

We can now sketch different types of freedom. The freedom of the will is contrasted with various doctrines about man or about time which say that our actions are determined by factors outside our control so that there is no point in our deliberating on what we ought to do. If physical determinism is true, then there is some antecedent state-description of the universe from which follows, in virtue of the laws of nature, what is going to happen in the future, and there is nothing I can do about it. If fatalism is true, then the future cannot but be what it will be, and is for this reason already fixed. If either of these or any other form of determinism is true, then we have no real freedom of the will, because even though we may think we are making up our minds what we shall do, it does not really depend on us or what we decide, but rather what we decide is itself determined by other factors apart from us, and outside our control. To say that the will is free is to deny that there are overwhelming reasons why things must happen in a particular way which leaves no room for our own decisions to alter the course of events, and makes it pointless for us to consider what we ought to do.

Legal freedom is contrasted with what I legally must not do. I must not do anything forbidden by a law, nor may I contravene a particular order made by an officer authorized to issue it. I am not legally free to commit murder, rape, or perjury, and if you turn me out of your house, I am not legally free to remain. Our exact conception of legal freedom will depend on our exact conception of law, and different men have different understandings of the law. For some men, law shades into morality, and in that case legal freedom will shade into moral freedom. For the most part, however, we draw a contrast between law and morality, and take it as characteristic of law that it should be external and specific; in which case it would seem reasonable to say that I am not legally free only if the reason against doing the action in question has been articulated in words, either as general law, recognized to be valid, or as a particular instruction from some person whose legal authority in this matter we accept. Law is exceptionally clear-cut, social considerations much less so, and moral considerations less so still.

There is no reason why the rules need have been articulated in some definite principle or instruction, nor, in the case of morals, is there any sense that the authority should be external. Often we find it very difficult to formulate the reasons for which we feel reluctant to envisage some proposed course of action: we have a vague sense of its running counter to some of our moral obligations, but we cannot spell them out in detail, and often simply say 'I don't feel free to do it.' Many of our practical unfreedoms are similarly vague. When I say that I am not free to go on a punting holiday with you next vac or that I am not free to give a course of lectures on probability next term, or that I am not free to take a couple of pupils for you next year, I do not mean either that there is some rule against it or that it would be morally wrong, but that, on balance, in view of my other commitments and the other plans I have already made and the other goals I have set myself, I cannot do this as well. I have not time for it in addition to the other things I have already decided to do. Of course, if I were to go back on those decisions, I could do what you suggest: if I were to be taken ill, and told by my doctor that I must have a break, I might very well be glad to go with you punting on the Upper Thames; or if it became vitally important that I should lecture on probability, or that your pupils should be taught by me, I could scrap my lectures on Plato, or postpone writing my book on Truth. But these unwelcome reappraisals I am reasonably anxious to avoid, and I am entitled to put them out of my mind as practical possibilities when the question of the holiday, the lectures, or the extra pupils, is first canvassed. It is in the nature of decisions that once having been made they need not be continually reconsidered. Having faced various questions about what I shall do and having decided them, I need not, except for some very grave reason, reopen the question. My decision is a datum, a *res judicata*, which itself helps to lay down what further choices are open to me. And where some choices are thus precluded, it is quite correct for me to say that I am no longer free to act in the way proposed.

We can now see why freedom seems illusory, and is elusive. It seems illusory, because there are many different sorts of reason against doing things. 'Everything I like is either illegal, immoral, or fattening.' As soon as one sort of reason against is removed, and we become in that sense free, we discover other reasons, equally cogent, for not doing it. When there is a law against it, we feel we are not free to do it *because* there is a *law* against it, but when the law is abrogated, and we are legally free to do it, we find we still cannot do it, this time because we have not the money to pay for it. So we say that legal freedom is not enough, and what we really need is economic freedom. But, as the rich down the ages have discovered to their cost, money is not enough either. Even if I am legally free to do it and am rich enough to be economically free to do it, I still may find myself not doing it for other, equally weighty, reasons. I may not have enough time, or enough patience, or enough aptitude. I may be legally free to stand for Parliament or marry the girl of my choice, and rich enough to afford it, but still feel myself not to be really free to stand for Parliament or to ask the girl to marry me, because I feel that what I really ought to be doing is to be a monk, or to explore the Amazon, or at any rate not to be fettered by ties of domesticity or party politics. And so it goes on. As we remove one set of conclusive reasons why a particular course of action cannot be taken, we often only succeed in making other reasons the conclusive ones. And if we remove those, yet others will emerge which still will appear to us overwhelmingly cogent against our actually doing it. Of course, this is not always necessarily so. We do succeed sometimes in finding things to do without there being any overwhelming reasons against. Nevertheless, since we are finite beings, with only limited capacities and only limited time, our ambition is always likely to outrun our actual achievement, and there are going to be many things we would like to do but cannot. And when, as often, we are asked to do something we cannot do, it is natural, both out of mental laziness and from considerations of politeness, to give the most immediately accessible and telling reasons for not giving it further consideration. It is easy and final to dismiss various proposals as being illegal, or out of the question financially, even though, if the truth were known, we would not consider doing them, however legal they were or however rich we were. And we do this not only in argument with others, but in internal dialogue with ourselves. Instead of telling myself that I do not want to go to Bermuda, because I should be horribly bored if I had nothing to do all day but laze, I just simply say to myself that I cannot afford it, and put it out of my mind. And with the passage of time I may come to think that the most obvious reason why I cannot do something which most people regard as desirable is because I am, in some sense, not free to do it, and may even blame currency restrictions or my own lack of wealth. And this phenomenon, generalized over a whole society, often leads us to embark upon a perpetual quest for freedom, which is perpetually eluding our grasp, just as we thought we had attained it. The case is worse when the time interval spans the generations. The fathers, who fought for some simple fundamental freedoms, such as freedom of worship or freedom of speech, may remember how terrible it was to live in their absence, and be correspondingly thankful that they have at least those freedoms, even if they have not many others. But the children never knew what it was to be unable to go to church, or unable to express or publish opinions, and are not correspondingly glad that there are no legal reasons against their doing these things. What they are conscious of are other reasons against their doing either these or other things. They will feel that they are too ill-dressed to be free to go to church, or that there are overwhelming social pressures against expressing unfashionable views. They will feel no sense of liberation, only a continuing sense of restriction and restraint. So, too, the immigrants to the United States found the Statue of Liberty a real symbol, and savoured the freedom they found there in contrast to the tyranny they had left behind in Europe: but their grandchildren no longer feel that America is the land of the free, not because the constitutional freedoms of American citizens have since been abrogated, but because they are conscious of other overwhelming reasons why they cannot do what they want to do. And, of course, there are. And they may be bad. But we cannot ever be totally free. By the mere fact of taking decisions and making plans and adopting goals, we are to that extent foreclosing the future, and making ourselves not free to do various other things we might have done. We shall never be entirely free. But this does not mean either that the freedoms we have are no good at all, or that we should simply be content with those that we already have, and never feel free to yearn for more.

Freedom, like justice, needs to be *specified*. Not only do we need to know what we are free to do, but in what way we may do it. I am free to wave my arms about – but not so as to hit you, or confuse the driver of a bus. I am free to go where I please – but not through your front door. I am free to say what I like – but not in front of an angry mob, inciting them to violence. When we confer a freedom we do not normally grant an absolute licence to perform the action irrespective of all other considerations. Rather, we say that there is no prohibition on the action *as such*, and often supplement this by imposing on other men various duties of not preventing a person from performing the action in any reasonable way. The more important the freedom, the more ways there are of exercising it, and the greater the weight laid on others not to interfere with one's exercise of it. But always there are some limitations. I am free to marry. The law protects this freedom very carefully. But if I want to get married, I have to do so in a certain way – I have to get my banns called, and can be married only at certain times and in certain places. My freedom to get married is specified in this way. It is largely by carefully specifying different freedoms, that the freedom of one man to do one thing is made compatible with the freedom of another man to do another thing.

The same analysis applies to political freedom. We need to know what political action a person has in mind before we can say whether he possesses the relevant freedom, and there is the same systematic elusiveness, in that as one obstacle is overcome, another, equally insurmountable, is likely to be observed. The fundamental concern of political freedom is with the communal actions of a community, although the means towards influencing communal actions will be individual actions on the part of those interested, and for the most part it will be these individual actions that may be prohibited if political freedom is absent, or facilitated if it is cherished. In some societies the rulers may not countenance outsiders entertaining any views about what the community should do. 'It is none of your business,' Stalin might say to a lorry-driver from Novogorod, 'to think well of the Western powers or to criticize my five-year plan, and if you presume to think on matters that are too high for you, I shall send you to Siberia for the next fifteen years.' Oriental despots have often taken the view that theirs alone is the right to hold views about public affairs; but that view is always subject to the erosion of practical necessity. Public affairs are necessarily concerned with what members of the public are to do, and what members of the public are to do depends essentially on what they can do and what they have done. The fact that there is no straw is highly relevant to Pharaoh's brick-producing programme, and if Pharaoh refuses to allow his subjects to tell him that the straw supplies are inadequate his future building plans are likely to come unstuck. Hitler and Stalin did not like being gainsaid and therefore their subjects feared to inform them of unpalatable facts, and their plans, based on false information, ultimately went awry. No government can impose a complete blanket of unconcern about public affairs on its subjects, for its very *raison d'être* is that it should make their concerns its concerns, so that they must be concerned with some of the things it does. I recognize the government as the body I can turn to for defence against public enemies and criminals, and for resolution of disputes I may have with my neighbour. If I cannot ask the government to intervene on my behalf or if it will not be bothered with me at all, and regards it as presumptuous for me to indicate to it what I think it ought to do, then I shall cease to regard it as my government at all, and think of it instead as an alien force with which communication is impossible, which may be taken into account or circumvented, but which cannot be negotiated with. To deny to subjects every sort of political freedom is thus incompatible with the purpose of government, and there is a constant pressure on rulers, from the very nature of government, to allow their subjects greater freedom of holding and expressing opinions, in order the better to secure their sources of information.

Even though rulers cannot afford to deny every form of political freedom to their subjects, they are not obliged to confer on them a legal right to hold opinions in general about public affairs. It is only communities which set a high value on the individual that are prepared to forgo the possibility of making it illegal to express at least some opinions. Even in Britain a convinced racialist could be prosecuted for expressing his sincerely held opinion, while in the United States, although in view of the First Amendment, a man may not be prosecuted for *believing* Marxist doctrines, he may be convicted for being a *member* of the Communist Party. These cases, however, are exceptions, and require exceptional justification. People are not prosecuted for holding views when it is none of their business to hold views, but because of evident dangers to either the ethos or the fabric of society which are expected to follow from the expression or the implementation of certain political views. It is clear that some such justification could be pleaded, speciously, for proscribing a large range of political opinions, since every form of criticism is inherently liable to erode unity of communal purpose, and in times of totalitarian enthusiasm people's courts or committees of public safety do not scruple to use such arguments for eliminating any hint of opposition. Lovers of liberty are therefore inclined to seek an absolute, constitutionally entrenched, right of free thought and speech, about political matters as well as everything else. It is difficult to accept the conclusion in its entirety, although we should sympathize with the argument. Every community depends on its members sharing values, some so central that they may not be gainsaid: treason must be a crime, and seditious libel illegal. Nevertheless, it is the mark of a free society to be extremely chary of having a law against the holding or expressing of any particular opinion about public affairs *per se*. The fact that a man wishes to see a certain communal decision taken ought not in itself to be sufficient reason for punishing him, and where it seems necessary to abridge freedom of speech in special circumstances, the restrictions should be narrowly drawn, and the subject left free to express himself in other, less objectionable, ways. If it is seditious libel to hand out pamphlets to soldiers alleging that their officers are corrupt, it should still be possible to test the truth in Parliament or the courts of law, and if it is a crime to belong to an organization advocating the overthrow of the American Constitution by force, it should still be lawful to advocate the same changes by constitutional means.

The minimal sense of political freedom is that there is no law against the subject engaging in political activity, that is to say, courses of action designed to influence communal decisions. But, as in the case of civil liberties, an absence of prohibition, although important, is not enough to secure an effective freedom. The fact that there is no law forbidding me to go to London is something that, had I been brought up under an alien regime, I might well be thankful for; but it would not make me really free unless there were other laws imposing on other people the duty of not obstructing me on my journey. If I am to have freedom of movement, not only must there be no law against my moving as such, but there must be other laws forbidding other people from incarcerating me in their private prisons, or from blocking my passage on the Queen's highway. Such supporting laws prevent me from being prevented absolutely from carrying out my plans. But – and it is important to stress this – they do not secure to me an unfettered right of achieving my aims any way I please. I can go to London, but not through your back garden. If I try that, I have no right of way, and you are entitled to stop me. Even on the Queen's highway, my wishing to go to London at 70 m.p.h. does not entitle me to run you down if you are going at 40 m.p.h. and are in my way. You must not try to stop me altogether from going to London, but you are not obliged to help me in every way possible. The same holds good of political freedom. It is not enough that there should be no law against political activity, though Russians would be grateful even for that; if people are to be effectively free to engage in political activity, we shall need supplementary laws, imposing on others the duty, if not of actively assisting them, at least of not positively precluding their efforts from ever achieving success. An enlightened despot of eighteenth-century Europe might well have allowed his subjects to entertain political opinions and prided himself on his toleration, without ever thinking it incumbent on himself to pay any attention to any of their views. Political freedom requires not only that a subject may hold opinions of his own and express them, but that he should have some real opportunity to ventilate his views, make common cause with those that are like-minded, and persuade others, who in turn may be able to persuade those to whom the decision is entrusted. Freedom of speech and the right of association are a beginning, but they need to be supplemented by some duty on rulers to listen, and some further provision that arguments and pleas are not only heard but sometimes heeded. Exactly what provision should be made cannot be laid down abstractly; it depends on particular circumstances and special considerations of practicality. It can never be entirely effective. Far more than in the case of individual freedom, conflict, and therefore frustration, is built into the foundations of political freedom. In the case of individual freedom, although my freedom of movement does require your not being free to obstruct me, it does not rule out your being generally free to move too. My being free to go to London is compatible with your being free to come to Oxford. But your freedom to campaign for nuclear disarmament cannot be fully effective alongside my freedom to urge the retention of the nuclear deterrent. We can both be free to try, but cannot both be free to succeed in our avowed aims. Communal action does not admit of division as individual actions do, and therefore admits of fewer easy resolutions. We cannot ever hope to secure that individual initiatives in the realm of communal decision-making will be generally successful. Nevertheless, we may regard them as valuable, and seek to prevent their being as invariably frustrated as they are at present. For we base one of the most fundamental arguments in favour of democracy on its being the best way of securing political freedom; and so only if it succeeds in realizing that ideal will our argument be valid.

8 Participation

Participation has come into vogue. It is on everybody's lips. But, like many vogue words, it is vague. Everybody wants it, but is not at all clear what 'it' is; and would-be participators are often dissatisfied with all attempts to meet their demands. This is not surprising. There is no one thing called participation, which can then be shown to be a good thing. Rather, as with freedom and justice, there are some pervasive considerations, which, in spite of counter-considerations that carry some weight too, establish a certain drift of argument, which we then need to specify in definite procedures and institutions to fit definite circumstances. We cannot lay it down simply, as part of the law of nature, that having the vote is a good thing or having a student assembly with the right to mandate its officers is a good thing, any more than it is part of the law of nature that I should be free to preach with a megaphone on the public highway at night, or that I have a right to compensation if I lose my job. As we saw in the previous chapter, rights have to be defined, so as to strike a balance between conflicting interests, under the guiding considerations of letting people do as they think fit and not trampling on their interests gratuitously. In the same way different participatory procedures may be established to take account of different needs and different circumstances, but in accordance with certain overarching arguments.

Participation can take many forms. Merely to know what decisions are being taken, and why, is to be in on them. In French the word *assister* means not only to help but to be present at, and when public affairs are being decided the two senses merge. But reasoning is typically two-sided. There are arguments against as well as arguments for. I shall not fully understand the reasons why a decision should be taken unless I also consider the reasons against and how they may be countered. If I am to internalize the dialectic of decision-making I need to hear not just the conclusion of the matter but the whole debate. Often other people are better at articulating arguments than I am, and I shall learn more by listening than talking; often, but not absolutely always. Very occasionally they may have overlooked a point which I have spotted, and more commonly it is only when I have formulated the matter myself and found what other people think of it that I fully understand what is at issue. We learn less by listening than by doing exercises for ourselves, and so too we participate more by actively arguing than merely attending a debate. But arguments about politics are, as we saw in chapter two, typically inconclusive. Although decisions are characteristically right or wrong, they are not necessarily right or wrong in view of the arguments adduced. Having heard all the arguments, I may judge differently from other people; hence, merely having taken part in the argument may be less than taking part in the actual decision. And therefore if I am to participate fully I may stake a claim to having a say in the final stages of the decision process. In particular, demands for more and more formalized participatory procedures arise when existing procedures produce unacceptable decisions. It is then that we want to know the reason why, and want the right to be heard so that we can argue back, and it is when good arguments are ignored that we demand not only a voice but a vote. But operating in the contrary direction is a tendency for real power to flow from formal participatory procedures to procedures that are more informal but effective. The more people we bring in on decision-making, the more formal our procedures have to be. We have to have notices of meeting, submission of motions and an order of business. If many people are to have a final say in the decision, it has to be a stylized say, a standard-form answer to a pre-set question. A lot of importance, therefore, attaches to the wording of the question, and this is for the most part decided by informal discussions before the meeting. The larger the meeting the greater the difficulty of amending motions or dealing with points of order in the course of formal business, and the greater the effective power in the hands of those who arrange the agenda and formulate the motions beforehand. A headmaster or a vice-chancellor with a governing body of twelve really has to share power with them: but let it be enlarged to sixty or seventy and it is reduced to docility by sheer weight of numbers. It is, as we shall see in chapters eleven and twelve, a reflection of our being finite and inattentive creatures who have difficulty in communicating with one another about the relevant factors. All forms of participation are subject to the fundamental constraint that the more people there are who have a say in a decision, the more formal and therefore the less real the decision will be. We have to strike a balance, different in different cases, between sharing power among few people effectively, and sharing it with many, but only nominally; and between giving participators only the right to know or only the right to speak at a relatively low cost in cumbersomeness and formality, and giving them a greater say at a much greater cost. Participation is not, as its advocates seem to suppose, all of one piece. It takes different forms, which may be incompatible with one another, and often we object to one particular form on the grounds that it precludes, or at least clogs, the type of participation which we really want as being most appropriate to our case. If there is some one form of participation, as with a Co-op or a Student Representative Council or a P.T.A., I can be told by the officials that I cannot complain, because the present arrangements were agreed to by the representatives; I am expected to abide by their concessions, even though they never consulted me, and, maybe, were elected before I came on to the scene. I may do better if I am allowed to represent myself, and make my own representations to the shop, the university or the headmaster. At the least, I can make sure that it is my views that are ventilated; and often the authorities will be willing to negotiate with individuals separately, if they do not have to be always looking over their shoulders at the official participators. Co-ops are not the only, nor uniformly the most successful, kind of shop. Private shops do well just because they are free to take more initiatives to try to suit the individual customer. Similarly I may get much more done by seeing the headmaster alone than by taking up time at a P.T.A. meeting. And student representation has notoriously failed to satisfy dissatisfied students, who feel cheated whenever, as sometimes, somebody else, claiming to speak on their behalf, settles for anything less than the whole cake. There are occasions when we are prepared to be represented by somebody else and allow him to make compromises and enter into bargains on our behalf; but we are not always so minded, and often want to conduct our own negotiations ourselves, or at least be free to hold our own opinions uncontaminated by other men's concessions. No form of participation is wholly satisfactory. There are always disadvantages as well as advantages. It is characteristic of participation that the case for it is only partial, and that the degree to which it should be practised is of necessity only partial too. Indeed, it is inherent in the concept that I should have cause for dissatisfaction. However fully I participate and have a say in deciding what we do, others also participate and also have a say; and my say is only some say and not a complete say, and may on many occasions be gainsaid and overruled by their say. The trouble with participation is that it is essentially incomplete, and the old Adam in me will never be content with less than complete control.

Arguments for participation are grounded in the nature of decision-making, of communities in general and of the state in particular, and its necessary commitment to justice and freedom, and sometimes in an ideal of men being autonomous agents who can affirm their own authenticity only if they decide for themselves what it is they are going to have to do. Arguments against tend to be less fundamental, but not necessarily less weighty, considerations of practicality. In assessing them we often need to view them from the standpoint both of the community as a whole and of the individuals separately. Simply because decision-making is what it is, participation may result in better decisions being taken in as much as they will be based on fuller information. Two pairs of eyes are better than one, and if everybody has been consulted, no relevant piece of information is likely to be overlooked. If I am a lonely autocrat, I shall often base my decisions on assumptions which will turn out to be wrong. Not only is the information available to any one man likely to be limited, but his judgement is fallible. Two heads are better than one. In talking over proposals with another, a man often comes to see the weaknesses in his original proposals. Even extreme autocrats have found it necessary to have some privy councillors to talk things over with. By making everyone privy to the counsels of state we ensure that no aspect is ignored, no consideration overlooked. In particular, if everybody participates, we maximize the chances of our having second thoughts about any scheme that may be unwise, and by the time the final decision is made, we shall have had opportunity to ponder every serious argument on either side. The more people, therefore, that are involved in decision-making, the more information and the more counsel there will be available, and this, it would seem, is a good thing. In the extreme case undoubtedly it is. Actions, particularly political actions, are responses to situations, and are not going to be appropriate or effective if the agents are ignorant of the essential facts. But not very much participation is needed to elicit essential information, and to involve people very fully in decision-making is neither the only nor the best way of securing the necessary flow of relevant information and argument. All that is required is a certain amount of openness on the part of the government. Proposals should be publicized before they are finally decided upon, and there should be an opportunity for anyone to apprise the authorities of any facts or considerations he thinks relevant. But there is no need for the authorities to take any notice of them. They may if they wish, but if they decide to push on regardless they are perfectly entitled to. We have this sort of participation in Britain. If the government wishes to build a road or change a school, it has to give notice of its plans, and provide opportunity for objections to be entered. Objectors can produce evidence to show that the proposals are bad, and it is always possible that the government might be so much impressed that it would abandon the proposals. If an objector could show that a proposed road ran over quicksands, his timely intervention might save the government from a great waste of public money. But it is very rare for anything like this to happen. Usually the government sticks to its own proposals whatever facts or arguments are adduced against them. Although objectors have an opportunity of stating their objections, the government is under no legal obligation to give them serious consideration, and in effect treats them with courteous disregard.

Arguments based on the nature of decision-making do not take us very far. They apply not to rulers only but to all decision-makers, businessmen, bishops, doctors and dons. We are none of us infallible, and suggestions from any quarter may prove fruitful. A few firms have a suggestions box, and many men try to be receptive to new ideas. But we do not for that reason feel it incumbent on us to solicit every man's views or submit our own judgement to his opinion. More powerful arguments for participation can be grounded on the nature of the community, and stem from the effect participation has on the atmosphere in which decisions are made and the understanding members of the community have of them. As we saw in chapter two, actions are not just events. We construe actions and respond to them not simply as bare, unintelligible alterations in the world around us, but as manifestations of a mind with a conscious purpose. If we do not know what the reasoning is that lies behind some decisions, we are liable to misconstrue it as something alien, and possibly hostile, to us. If we have taken part in reaching it, then, as we saw in chapter three, we shall understand it and may construe it as our own, and therefore regard it not as an alien event, to be resisted, circumvented or manipulated, but as an expression of our own personality and aspirations, to be supported and defended. A decision publicly arrived at is better understood and likely, therefore, to be better carried out. Even when a decision is not wholly agreeable, we may be the more willing to accept it for having had some part in the discussions which preceded it. At the least, we understand the reasons that led to its being adopted. We may not agree with them or we may feel that other more cogent considerations have not been given the weight they deserve, but we have some appreciation of the force of the arguments which were finally adopted; the decision may still seem misguided, but is less likely to appear utterly irrational or wrong-headed. Often a further factor will assuage our disaffection: even though the arguments themselves carry no conviction, the persons who put them forward are worthy of respect. On some previous occasion they may have been allies, or at least shown themselves not to be complete bigots. And therefore, although we may still regard them as having been wrong on this occasion, we do not conclude that they are altogether wrong-headed and all their work a manifestation of ill will towards us. More generally, we may say that participation is both a corollary and a cause of our speaking of communal decisions in the first person plural rather than the third, and that a society in which this is the case is more united and cohesive than one in which most people regard themselves simply as subjects, passively obedient to the powers-that-be, but not active supporters. If everybody feels the laws to be enacted by himself and manifestations of his own will, then not only is the problem of political obedience solved at a stroke, but the body politic is made immeasurably stronger and more effective.

So important is it to involve individuals with the decisions of the community that the decision-makers of every community go to some considerable lengths to explain their decisions to their public. Parliament largely originated from the king's need to communicate with his subjects and mobilize their support for his policies. The annual general meeting of a voluntary society is very seldom the occasion of the committee's being called to account by the ordinary members – the chairman positively begs somebody to ask a question so as to liven up the proceedings and give the committee a chance to explain what it has been up to. Even the various branches of the Christian Church which have not been noticeably keen on lay participation have been at great pains not merely to publish the reasons for their decisions but to ram them down the throats of the all-too-apathetic faithful; and many catechisms should be seen as fossils bearing witness to the fact that, since reasoning is essentially dialectical in form, the method of question and answer is the best way of achieving real understanding.

Participation not only helps people to construe the phenomenon of government as a form of action rather than merely a kind of event, but leads them to criticize from the standpoint of agents rather than spectators. It is easy to criticize. It is easy to find fault with what the government actually has done. What is much more difficult is to suggest feasible alternatives. Those who have taken part in making decisions will know the immense difficulties decision-makers face, and will judge the performance of the present incumbents, if not with indulgence, at least with a tinge of realism. They will criticize, not as mere consumers conscious of every imperfection, but as those who have also tried and also failed, and who are correspondingly more ready to recognize what has gone right as well as what has gone wrong. The captious critic is soon silenced. 'If you don't like the way things are working out,' we ask him, 'what did you do to remedy them while there was yet time?' Where opportunities are open for anyone to ventilate views, make proposals and canvass support, those who do not bother to take any steps to ameliorate the state of affairs forfeit their right of complaint. Participation does not stifle criticism – far from it. But it does show up idle criticism for what it is. Such criticism as there is will at least be informed criticism, put forward by people who are proposing serious alternatives to the policies at present being pursued, and who are aware of the difficulties and drawbacks attendant on any course of action. The criticisms they make will be telling. If the government is found wanting, it will be found wanting in respect of real defects realistically assessed and not for a failure to live up to some imaginary standard of excellence. The language of criticism will be carried on, not grandiloquently in the optative mood, but more humbly, making allowances for the awkwardness of facts, and always acknowledging that decisions are essentially choices between alternatives, and often all the available alternatives are evil, and that to have succeeded in choosing the lesser evil is the most that any government can hope to achieve.

These arguments apply to any community. There are others which apply peculiarly to the state. The most important follows from the principle argued for in chapters six and seven that the state is necessarily concerned with the interests of its individual members. This point once granted, some forms of participation are inevitable, for, with regard to at least some of their interests, the individuals concerned are the best authorities. On all sorts of other matters other people are more authoritative than I, but on what I want and what I think I am *the* authority. And since the concept of interest cannot be entirely third-personal, but always depends on first-personal avowals somewhere along the line, the state cannot look after its subjects' interests well unless it finds out from them what they think. Participation may or may not be the best way of eliciting other sorts of information, but it is the only source of information about the opinions and desires of the individual, and this information is essential if the government is to know what the interests of the individual are. Although often paternalistic, as it must be, in its assessment of the interests involved, the government cannot assess them altogether vicariously. Only the wearer knows where the shoe pinches, and only the governed can say how the activities of government bear on the values they care about most.

A more practical consideration was dominant for many centuries in English political thought. Participation is the best guarantee against tyranny. Where people give freely of their time and energy in carrying out the processes of government, no elaborate machinery of paid state officials is required, and therefore this machinery is not available for misuse. A government with a large retinue of paid retainers is in a position to push through its decisions, however bad, but where it largely relies on the voluntary cooperation of members of the public whose jobs are not in jeopardy if they refuse to carry out instructions they believe to be unwarranted, the government's ability to implement its decisions depends largely on their being tolerable to the people at large. Participation constitutes as it were a built-in clutch in the transmission of power in the body politic, which will remain effective so long as the power is being used aright, but will begin to slip if the government seems to be over-stepping its limits, and will entirely disengage if it embarks on unconstitutional action.

One disadvantage of professionalism in public administration is that it leads to staleness. The very advantage of professionalism, that it enables policies to be coordinated, has as a concomitant disadvantage that decisions are taken today in the light of the decisions of yesteryear, long after the circumstances of yesteryear have ceased to obtain. Participation brings in fresh blood, and so, sometimes, a fresh outlook. Merely in explaining to the new incumbent why old remedies are best, the advocate of the old is forced to restate, and thus given the opportunity to rethink, his position. Often he will be right. But it will be a reasoned rightness. The dead hand of precedent will be loosened, the cocoon of habit unwrapped, old rigidities relaxed and ancient errors silently abandoned. A permanent full-time official in a position of power has been a permanent full-time official for a very long time, and has succeeded in the race for promotion largely by virtue of internalizing official attitudes of mind with exceptional success. It is difficult for him to see things from an outsider's point of view or to remember what it was like not to know all the things officials know. A temporary decision-maker was only last month the other side of the desk, and a part-time decision-maker often finds himself there still. Each can bring to bear on his decision-making a range of sympathies, as well as often a width of experience, denied to the professional administrator. Participation makes government less hidebound, more sympathetic to the viewpoint of the governed, and less likely to alienate those it exists to serve.

Participation may be good from the standpoint of the individual too. Apart from any benefit my counsel may bring to the community at large, it may benefit me personally if I am in on the taking of the decisions. I may be able to see that they go the way I want them; or at the least, I may be able to ward off the most adverse ones from being taken. In my absence people may say things about me which will lead to my losing the chance of promotion, or losing my job, or even, under some regimes, losing my home, my liberty or my life. If I am there, I can challenge what is said, or explain my actions as being not at all objectionable, or bring forward counter-considerations which will incline people not to visit harsh consequences upon me. Although in certain sorts of cases, as we shall see later, my exertions on my own behalf may be counter-productive, it is in general true of any society that a person is more likely to get what he wants if he is able to urge its merits on other members of society than if he cannot, and therefore if everyone can participate, everyone will tend to be in a better position to get his own way; and this, at least from his point of view, is a good thing.

There are many other reasons for which I may want to participate in public affairs. I may have an unselfish interest in seeing my country take one particular decision or adopt one particular policy. I may be agitating that the United States should make Winston Churchill an honorary citizen, or I may want legislation passed to make the wearing of seat belts compulsory, or I may want more aid to be given to the Third World. These crusades have limited objectives, and I want to participate in order to achieve these aims. Participation is a means. If congress agrees at once to pass the requisite bill, if the government is already in process of enacting a law about seat belts, if everyone accepts my proposals for more aid, then I can pack my bags and go home. It is only because the wrong decisions, as I see it, are being taken, that I want to have a say in them. I participate merely in order to secure that certain fairly specific decisions are taken, and provided they are taken I am content. The demand for participation most commonly arises from discontent with decisions actually taken, sometimes, as in the examples given above, because of a failure to achieve some valued aim, but more often because of their being positively unwelcome. We want to participate because we have grievances which our rulers are slow to redress. We demand a say, because their say has said wrong, and we want to be able to gainsay it in order that it may be unsaid.

Although the commonest cause of the demand for participation is discontent with the decisions being taken, it is not the only one. Men may want to participate, not as a means of securing special ends, but for much more general reasons. They value not just the end-result – they do not know in advance what they want it to be – but the whole business of being in on decision-making. Some want to be full-time rulers – politicians and civil servants. Many feel impelled to give some of their time and energy to public affairs – councillors and magistrates, members of Royal Commissions and statutory bodies. Most acknowledge a duty to vote, at least in parliamentary elections, and serve on juries. Their motives are many and mixed. We need, so far as we can, to understand them if we are to cater for the demands for participation that are grounded ultimately on our ideal of freedom, which regards it as good that each man should be free to follow his own bent, and, if he so wishes, be free to enter public life.

Why should a man want to engage in public life? For many

people, perhaps, it is money. In some societies politics can be very profitable, and an able man anxious to acquire wealth can make more money out of politics than any other occupation. Even in present-day Britain a man might go into the Civil Service simply in order to earn a living, reckoning that an office job in Whitehall would provide a more reliable income than being a stockbroker in the City or a businessman in Birmingham. But it would be inaccurate to suppose that money is the only motive. Money can be earned more easily and with equal security in many other ways in modern Britain. It is, indeed, a merit of a society to offer those who love money opportunities of obtaining it by other means than going into public life. Moreover it would be unduly cynical to discount entirely the account civil servants and politicians themselves give of why they devote themselves to public affairs. Money is not the main motive, they say; and we should, at least to some extent, believe them.

Some people are ambitious to rise to positions of importance and power. It is easy to castigate ambition. It can be a vice; but the desire to serve, and the desire to make a contribution to public life are estimable motives. They can be corrupted, as can other estimable motives; but if we are to understand clearly the reasons that lead men to enter public life, we must avoid gratuitous imputation of bad motives, the more so because mud will often be thrown in the rough and tumble of political controversy. We should not automatically condemn all those who participate in public life as power-hungry types with a liking for the limelight, any more than we condemn ourselves for eating food. We can be greedy, and so can they. But it is not to be taken for granted that either we or they must be or always are.

Politicians like publicity. They are gratified when the newspapers carry pictures of them, and are happy to think of their name being on men's lips. They seek power partly because they adore glory, and because the possession of power, together with its wise exercise, is the means whereby they may win for themselves immortal fame. But reputation is parasitic on achievement. Other men will think well of me because, in their opinion, I have done well. They may be wrong, and many men, particularly now in the age of public relations officers, enjoy a reputation they do not really deserve. But the connection between image and reality is not purely contingent. I cannot rationally want to be well thought of except deservedly. I may be inordinately keen that other men should know that I have done well, but I must then desire actually to do well. And many civil servants make a point of shunning the limelight and seeking for themselves only the power without the glory.

Why should one want power? Political power is in many respects much more circumscribed than financial or even physical power, and is less relevant to achieving the immediate objects of desire. Yet, almost instinctively, we think it more important. A very rich man can gratify his appetites more readily than a king or president, but a king or president matters more, because the decisions he takes determine the future of our whole society. If I affect the course of public affairs I act on a bigger scale than if I arrange my private affairs to my own liking. I have done more, although it may affect me personally less, if I get a new law passed than if I choose a new wallpaper for my bedroom. The people who decide on the Budget do not benefit personally from it, but their decisions have a wide inter-personal significance that private money-making lacks. They can feel that they are leaving their imprint on the sands of time in a much more definite way and on a far larger scale than if they had merely cultivated their own gardens. The sense of insignificance which besets the isolated self they escape in the more incontrovertible importance of the collective affairs of all. Not only is the scene larger, but it is constitutive of the individual identity. I am an Englishman. Being English is an essential part of being me. And therefore it matters to me most intimately how England fares. At the least, I shall want to serve, and do some things which could well have been done by someone else but are in fact done by me; I am then doing my bit, whether as a parish councillor or in helping Meals on Wheels or as a full-time public official, to keep things going, and am an active member of the community, not merely a passive consumer of community benefits, and being myself a contributor can properly take the first person plural on my lips, and say 'we' rather than 'they'. I cannot help being English. But it is up to me whether what being English consists of depends at all on my own actions or is something entirely determined from outside. For most people being English is simply a matter of making an already existing communal identity their own through doing their bit to maintain it. But although the English way of life, the Scottish way of life and the American way of life are already going concerns, and very largely require only maintenance, they are not completely determinate, and require some innovation too; consequently a few people are drawn to public affairs not in order to do themselves what could equally well be done by others, but to make an individual contribution which is peculiarly their own. Politicians and senior civil servants do not regard themselves as dispensable. Other people would do the job differently, and that would in their eyes be a bad thing. They want to feel that it is their decisions, their own unique decisions, which are moulding the country's future. It is up to them what the U.K. or the U.S.A. shall do, and therefore it is they who decide what the fact that they are British or American is going to mean. They not only are identified with their corporate identity, but are in a strong sense deciding what is going to constitute that corporate identity in time to come.

The love of power is often made out to be selfish. Certainly there is something self-centred about political ambition. Plato spoke less than the full truth when he said that the real reason which drove good men into politics was the fear that otherwise they would be ruled by men worse than themselves. It may be one reason, especially to those just beginning, but to those who have once tasted power the driving motive is not the fear of unworthier men, but simply of other men, possessing it. It is me that matters, me being in office, me being important, me having the decisive say. If my opponents do well in office, I find it difficult to rejoice in the country's good fortune in being well-governed, and the only time I can sincerely sing their praises is when the House adjourns as a mark of obituary respect. Political power enlarges my ego, and the pursuit of political power is naturally seen by others as a form of self-aggrandizement, and a not very estimable one at that. Yet this is too simple a view. If infirmity it be, it is the last one of a noble mind. The desire to do well and to deserve well is not an adventitious acquisitiveness on the part of some men but part and parcel of our human condition. An autonomous agent must be conscious of himself as an entity different from everybody else, and must be anxious to attain his own aspirations. That is why we value liberty. Equally, that is why each man must seek some sort of success, and have some aims he is ambitious to achieve. The point at issue is not whether a man should strive to succeed – everyone should – but what he ought to count as success. The ambitious politician too readily confuses the show for the substance, and values power for itself rather than for what he will do with it. Political power, like political liberty and like liberty generally, is a good thing in as much as it is a necessary condition of a certain important sort of human achievement. But, again like liberty, it is not by itself enough. It is no good just being free: being free is valuable because it is being free to do things the doing of which is itself valuable. Political power has been a great boon to great men, who have thereby been enabled to achieve great things, but it has shown up many others, who would have been reasonably successful and enjoyed a good reputation, had they not succeeded in obtaining a power they proved unworthy to exercise.

Not only do some people want to participate, but it is good for them that they should. J. S. Mill speaks eloquently of what we might call the educational effects of a form of government in which everyone participates:

Very different is the state of the human faculties where a human being feels himself under no other external restraint than the necessities of nature, or mandates of society which he has his share in imposing, and which it is open to him, if he thinks them wrong, publicly to dissent from, and exert himself actively to get altered. No doubt, under a government partially popular this freedom may be exercised even by those who are not partakers in the full privileges of citizenship. But it is a great additional stimulus to any one's self-help and self-reliance when he starts from even ground, and has not to feel that his success depends on the impression he can make upon the sentiments and dispositions of a body of whom he is not one. It is a great discouragement to an individual, and a still greater one to a class, to be left out of the constitution; to be reduced to plead from outside the door to the arbiters of their destiny, not taken into consultation within. The maximum of the invigorating effect of freedom upon the character is only obtained when the person acted on either is, or is looking forward to becoming, a citizen as fully privileged as any other. What is still more important than even this matter of feeling is the practical discipline which the character obtains from the occasional demand made upon the citizens to exercise, for a time and in their turn, some social function. It is not sufficiently considered how little there is in most men's ordinary life to give any largeness either to their conceptions or to their sentiments. Their work is a routine; not a labour of love, but of self-interest in the most elementary form, the satisfaction of daily wants; neither the thing done, nor the process of doing it, introduces the mind to thoughts or feelings extending beyond individuals; if instructive books are within their reach, there is no stimulus to read them; and in most cases the individual has no access to any person of cultivation much superior to his own. Giving him something to do for the public, supplies, in a measure, all these deficiencies. If circumstances allow the amount of public duty assigned him to be considerable, it makes him an educated man. Notwithstanding the defects of the social system and moral ideas of antiquity, the practice of the dicastery and the ecclesia raised the intellectual standard of an average Athenian citizen far beyond anything of which there is yet an example in any other mass of men, ancient or modern. The proofs of this are apparent in every page of our great historian of Greece; but we need scarcely look further than to the high quality of the addresses which their great orators deemed best calculated to act with effect on their understanding and will. A benefit of the same kind, though far less in degree, is produced on Englishmen of the lower middle class by their liability to be placed on juries and to serve parish offices; which, though it does not occur to so many, nor is so continuous, nor introduces them to so great a variety of elevated considerations, as to admit of comparison with the public education which every citizen of Athens obtained from her democratic institutions, must make them nevertheless very different beings, in range of ideas and development of faculties, from those who have done nothing in their lives but drive a quill, or sell goods over a counter. Still more salutary is the moral part of the instruction afforded by the participation of the private citizen, if even rarely, in public functions. He is called upon, while so engaged, to weigh interests not his own; to be guided, in case of conflicting claims, by another rule than his private partialities; to apply, at every turn, principles and maxims which have for their reason of existence the common good: and he usually finds associated with him in the same work minds more familiarized than his own with these ideas and operations, whose study it will be to supply reasons to his understanding, and stimulation to his feeling for the general interest. He is made to feel himself one of the public, and whatever is for their benefit to be for his benefit. Where this school of public spirit does not exist, scarcely any sense is entertained that private persons, in no eminent social situation, owe any duties to society, except to obey the laws and submit to the government. There is no unselfish sentiment of identification with the public. Every thought or feeling, either of interest or of duty, is absorbed in the individual and in the family. The man never thinks of any collective interest, of any objects to be pursued jointly with others, but only in competition with them, and in some measure at their expense. A neighbour, not being an ally or an associate since he is never engaged in any common undertaking for joint benefit, is therefore only a rival. Thus even private morality suffers, while public is actually extinct. Were this the universal and only possible state of things, the utmost aspirations of the law-giver or the moralist could only stretch to make the bulk of the community a flock of sheep innocently nibbling the grass side by side.

From these accumulated considerations it is evident that the only government which can fully satisfy all the exigencies of the social state is one in which the whole people participate; that any participation, even in the smallest public function, is useful; that the participation should everywhere be as great as the general degree of improvement of the community will allow; and that nothing less can be ultimately desirable than the admission of all to a share in the sovereign power of the state.*

We should add to these, as an argument for participation in a different key, that we owe it to people as human beings to consult them about what is going to happen to them and what they are going to have to do. Otherwise, we are merely pushing people around, as if they were things not men. Men are rational agents, and ought to be reasoned with about what they are going to do, and all the more so about public legal enactments they are going to be obliged to carry out. Since nobody can contract out of the body politic, and all are required to conform to regulations, we show disrespect to man's rationality if we expect any one to hearken to our laws but are not prepared to listen to his views. Only if each man is himself a legislator and able autonomously to

* J. S. Mill, *Representative Government*, Everyman, 1910, chapter 3, pages 215–17.

enact by fiat of his own will the laws he must obey as being his own, do we witness to our view of him as an end in himself and enable him to reach his full moral stature. More modestly but more insistently we repeat the argument of the previous chapter, that the state is necessarily committed to the ideals of freedom and justice, which carry with them a recognition of some right for some people to participate in deciding some sorts of question.

All these arguments have force in them, but are eloquent rather than exact. It is difficult not to be stirred by them, but when we reflect we begin to feel that they are exaggerated. They seem to be remote from the realities of life, in which people are often ignorant and partial, and time and temper are often short, and men more bent on obstinate obstruction than the rational exercise of their highest faculties. It may be that the Athenian jury system did much, as Mill alleges, for the education of the citizens – but at what cost in injustice and insecurity to the litigants? The noble vision of the citizen freely legislating the laws he will be obliged to obey seems not only unrealistic but false to much of human nature. Even where the arguments adduced for participation have considerable merit, practicalities often preclude our paying it anything more than lip-service. It may, indeed, be effective in eliciting information and argument, but we can understand why governments are seldom enthusiastic. For one thing, not all the information elicited is relevant, nor all argument advantageous. A great deal of the information churned out at public meetings – even in Parliament or in Congress – has little bearing on the question at issue, and much of the debate is threadbare and repetitious. Essential facts are fairly easily found out, and on most issues the number of relevant arguments that can be adduced is limited. Quite apart from the impracticality of it, there is no need to solicit opinions from all and sundry: a far more limited inquiry would be enough to ensure that all serious arguments were ventilated. Plato's Guardians would have been as zealous as any modern democrat to see that every aspect of public policy was properly discussed; and, because they avoided needless repetition, far more effective. Even so, it may be countered, any body of bureaucrats is liable to unconscious bias, and only by casting the net wider can we ensure that no considerations are overlooked.

This may be so. However high-minded, those closely involved with the business of government have a systematically different way of looking at things from those who are outside. We sometimes need the outsider to open our eyes to the truth about the Emperor's new clothes. But this is an argument, it will be said, not for participatory democracy but the freedom of the press. We do not, so far as this argument goes, need to consult everybody about everything, but only to ensure that if anybody has anything new to contribute, he can put it forward for discussion. If on consideration the contention seems cogent, it can be adopted, while if it does not stand up to detailed examination, it can be dropped with no harm done.

Governments have another reason for being unenthusiastic about public participation. Too much information is almost as bad as too little. It clogs the system and submerges the important messages with irrelevant noise. Even relevant information can on occasion be a disadvantage. For actions are homeostatic, and issue in success because they are carried through irrespective of alterations in circumstance. Often, therefore, it is more important that we should plough on regardless, than that, having once put our hand to the plough, we should reappraise the situation in the light of fresh information, and decide that really some other furrow would be a better one to cultivate. A person who is too responsive to changes in the situation becomes hesitant, and he who hesitates is lost in ineffectiveness. This was one of our arguments for delegation. To get things done, we give a man the power he needs and leave it to him. He can shut his ears to adventitious considerations better than can any corporate body, and push on regardless of any difficulties.

These counter-arguments are weighty, but not conclusive. They show that what we should seek to maximize is the availability not of all the information, but of the relevant information, and that there are occasions when we need to insulate some centres of decision-taking against some sorts of information. We need to prevent irrelevance and irresolution, but must be careful not to go too far. Many things which seem irrelevant from one – usually the official – point of view, seem highly relevant from another, and it is more important not to suppress them altogether than to avoid boredom on the part of those who have to listen. Equally, although we do not want to be always having second thoughts, we must not shield ourselves too securely from unpalatable facts: some governmental enterprises are so wrong or so futile that the sooner they are abandoned the better; and although we should not achieve anything if we were always reviewing decisions that had been already made, we need some procedure whereby at least the worst mistakes can be reversed in time. We need filters and we need safety-valves: filters to screen the important signals from irrelevant noise; safety-valves to blow when the public authorities seem set on a disastrous course of action. In the case of the state, the danger is that if it is left to the government to set the controls, it will set the filters to cut out too much information – especially that about their own views and values, which only the governed can provide – and not set the safety-valves to blow readily enough. Although sometimes in public affairs it is important to exclude certain sorts of information, and civil servants try hard to shield their minister from what they regard as irrelevancies, the results are not entirely happy. Whitehall has a formidable reputation for getting its own way, and pushing through its programme come hell or high water; but often what is believed there to be an exercise of political will is seen by the outsider as the insensitive exercise of power, and an insistence on yesterday's solutions to tomorrow's problems.

Participation was argued for not only on account of the decisions it yields but for the atmosphere it engenders. But often that can be achieved more economically, and sometimes, even, participation will do more harm than good. Monarchs are often more charismatic than democratic assemblies: people find it easier to identify with a single person than a corporate body, and may be more ready to obey the commands of a king than the resolutions of some amorphous committee. As a matter of social psychology, it is not universally true that participation engenders a greater feeling of identification than other forms of government. The Fascist and Nazi regimes succeeded in whipping up more popular support than their democratic predecessors, although giving a far smaller part to the people in actually making decisions. We may go further, and point out positive disadvantages in participatory forms of government. Not only is it extremely time-consuming and often ineffective, but it can poison the atmosphere if every decision is taken publicly in a blaze of publicity. Many people prefer to settle their affairs in the relative privacy of a face-to-face discussion with a single person. The Christian Church soon came to adopt the principle of the monarchical episcopate whereby there was one man in authority over each diocese, because it was much easier then for the authority to be exercised in a personal, paternal way. If every matter is decided publicly, then many people will be inhibited from discussing their problems freely, and decisions cannot take into account the particular personal circumstances of each individual case, but must be made with a view to all cases, since they are bound to be regarded as a precedent. Nor am I going to be inhibited only by my problems being brought forward for general discussion: I may be equally unwilling to express myself candidly about other people or other matters in public. People are often only willing to speak frankly if they can do so confidentially – we except discussions of appointments and promotions from our general rule of full publicity – and in so far as we value full and frank advice, we shall have to accept some degree of secrecy in some parts of public life. Parliament is public, but the Cabinet highly confidential.

Participation may also foment discord rather than assuage it. Apathy is often an advantage. If the government takes decisions for me, provided they are not grossly unreasonable, I shall probably acquiesce. But if I am to be consulted, and have to give my mind to the matter, I may well form an opinion of my own, differing from the generally accepted view, which, being my own, I shall tenaciously defend. Instead of my dissent being assuaged by the fact of my having taken part in public deliberations, it may by that very fact have been aroused. Civil servants are often secretive for this very reason. If the public does not get to hear about what is being done, it cannot protest until the decision has been both taken and carried out, by which time protest is futile and will therefore be only half-hearted. If the public have to be informed, it will only encourage them to object, and the last state will be worse than the first. Not only will the naturally cantankerous be given more issues to be difficult about, but often the whole nation will be divided. Participation can engender partisanship. People enjoy taking sides anyhow, but instead of merely supporting Arsenal or Wolverhampton Wanderers, they will inject their passions into politics. It is inherent in the idea of participation that different people will take different sides on occasion; and if, as sometimes, the issues are ones on which people feel strongly, they may well polarize opinion into two entirely separate and hostile groups. Those who oppose me on some cherished plan of mine will be my enemies, and I shall oppose them on their proposals, just because they are theirs, even if they are, in themselves, a matter of indifference to me. In order to protect and forward my interests, I shall form alliances which may well become permanent, and will judge everything from the point of view of the alliance rather than of the country as a whole. Parties will be formed, and party spirit fostered. At the best, national unity will be weakened; at the worst one part of the community, finding itself always defeated on every issue, will become altogether alienated.

It is very difficult for party leaders to be impartial. Sometimes, as in Britain and the U.S.A., a convention is established that, after the party conflict to determine who shall form the government or be the president, the successful contestants should regard themselves as responsible for the welfare of the country as a whole and not only for that of their own supporters. But it is a convention difficult always to obey, and even when obeyed not always believed in. Even if the prime minister or president wants to act in the public interest, he may not be able to do so for fear of offending his own party supporters, on whom he ultimately depends for the continuance of his power. The party system rules out many possibilities of desirable political action for just the same reasons as 'the prisoners' dilemma' precludes the possibility of certain sorts of individual action. Often a non-party government can knock the party leaders' heads together and impose compromises which the leaders could never reach by themselves because neither side could afford to make the necessary concessions to the other if it had a free choice. A party leader who seems to be selling his own side down the river will lose his supporters:

he must be seen to be doing his best for them. The position of a monarch, who can claim to be above party, or a permanent under-secretary, who can claim to be non-party, is much stronger. Not only can he claim to be acting in a higher interest, but often he can succeed in delivering the goods which the party leaders had been unable to provide. After the Wars of the Roses the Tudors, after the Wars of Religion the Kings of France, after the French Revolution Napoleon, all owed a lot of their strength to their being able to ensure that the course of events, although not exactly to the liking of any partisan, was at least tolerable and at any rate far preferable to what might be expected were the other party to come into power. The deep logic of the theory of games, which gives from one point of view the underlying rationale of there being a state at all, provides also a theoretical limit to the degree of participation that can be demanded or allowed. At some stage or other, participation, just because it is inherently partial, prevents the interests of the nation as a whole from being secured or even pursued.

Participation is reckoned to work out to the advantage of the participator, and often this is so: but not always. In addition to the cases where a man turns out to be a bad advocate of his own cause, there often operates a subtle shift in the background understanding of the context of decision-making and in the psychology of those actually deciding. It very much changes the game what part a particular man is given to play in it. If he is not allowed to make any moves, it is impossible for any of the rest of us to see our activity as 'playing against' him; whereas if he is himself a player, we may see the game as a competitive one, in which he is playing for himself and we should play to counter that strategy on his part, regarding him as an opponent. We feel feudal towards our dependents but pugnacious towards our rivals. If I am just and merciful to those in my power, I magnify my role and my own self-esteem: but I count it equally to my credit to be a good businessman and drive a hard bargain when it comes to doing a deal. If it rests entirely with me what shall happen to those under me, then no forbearance or generosity on my part can be construed as a concession to weakness. But if the decision is not entirely mine, but one in which you have some part too, then I shall be inclined to minimize your benefit in order to maximize my achievement. There are many examples in politics. Many a monarch has loved justice and taken pride in dispensing it freely and fairly to his subjects, while being a terror to his nobles who were in a position to gainsay him. Modern departments of state have in theory absolute power over the careers of civil servants and the part they can play in the making of decisions, and ought in theory to allow Members of Parliament an independent part in the formulation of policy; but in fact give more and more say to the former, and are always trying to exclude the latter from being able to interfere. Participation thus does not always or naturally work to the advantage of the participant, as regards his being able to have the decisions go the way he wants them. It depends on the question being decided and the frame of mind in which a decision may be reached. If the accused always retired with the jury, and took part in their deliberations and had a vote the same as all the jurymen, we can be sure that nobody would ever be found guilty by a unanimous vote; but many more majority verdicts of guilty would be returned, with the accused as the sole dissentient.

Most of Mill's arguments for participation are based on the good effects it has on the individuals who participate. Undoubtedly there can be such effects. But they are not as great as Mill makes out. To participate on occasion in public affairs undoubtedly enlarges the horizons, deepens the understanding and extends the sympathy of some men, but there are others who have no talent for public business, and will gain little benefit from having to do badly what they would rather not do at all. We may, for sufficient reason of the public interest, compel the sportsman to leave his game, the artist his studio, the visionary his contemplation, the housewife her cakes, and take their turn on the jury or the parish council; but must be wary of assuming too readily that it will be for their own personal benefit. It may be. It may be good for most people to learn the higher mathematics and the Greek language, but a certain degree of caution is necessary before insisting that everybody shall be made to devote himself to differential equations and compulsory Greek. Participation takes time, and life is short. Most people have their own private ends, and find fulfilment in achieving them rather than in exclusively public activities. There are better things to do, in most people's estimation, than taking part in endless debates about the siting of the public conveniences. Some people, perhaps, have a taste for that sort of thing. We are glad that they exist, but repudiate any suggestion that they are examples we all ought to emulate. On the contrary, if the question is canvassed, we may counter with the suggestion that it is really a symptom of some inner inadequacy to be too much concerned with minding other people's business. A man who immerses himself in public affairs is really, we may say, taking refuge from frustrations or failures in his personal life. Because he cannot come to terms with himself he bolsters up his self-esteem by being an important busybody. Because he does not know what to do with himself and has not got anything better to do with his time, he occupies himself with the trivia of public business. It is an unkind suggestion, and largely untrue. But it has a grain of truth – otherwise it would not wound – and should make us wary of welcoming too warmly proposals for everybody's greater involvement in public affairs. Decision-making can be a chore, and should be recognized as such. Many people do not want – and should not be told that they ought to want – to devote more time and energy to it than they have to. They have their own lives to lead, and should be allowed to do so without undue pressure to participate very much in public affairs.

Mill draws a contrast between the active energetic frame of mind of the participator, and the passive acquiescence of those accustomed to be governed without any say in the fate of their society. But again, the argument is not entirely one way. A society can be too agitated as well as too torpid. If everything is open to change by the energetic, it imposes on everybody else the burden of exerting himself in order to prevent the energetic from always having their own way. People are compelled to spend time stopping planning permissions being given to suit the interests of the local builders and estate agents. Even where the energetic are not out to feather their own nests, other people may have to waste time preventing them from achieving their aim of, say, compulsory euthanasia for all at the age of seventy. Freedom for some to organize their own pressure groups forces others to bring countervailing pressure to bear; and to that extent can constitute an un-freedom for those who are not free to go their own ways if they want society to be safe from the activists. Against Mill's rosy picture of brisk, energetic Victorian society should be set the somewhat harassed Anglo-Saxon of the twentieth century, pressured into an unhealthily defensive frame of mind as a member of innumerable preservation societies and with an uneasy conscience as he flits from one committee to another in his endeavours to save himself and his society from the initiatives of others.

Participation not only takes time, but involves the personality and seeks commitment. This is why we value it, but also constitutes a reason for not valuing it too much. Sometimes it is important that people should not be too much involved and not feel committed. It may be in quite trivial matters – it is good to be able to shop around and not feel obliged to reserve one's custom for the corner shop which has always been so obliging or the old-established firm in which uncle served for fifty years – but it may be in much more important matters too. The argument that participation counters the criticisms of the captious is two-edged. We may be too successful in stifling criticism with the rejoinder 'Well, why don't you do something about it?', and by tying ideas to action too closely drag many *ballons d'essai* down to earth for each practical project we get off the ground. For many years the English participated while the French did not; and the English were commonsensical prosaic dullards, altogether lacking the brilliance and penetration of the free-ranging Gallic mind. The leaders of the student movement demanded total participation in all university affairs, without realizing that what students most needed was to be uninvolved and uncommitted so that they could make up their minds for themselves what sort of person they wanted to be. Participation both is justified by and produces the identification of the individual with the community. But too much identification is a bad thing, especially when the individual is trying to discover and create his own identity. More generally, we need to beware of seeking always to internalize obligations. Although at present we are properly much more aware of the

alien face that externalized obligations present to the individual,
we should see that they are in part the other face of freedom. If
I am to be free to make up my mind for myself, then I must
know myself to be different from other people, and other people
to be different from myself; and the ways in which the existence
of others limits my own freedom of action will be seen by me as
external restraints on what I can do rather than inner obligations arising out of the bare fact that I am who I am. In the
theory of the state there is an important argument from freedom
to legality based on the need the individual has for a certain
separation between his own thinking and that of the state if his
individuality is to be preserved. Total non-alienation, that is
total identification with the community, would stultify the individual's development of his own identity, and might suffocate
him altogether. We often complain about the alienation modern
man feels, especially in relation to the state, and with justice; but
we should not seek to do away with all sense of being a stranger
and of having no abiding city here, or we shall be prescribing
a political panacea for a metaphysical malady.

These counter-arguments are not decisive. They do not refute
the arguments for participation, but they limit their application.
We cannot give blanket approval or blanket disapproval of participatory procedures, but need to consider what the question at
issue is, whose interests are involved, in what frame of mind the
decision-makers will approach their task, what costs are likely
to be acceptable, and how far we should aim for the best or seek
to avoid the worst, before settling on any form of decision-
procedure. Beneath the welter of conflicting considerations the
two underlying themes of justice and freedom persist. Issues of
justice arise where a proposed decision would adversely affect
an individual's exclusive interests, and then we lay on decision-
makers a duty to be reluctant to harm that man's interests, and
to do so only for adequate reasons of an acceptable sort. The more
central the interest the greater the reluctance, and the more
readily we call on his aid to avoid our being led to take that
decision. With more peripheral interests it is reckoned enough to
inform him of our intentions – we merely post notices in the area
before making it a smokeless zone – or give him an opportunity

to state his case – as when we invite applications for a job; but always we have some compunction in deciding against a man, and reckon, special considerations apart, that he will be the best advocate against an adverse decision, and therefore should have a say in the process of taking it. But also, since he is *parti pris*, he should have less than a full say. We hope that if we enable him to cite every fact and adduce every argument in his favour, and he hears all the arguments on the other side, and sees that the decision-makers are eminently fair-minded, he will be reconciled to the decision should it in the end be an adverse one; we hope, but cannot rely on it. It would be incoherent to give him a Lockean veto, and pointless, as we have seen, to give him a Rousseau-style vote. The form of participation appropriate for him is as an advocate, not a judge; and beyond that, we hope to secure his – and many other outsiders' – identification with the decision by having the procedure evidently fair, and the decision itself reached as rationally and impartially as possible.

Where the interests involved are not exclusive, the argument for participation is based on the ideal of freedom. We have to leave everyone free to express an interest because only so can such interests be identified. We cannot assume that there are adequate reasons of an acceptable sort either way, or that all men of good will would tender the same answers, provided they were apprised of all the relevant considerations, but neither need we reckon any one man's cause so exclusively his own that his judgement is too biased to be valuable. In the first place, since many interests cannot be imputed but depend in some degree on first-personal avowal, we cannot determine merely from the nature of the proposals who should have the right to be heard. The initiative must come from the interested parties to declare their interest. Every one must have an opportunity of entering an objection or airing an opinion, and therefore the problem of 'noise' becomes much more acute than where participation is governed by the canons of justice, and we can hear the parties at length because they are few. Rather than require decision-makers to listen to all those interested in every question, we reckon that those who share a common interest should make common cause and present their arguments together by means of one man who should represent them all. Under the aegis of justice, for each question there may be some few individuals with a *locus standi* – because their exclusive interests are affected – which gives them a right to be heard in full; under the aegis of freedom, for every question those who feel an interest in it should have some opportunity to make some representation about it, but there is no obligation to secure that every opportunity is open to every one of them to represent his views in full. Since they are self-selected, the number of would-be participants may be large, but since they select themselves by reason of a common interest, considerable economies of scale may be imposed on their mode of participation.

In the second place, freedom, unlike justice, lays no claim to complete rationality. No matter how reasonable my colleagues are, they may not be convinced by the arguments I adduce. It is not enough, therefore, merely to have the right to be heard; I need to be able to throw into the scales not only my arguments but my judgement, and have them register not only my reasons but my wishes. Nor can I, thirdly, be debarred from helping to decide in my own cause, for then everyone might have to be disqualified. We can afford to disqualify those with exclusive interests involved from adjudicating a dispute because they are necessarily few, and disinterested judges are available; and though some men are sufficiently disinterested to give a fair decision even if they had some interest at stake, we still disqualify them because their having an interest will enable other men to impute bias and impugn their decision, however fairminded they have been, and we are anxious that justice be seen, even by the disappointed or suspicious, to be done. Shareable interests, however, can be shared by many. We might be unable to find a disinterested decision-maker, when a shareable interest was involved, and we could not always know in advance whether a man had the relevant interest or not. If we want to set up a royal commission on capital punishment, we may know some committed abolitionists or retentionists who for that reason are unsuitable to serve on it, but we cannot rely on finding a sufficiency of men with an entirely open mind on the matter, and their opinions may be discovered only after they have been appointed. All we can do is to choose fair-minded men who are not completely prejudiced and who will listen to reason. But they cannot avoid having formed opinions antecedently to their commission and coming to it with a preliminary judgement already in mind. Of course, we may take antecedent opinions into account in deciding what store to set on a man's final judgement. If you are an ardent enthusiast for euthanasia, I may discount in part your being against our building a geriatric ward, and wanting a new crematorium instead. But I cannot dismiss your whole position as mere self-interest, and must allow that you have your reasons, even if not, in my view, very good ones, for wanting to recycle, rather than rehabilitate, the elderly. You may believe me similarly prejudiced, and although we cannot both be right, neither is so evidently wrong that his opinion ought to count for nothing. Political thinking, although seeking to be rational, is not governed by any decision-procedure, and, rather than lay down rules, we have to rely in the end on the judgement of reasonable men; and nobody can be safely accounted altogether unreasonable in advance. From this it follows that the mere fact that a citizen holds an opinion ought to carry some weight. This conclusion is both encapsulated and reinforced by the ideal of freedom, and in so far as public decision-making is to be guided by the canons of political liberty, it should take into account not only the arguments adduced, but the opinions actually held. It is therefore appropriate that forms of participation grounded on the ideal of freedom, rather than that of justice, should include not only the right to know and the right to be heard but the right to vote.

9 The Value of the Vote

Most men do not want to participate much. The cost, in time and energy expended, of participating in even a small way is considerable. And, in the absence of some burning grievance, many men are content to let others take decisions for them. But they do not want to opt out entirely. Nor need they in democratic societies. For it is characteristic of democratic societies that every adult citizen has the vote, and the vote constitutes a form of minimal participation, which is made available to everybody and is so easy to exercise that nobody can plausibly maintain that it takes more time or trouble than he can afford to give. By giving people the vote we enable them all to be participants. But often we engender discontent, because we fail to make clear what the institution of voting really is, or what logical constraints there are upon its exercise, or how minimal a form of participation voting by itself really is.

Votes, as we saw in chapter three, are stylized answers to standard questions. Voting is therefore a somewhat passive activity. Other people propose, and the voters can do no more than dispose. They do not have the initiative but only a say in the penultimate stage of decision-taking. Often, much depends on the terms of the question put, and those who frame the motion have a much greater say than those who merely vote. But those who vote may understand the question in a different sense from that in which it is formally expressed. For votes decide what action shall be undertaken, and actions, as we saw in chapter two, can be characterized in many different ways. Different voters can construe the question put to them differently, but there are pervasive pressures on voters to adopt certain common interpretations. Voters have limited information and limited intelligence. It is difficult to find out things about a stranger, but if I know that he is the official Liberal candidate then I can base my decision on that fact alone. It is difficult to go into an issue thoroughly and see the arguments on both sides and strike a balance, but if I know that you are a sensible man and have been into the question properly, then it is rational to be guided by your judgement. In particular, as we saw in chapter five, actions are subject to a coherence condition which large decision-making bodies find it difficult to satisfy. In order to prevent different questions being considered separately they need to be presented as parts of an integrated programme, with voters being asked to vote for the individual items not on their individual merits but simply as part of the package. These three considerations re-inforce one another, and together lead to the formation of parties. If we were all fully-informed, perfectly rational, and able to make each decision within the context of all the other decisions already taken or in prospect, there would be no need for parties. But we often lack information, and, knowing ourselves to be imperfectly rational, it is rational for us to look for guidance from some one we believe blessed with a better judgement than our own. Having followed a leader on one issue, we are inclined to follow him in all; for not only is his judgement likely to be better in each case, but he is better able than we to see that all the separate decisions together constitute a coherent policy. In the absence of unanimity we need to polarize to ensure stable majori-ties for the separate parts of coherent policies, and since we tend to follow leaders, we naturally polarize around them. Thus in spite of many and authoritative warnings against there being parties, parties have sprung up wherever democratic forms of government have been established; and this is due not only to size and the need to economize time but to the equally pressing need to economize thought.

Parties are required to secure coherence in decision-taking, but once they have grown up, they tend to integrate decisions more monolithically than necessary. Although some of my de-cisions are relevant to others, not all are. Decisions on education are fairly easily separated from those on health and transport. But once I realize I am one imperfectly rational member of a com-munity composed of other imperfectly rational members, who do not decide each case on its merits but in accordance with a party line, I shall attempt to bargain my support for their proposals in return for their support for mine. Again, it would not happen if we were all perfectly rational. Then I could only hope to influence the votes of others by addressing cogent arguments to them on the merits of my case, and I should be unwilling to mortgage my judgement on any other issue. But being of limited rationality, I can only give my mind to some questions, and am bound to find others of relative indifference to me; and if this is true of others too, there is an opportunity and natural incentive to start trading votes on different items, and to build up coalitions for the mutual support of their different interests, and to continue the process until a majority is achieved. This is entirely rational, if not totally estimable. In addition, partisan behaviour is emotionally self-reinforcing. It is a sad fact, but a true one, and for politics highly important, that a shared dislike is usually a more powerful bond than a shared liking. It is in the face of a common enemy that we discover the real depths of fellow-feeling. A party system institutionalizes antagonisms and therefore also feelings of fellowship. In labouring to defeat the machinations of the other side, I come to identify with members of my own party far beyond what is required by prudent calculation or co-incidental coalescence of interest. The very same experiences which lead people to value the group-dynamics of small-scale democracy lead them equally to value the solidarity engendered by 'the movement' or 'the cause' in its fight against its opponents, and we come to see ourselves no longer as citizens of Verona but as Montagues or Capulets instead.

There are many things wrong with the party system just as there are many things wrong with the profit motive, and thinkers often inveigh against both with equal fervour. But before we condemn we should understand. Each, although a regrettable concession to imperfection, represents an accommodation to the facts of human nature which it would be unwise as well as inhuman to ignore. We form parties, as we seek profits, because we each have interests which are not the same as those of everybody else, and which we feel bound to look after to the best of our ability. Rousseau thinks this is wrong. Voters, he says, should vote not in order to advance their own interests, but as trustees for the common good. In one sense he may be right. Although some thinkers have put forward an economic theory of democracy in which the voter sells his vote to the party whose programme appeals to him most, just as he exchanges his money for the goods that he likes best, voting is intelligible only as part of a procedure for taking a communal decision, and therefore carries with it a duty to evaluate the alternatives from a communal point of view. And in point of fact men often vote for a policy which will affect their personal exclusive interests adversely but will be, in their view, of benefit to the community at large. As we saw in chapter six, the concept of interest does not allow us to make Rousseau's antithesis between interest and unselfishness. I may be very altruistic, and entirely ready to vote against my own financial interest, but have other interests I share with some of my fellow citizens, which I can best pursue by forming a party and following a party line. If I want – for entirely altruistic reasons – to get Britain out of Europe, I had better join the Labour Party, and vote the Labour ticket on nationalization and education too; and, equally, if I am very keen on the Common Market, I should be wise to vote Conservative, and put up with growth, inflation and the destruction of the environment. Even though my interests are not self-interested, they are still my interests, and in a world of imperfectly rational men I am often going to need to supplement argument with a certain amount of vote-trading. It is one of the reasons why a vote is valuable. But it means that to vote is not nearly as simple as it seems. My choice is not an unfettered one between competing candidates or alternative courses of action, but is subject to many subtle pressures, which often make voting seem much less satisfactory than we had at first supposed. We felt – we were encouraged to feel – that to be enfranchised with the vote was to be masters of our own destiny, but we find that it gives us an absolutely minimal say in public decision-making, and, when we reflect, we see that this is not so much the fault of our institutions as part of the logic of the vote itself. We are easily disillusioned with democracy thus institutionalized, and conclude that elections are an elaborate charade, and voting entirely valueless. But this is wrong. The vote is not everything, but it does not follow that it is valueless. It has many virtues, some symbolic, some practical. They need to be seen for what they are, rather than over-praised, and then in disenchantment dismissed, for what they are not.

Votes have a symbolic value. To give a man a vote is to enfranchise him as a citizen and to make him into a person who counts. It is easy, especially in modern society, to give people the impression that they are nobodies. The admass economy is not a respecter of persons. In the old days, if my shoes did not fit, I could go and give the cobbler a piece of my mind, but now the sales lady does not want to hear if none of the shoes fit, and merely repeats that there is no demand for my size, and clearly has no control over what sizes are stocked, and to the manager I am only one marginal unit among thousands. Work is equally impersonal for many. Our economy seems to say that workers are but hands, consumers but gullible fools to be manipulated into parting with their money, and that nobody really matters. It is all the more important, then, that our political institutions should say the opposite, that each man is valuable not merely for his hands or his money, but for his opinions and choices. By giving people votes, we make them matter. They are entitled to have opinions in the pubs, not merely by way of pastime, but as part of the role accorded them by society. It may not be everything, but it is something. And something is a lot better than nothing.

Giving people the vote has a symbolic value in showing that society thinks they matter. Exercising the vote has a symbolic value in enabling the voter to identify with society. The communist countries know this well. They have not the slightest intention of allowing the inevitable progress of the Marxist dialectic to be deflected by the real preferences of the unenlightened masses, but they find it useful to organize periodic elections to enable the voters to muster massive votes of confidence in the regime. We should not laugh. Many societies have similar institutions whereby decisions already made are ratified by the expressed assent of the whole body politic. We go to hear the new monarch proclaimed, sleep on the pavements to catch a glimpse of the procession to the Coronation, or watch the service in the Abbey on our television sets. It is a natural instinct to want to identify oneself with one's society, and the ritual of voting for the government is a peculiarly apt and explicit form of expressing personal commitment and support.

Where the result of the vote is not a foregone conclusion, the actual casting of the vote has both a symbolic and a practical value for the voter. He has taken part, and whether his vote was successful or unsuccessful, he is to some extent committed to the political institutions of his society. They have played ball with him, and even if he did not win that game, provided that it was a real game with a real possibility of his having won, he will be inclined to play ball with them. This argument will not weigh where the elections are rigged or where some voters perceive themselves as being always in a hopeless minority. But in many circumstances, voting, even when unsuccessful, will still have some value both in expressing and inducing support for the institution, if not for the actual outcome on that occasion. It depends on the whole tone and underlying assumptions of society as well as the bare exercise of the right to vote; but the actual exercise is an essential part of that vision which sees democracies as having a special claim for allegiance that no other form of government can have. Moreover, in most systems of voting, a majority, or at least a plurality, of voters are successful. If the winning side is that which has most votes, most voters are on the winning side. They therefore are to some extent committed to the government. Even though the choice presented to them may not have been posed in the terms they wanted, when it came to the crunch they decided that one alternative was preferable to the other, and having got what, to that extent, they wanted, they will be inclined to see the government as their government and to give it a great measure of support. Even if it proves to be far from ideal, it may yet be less bad, in their eyes, than the other one they might have got, and for that reason alone worthy of support. The mere fact of having voted forces the voter to face up to the practical alternatives available to him, and to plump for one; and in the majority, or near-majority, of cases, the voter will have plumped for the party that actually forms the government after the election, and will be to some extent its supporter.

Votes are also important because Members of Parliament and ultimately governments depend on them. Politicians sometimes are corrupted by power at least to the extent of thinking of themselves more highly than they ought to think. But whereas other pompous people need never allow unpleasant thoughts to disturb their contemplation of their own importance, a Member of Parliament can never entirely forget that he owes his position to the suffrages of his constituents and that if he does not mind his step he may not be returned at the next election. In particular, when listening to a constituent, he has a healthy feeling of dependence. Most people in most walks of life are courteous to casual inquirers, but their courtesy need not extend all that far; but a Member of Parliament has an added incentive to be polite. Although I may not have voted for the successful candidate at the last election, he does not know that I did not, but only knows that if he made such an assumption in general, he would in general be wrong. Perhaps even more important are the feelings of the constituent. I can approach my Member of Parliament with a certain degree of confidence that I have some claim on his time and that he will be favourably disposed towards me. Although I individually may or may not have had a hand in sending him to Westminster, we collectively most certainly did, and I, as one of we, can properly presume on what he knows we did for him, as well as trade on what he hopes we shall do for him again when next there is an election. I come not as a suppliant, like a peasant to the court of a medieval king, but as a man having himself done a service and now seeking one in return. Every constituent is entitled to call on his Member's attention and aid in any matter on which his interests are affected by government action, and the Member feels obliged to give the matter his sympathetic consideration. Of course, it does not mean that every Member of Parliament must take up every constituency issue and pursue it to the bitter end. Rather, he exercises his own judgement about the merits of the case, and often he will do no more than refer the person aggrieved to the remedies already available; and even when there is no other recourse the Member will content himself with writing a letter to the minister, and will receive a standard reply composed by a junior civil servant, which will carefully avoid the question in issue, and the Member will be too busy to press the matter. Nevertheless, the institution of elected representatives does give to every elector a voice. Although he cannot ventilate his views in person to the decision-makers, he has got someone to whom he can address himself with a fair prospect of being heard and to whom the decision-makers will themselves attend. For a Member of Parliament writes to Whitehall as being also himself the possessor of a vote which the minister may need to woo. Perhaps now it is no longer as true as it once was – this may be one of the root causes of our present discontents – but according to one cherished view of Parliament, the government depends for its existence upon the support of M.P.s, and will always aim to avoid gratuitously alienating them. Even though it might seem safe to snub an opposition back-bencher who did not command much respect, he would be likely to talk about the case in the smoking-room, and it soon might get around that the department was getting out of hand, and a movement of opinion might begin that could have untoward consequences at a later date. Not every Member of Parliament will be satisfied by every answer the government gives him – no government could achieve that – but every Member of Parliament will be given an answer, and as good a one as the circumstances permit. The voter can make his views known, and the government has some incentive to attend to them. And thus the possession of a vote secures to the elector, at one remove through his parliamentary representative, some sort of voice.

The value of the vote to the individual considered solely as an individual is inevitably limited. Although it gives him a part, it is necessarily a very small part, in the making of decisions. Other people also have votes, and the vote of any single individual will seem negligible among the enormous number of votes normally cast. Perhaps in Peterborough in the 1960s when two or three were gathered together, they were conscious of the momentous significance of their ballots, and that if they had voted differently the composition of the House of Commons would have been

10 Representative Government and Elective Autocracy

The value of the vote depends on the actual working of the institutions in which we exercise the vote. But there is no adequate account of how our votes affect the processes of government. For our purposes it will be convenient to distinguish two paradigms, in much the same spirit as we distinguished two ideal forms of democracy in chapter three. There is a weak analogy between the thinking of Locke and the first, somewhat fuzzy, paradigm of representative government, and a stronger one between Rousseau's approach and elective autocracy.

Representation was almost unknown in the ancient world. It grew up in the Middle Ages as a way not only of obtaining information about what the various communities of the realm wanted, but, more importantly, of securing their cooperation in carrying out those policies, notably the waging of wars, the enactment of statutes and the raising of taxes, for which their assistance was particularly needed. In the course of the seventeenth century supreme power in Britain passed from the monarch to Parliament, and since the American and French Revolutions an assembly of representatives, usually elected by constituencies geographically defined, has become a standard political institution. By means of this device, every elector is assigned a representative, who stands in a special relationship to him and his neighbours, and will ensure that their interests are defended in the counsels of state. Thanks to representation, the huge numbers of modern nations can be reduced to manageable compass without anyone having to be entirely excluded. There are far too many of us for us all to be present at parliamentary debates; but although we cannot all be really present, we can be represented by our Member of Parliament, who in some sense does duty for us all, only taking up much less room. But in what sense? The word 'representative' is used in many different senses, none of them quite adequate to present-day practice. A barrister represents his client by bringing forward evidence and adducing arguments to win his case for him. An agent represents his principal by bargaining and entering into contracts on his behalf, with the principal being bound by his agent's undertaking. An ambassador represents his country by making its views known to a foreign power, and keeping his own government informed of the state of affairs in the foreign country, and, if he is a plenipotentiary, by negotiating treaties. In a very different sense, a monarch or a flag or an emblem represents a community by being symbolic of it. In a different sense again, a man may represent a particular type or class of people by being a typical or characteristic member of it.

Each sense contributes something to the political concept. The eighteenth century was fond of arguing that Parliament rather than the monarch should be sovereign, because Parliament, being composed of many men, could reflect differences of opinion and deliberate on the different sides of the case much better than a single man could. Parliament represented the nation by being a microcosm of it. In the same way we think of a jury as being a representative sample of our fellow countrymen; and the Ancient Athenians selected their council, the Boulé, more or less by lot, to be a scaled-down version of the whole Assembly. On this theory, it does not matter very much *how* the representatives are chosen, so long as they are typical of the country as a whole. Infrequent elections and highly anomalous constituencies were acceptable, so long as the House of Commons did its job of reflecting the national mind, and bringing into the debate all relevant considerations. In the same vein, we often defend the House of Lords today, because, although the hereditary principle is out of fashion, it produces a chamber which contains more 'ordinary chaps' and articulates more points of view than does the present House of Commons. Parliament is the national forum of debate, and every significant opinion should be voiced there, and every shared interest should find someone there to defend it.

Even communist countries reckon representation important, as symbolizing the legitimacy of government. Their elections do not produce representatives who reflect opinion at all, nor do they give the voter any opportunity to exercise a choice; but besides giving, as we saw in the previous chapter, the voter an occasion to feel that he has played his part in the political process, they express the claim of the regime to be a people's government, which exists for the benefit of the people and is what the people really want. So too, in western democracies, we think that a new parliament or congress or assembly has more authority than an old, and that the government, having the support of the representatives of the nation, ought for that reason to be obeyed. People often complain that parliamentary proceedings are very largely just play-acting, but this is part of their function: they are a ritual to be explained in terms of social anthropology, and should be compared with the challenges and championships and joustings of a medieval tournament marking a royal wedding or the accession of a new king. The government acquires authority over us through our representatives being there to acknowledge it, and through them it tells us what we ought to do. As a theory of political obligation it is inadequate, but as a fact it is effective. Authority rests not on autonomous choice, but on generalized acquiescent acceptance: symbolic representation both reinforces and is reinforced by the half-formulated public conventions whereby we collectively and individually recognize the government as the authority we all agree to accept and whose decisions we shall acknowledge as our own. For this purpose, representative institutions do not have to have the form they have come to have in Western democracies; but, having the form that they have, they also serve, and are shaped by, very deep primitive needs common to all societies.

Originally, members of the House of Commons represented the communities which elected them as agents, spokesmen or – almost – ambassadors. Great importance was attached to their being plenipotentiary, and having power to enter into binding agreements on behalf of their constituents. Inevitably they could not consult their constituents very closely, and had to exercise their own discretion, but this is what an ambassador used to do, and what a doctor or a barrister still does. It is possible to represent without having detailed instructions, because the concept of interest is third-personal. Within a given context and on the basis of shared values, one man can act on behalf of another man or group of men or corporate body, because he can know what their interests are without continually needing to consult them. Because he can take their values to his heart, he can act as they would have done, had they been in a position to do so. Common values make vicarious action possible, and also enable many men to have their cause presented by just one man. So long as we are a community and have certain values in common, we also have common interests which can be represented by a man of good will in a fairly straightforward way. But parliamentary constituencies now are seldom the homogeneous communities they once were. At one time there was a reasonably well-identified local interest in each shire and borough, and on the questions that touched those interests the knights and burgesses could represent them fairly effectively. Similar questions arise still, where there is a local interest at stake on which nearly every constituent who gave the matter his attention would reach a common view, and the M.P. in expressing this view is representing his constituency in as real a sense as an ambassador represents a nation; but these questions play a much more subordinate part in the business of government, and on most questions the divisions are inside each constituency rather than between one constituency and another, and there is no basis of shared concern which enables the Member of Parliament to represent his constituency in an ambassadorial sense.

Behind these different senses of representation lie certain underlying themes which can guide us further in elucidating the political concept. Representation is concerned with identification, either of action or of argument. A symbolic representative acts for us all: when the Queen went to Churchill's funeral, it meant that we all through her were paying our last respects to him. A typical representative acts and argues like us all: if the man on the Clapham omnibus is offended at an obscenity, we reckon that most of us would be similarly offended. A spokesman adduces the same arguments as those he represents would, were they able and articulate enough to do so, and an agent is a person whose actions are deemed to be those of his principal. In politics part of our concern is that the actions of the whole community shall be ones that everyone can acknowledge as his own. To this end it is important that those who make decisions shall be moved by many of the same arguments as other people. Above all, we need the arguments which people would adduce if they were in on the making of decisions actually to be adduced in spite of their inevitable absence. We need this not only as a means of securing the greatest possible identification with the decisions ultimately reached, but also to accord with the canons of justice and freedom, and further as a consequence of our view of the state's activity as being, to some extent necessarily, a function of the community as a whole, and not merely of the government. And arguments have the same logical characteristics as reasons and values which, as we noted in chapter two, can be identical even though adopted by different people. My reasons can be the same as your reasons. Whereas with persons and actions it always seems something of an artifice from the strict logician's point of view to talk of anybody's being identified with anybody else, or performing the self-same action as anybody else, there is no metaphor at all in saying that I have the same values or the same views or am moved by the same considerations as you. Hence it is that the concept of interest, which enables views and values to be presented vicariously in one's absence, is fundamental to the concept of representation. But interests, as we saw in chapter six, cannot always be ascribed third-personally. If one man is to represent the interests of many, it must be mostly their shareable interests he represents, and shareable interests are less easy to impute than exclusive ones and more dependent on first-personal avowal. Only by sometimes consulting people or corporate bodies can a representative know what these interests of theirs actually are. Moreover, interests, whether of an individual man or corporate body, often conflict, and these conflicts cannot all be altogether resolved third-personally. However loyal a friend I am of yours, I cannot look after all your affairs and take all your decisions for you. Sometimes only you can decide how far to jeopardize your health for the sake of your bank balance, or whether to move to a less good job for the sake of your family. Similarly, no matter how dedicated a spokesman is to his constituency's interests, he cannot always know without asking how they are to be weighed against one another. He cannot speak for others, unless he sometimes speaks with them. The same concept that makes representation possible makes consultation necessary, and occasionally requires that definite decisions be taken. And therefore in political contexts, where unanimity cannot be assumed, any system of representation must provide for the taking of a vote.

Voting is essential to the concept of representation in political contexts, but voting has also undermined it. Voting enables each voter to give his answer to a certain question that is being put to the vote. But the question as put may not be the question the voter wants to answer, and, as we saw in the previous chapter, he may reinterpret it to meet his own standards of relevance. Votes on particular measures are often seen as votes of confidence, and the election of a local representative is seen as a choice between parties. Although formally at a general election we elect particular persons to serve as Members of Parliament, and until recently no affiliation was stated on the ballot paper, the election is none the less regarded not as a way of selecting good men to serve in an important organ of government but as a choice between two or more possible administrations, each with its own personnel and policies. People say they vote Conservative or Labour, rather than for Mr Woodhouse or Mr Luard, and Members of Parliament are seen much more as bearers of party-labels than as persons in their own right. Although many Members of Parliament find 'constituency work' the most satisfying part of their duties, and some devote themselves to it with great vigour and attention, few people see them as top-level social workers, and it is generally reckoned – although falsely in a few cases (e.g. Rugby in 1970) – that no matter how assiduous a Member is in taking up his constituents' cases, it will have little effect on the number of votes cast for him at the next election, which most electors will see primarily as a choice between parties, with the person of the candidate being much less important than his party affiliation. Candidates represent political parties, not geographical communities, and representative government has become a form of popular government, where the procedure for choosing who shall govern is indirect and complicated, rather than a straight vote in a direct election. This can be seen most clearly in American presidential elections. It was the intention of the Founding Fathers that the president should not be elected directly by the people, but by special electors, chosen for the purpose, rather like the electors to a professorship in a British university, who were supposed to choose the man best qualified in their opinion for the office of president. What actually happens is that these electors are themselves elected not as men qualified to form an independent judgement about who would make the best president, but as committed supporters of one or the other candidate. The voters have insisted on reconstruing the question put to them by the American Constitution, namely *Who would be the best qualified people from your state to help choose the next President?* as being the question that they really want to answer, namely *Who shall be our next President?* In a similar way, British voters tend to reconstrue the question *Who would be the best person to represent your area in the next Parliament?* as being instead *Do you want the Conservatives or the Socialists to form the next government?* or more recently, *Do you want Mr Heath or Mr Wilson as the next prime minister?* Of course, the House of Commons is not exactly like the Electoral College of the United States, which is not a continuing body and has no other function than to elect a president for a fixed term, and which therefore provides no way of enabling the interests and views of American citizens to be represented to the government. Nevertheless, the parallel is pertinent. The most important thing the House of Commons does now is to get itself elected – it is very rare for a government to change except at a general election. And for a number of different reasons, the role of the House of Commons and its individual members in the intervening years is continually diminishing.

Many factors have brought about this result. The most important is that it is what the voters have wanted. They are not content to pick a good representative and leave it to him to vote for or against the government, but have wanted themselves to say whether Gladstone or Disraeli should be prime minister, or whether Home Rule was a good thing. Not only does this seem to be a more important question than any other, but it is the only one that can be asked of the nation as a whole. With the growing ease of communication, the isolation of separate geographical constituencies has been much diminished, and so too their sense of identity and individuality. I live in Oxford City but many of my colleagues and friends live in Oxfordshire or Berkshire, and I read newspapers and listen to wireless programmes that are meant to be read or listened to by people living in all parts of the country. A discussion on the rival merits of Mr Woodhouse and Mr Luard would be of no immediate practical concern to them, whereas everyone can follow an argument in terms of the competing claims of the Conservative or Labour Party; and so any discussion of political issues which is not to bore a lot of people must be in terms of national, not local, divisions. Such divisions as there are in the country are likely not to be geographical ones. When communications were bad, almost all my business and almost all my conversation was with my neighbours, and the neighbourhood formed a natural community. But now a man is much more likely to think of himself as a schoolmaster, as a skilled craftsman, or as a worker on the production line, than as a resident in Selly Oak or Perry Barr. How many secretaries in London as they flit from flatlet to flatlet are aware of whether they are in Hammersmith North, or Hammersmith Fulham, Marylebone, or Holborn and St Pancras South? Geographical divisions seem irrelevant and often are artificial, and the effect of our continuing to have Members of Parliament representing constituencies defined in geographical terms is to encourage us to understand the business of electing a Member of Parliament in some other way that does make sense to us. Once elected on this basis a Member of Parliament finds it very hard to maintain any independence of judgement, and therefore we in turn are all the less likely to see his election as anything other than a choice between parties.

Egalitarian sentiments also militate against parliamentary emphasis on the different representatives of different constituencies. For if everybody is really to count as one and nobody for more than one, then not only must each have one and only one vote but each vote must be equally effective. The most important thing about constituencies is no longer that they are constituted by some common interest but that they all should contain the same number of electors. The ancient distinction between shires and boroughs has been obliterated, and it became intolerable to egalitarians that there should be separate representation of universities. Equality in size of constituency, however, is not enough. The country is not so homogeneous that every constituency is exactly like every other, and the nice calculations of the psephologists about percentage swings and marginal seats are as abhorrent to the egalitarian as were the rotten boroughs of the unreformed Parliament. It is unfair that the marginal voter in Brighouse and Spenborough should have a more effective vote than his brother in Bournemouth or Ebbw Vale, or that a party can win a majority of seats in Parliament having obtained fewer, although better placed, votes in the country than its chief rival. The United States suffers from similar defects in the eyes of egalitarians. Not every vote is of equal value. In presidential elections a few votes in New York or California can make all the difference, whereas in the Senate the voters in Delaware or Nevada are given far greater weight than those of more populous States. Once the question being voted on is seen as a national question, only a nation-wide vote subject to a simple aggregation rule is appropriate. If everybody is to count the same, then exactly the same question must be asked of every voter, and their answers must all be treated exactly the same – they must all be added together as part of the same sum. Anything else is felt to be artificial and unfair. It may be accepted for the time being, but in times of crisis, when the decision is open to dispute, it will be criticized and will fail to win full acceptance from those disappointed by the result it yields.

These factors have contributed to the erosion of the traditional ideal of representative government. It would be an exaggeration to make out that it had entirely faded, but the tendencies are all towards playing down the role of the representative and playing up the importance of the electoral vote. The end-result is the mandate. The people are asked to entrust themselves to a person or a party for a term of years, and in their answer will be either approving or disapproving of the existing government's conduct of affairs during its term of office. Sometimes the choice will be between programmes, although with the advent of television it has become more a matter of the personalities of the two leaders. Democracy becomes an autocracy, in which all decisions save one are taken by the autocrat, and the only decision left to the people is the occasional choice of autocrat. We are once again a monarchy, but we do wrong to think of Queen Elizabeth II as the monarch. She is the Archbishop of Canterbury whose function it is, by the kissing of hands rather than the placing of the crown, to register and proclaim who our lawful sovereign is. Edward and Harold now take it in turns to be our king, as five hundred years ago Edward and Henry did in the Wars of the Roses. Only, we are more civilized, and confine our skulduggery to party conferences, and our battles to words. General elections decide who shall reign over us instead of the arbitrament of arms at Towton or Tewkesbury, and would-be leaders forfeit only their deposits and not their heads if they choose the losing side.

Many advantages are claimed for elective autocracy. It is held to be the most democratic form of government, the only one which gives everyone an equal say in public affairs. It is simple, and assigns responsibility clearly. It encourages those in authority to promote the public interest, and if it does not in fact work out all that well, it cannot work out all that badly either. In spite of these advantages, however, elective autocracy enables people to participate in government only to a derisory extent. In the name of equality it effectively denies political liberty, and makes the government singularly insensitive to the wishes of the governed and the requirements of justice.

Elective autocracy gives everyone a say. We all have a vote, and all can vote. Most of us are lost in a court of law or an administrative tribunal. But voting – putting a cross against a name – is something anyone can do. The paradigm of parliamentary representation outlined at the beginning of this chapter is fine for the ardent activist who likes writing letters to his M.P. and enjoys going to committees for the promotion of this and that, but it necessarily disfranchises the dumb majority who do not know how to write letters and do not relish being torn away from their television sets of an evening to go to public meetings in draughty village halls. More participatory forms of government, as we shall see in chapter twelve, favour the energetic, the educated and the economically well-off just as Locke's paradigm worked out in favour of the landlord and the entrepreneur. If we care for equality, and want to ensure that everybody can take part and nobody need be excluded, then we must bring the question within the reach of everybody. It is a reasonable tax on people's time to make them go to the polls once every four or five years, but more than this we cannot demand without in effect preventing some people from having as much a say as everybody else. Only by cutting everybody's say down to this size, can we be sure that everybody's say is the same.

Elective autocracy is effective in promoting the general public interest. Although different voters may understand the issue at a general election in different ways, anyone can understand it in a minimal sense as being a vote of confidence, and can form an impression whether he ever had it so good as under the present government. *How are you?* is about the simplest question that can be asked, and almost the only one that can be asked of everybody. Thus, if the question is put to every citizen, there will be a tendency to construe it in terms of general well-being. All contenders for power, therefore, will be seeking the greatest interest of a majority of voters, and so, although the choice of the voters may be somewhat unintelligent or uninformed as between the different ways of promoting their greatest interest, the alternatives themselves will have been framed by highly motivated professionals, and will thus be pretty good. Competition for political office, like economic competition generally, is highly effective in improving the standard of services on offer. Moreover, whichever alternative is adopted by the electorate, there is a fair prospect of its being carried out. Just because we are giving one man the power and letting him get on with the job, we can hold him responsible for what happens and judge by results. If we all insist on having a finger in the pie, then we cannot blame the cook if the pie turns out uneatable. If, on the other hand, we do not tie the government down but give it all the rope it wants, then it is quite clear whose fault the resultant hang-up is. More generally, if it is results that we want, then the best way to obtain them is to delegate full authority to the government and not fetter its discretion, but to hold it accountable at the end of its term of office for the general state of affairs obtaining then. The government once elected will seek to ensure that the general state of affairs is as good as possible. Moreover, it will be the general state of affairs as perceived by members of the general public. There will be no temptation to prefer special or partial interests to the public interest, because special interests appeal only to a minority of voters, and it is the majority who must be wooed. Measures which offend powerful interests will still be worth promoting if they conduce to the public interest, because on the day of judgement it will be the general impression of the general welfare formed by the general public that will bring in the votes and win the day. The autocrat knowing this, and wanting to be re-elected, will have every incentive to use his power for the general benefit. The traditional arguments for monarchy reappear under democratic guise. Kings are best, provided the people are the king-makers.

Even if these arguments fail, and elective autocracy is not the best form of government, still it is necessarily not the worst. It has a built-in safety-valve. If we do not like the present incumbent, we can replace him by the other man. Hence, however sub-optimal it may be, it has the more essential virtue of being 'super-pessimal'. The worst in politics is so bad, that it is well worth forgoing many excellences in order to ensure that it cannot happen here. Here, more than anywhere else, we need to pursue a 'minimax' strategy and choose that system which, even if everything else goes against us, will yield a result less disastrous than could have occurred had we made any other choice. And on this test elective autocracy comes out well. We shall always be able to avoid the worst excesses of government by reason of our being able to replace bad rulers by others, whom we may hope to be less bad. At the least, they will be other, and so constitute a salutary reminder to those in power that if they are reckoned to be bad they will not be re-elected; and even if the competition between parties at elections cannot be guaranteed to promote consumer satisfaction in the way the classical economists supposed, it does provide an effective remedy in the case of extreme dissatisfaction. Elective autocracy may not serve the long-term interests of the nation as well as a benevolent despot or Platonic meritocracy might: but it cannot continue being as bad as a Roman emperor or caste oligarchy could. And that, where the control of the coercive machinery of the state is involved, is far more important.

These arguments are not conclusive. They establish the case for there being some democratic element, so that everyone can have some say and unpopular regimes can be removed without bloodshed, but not for concentrating all power in the hands of the central government. Even within the terms of the economic analogy the argument is broken-backed. In particular, we need to be wary of the concept of general well-being which governments, under a system of electoral competition, will be encouraged to promote. True, we can ask people how things are going, and they may all give the same answer. But there is no single measure of the public interest that they are all applying. Nor are conditions favourable for assessing the performances of governments from a consumer's point of view. After all, even with cars, where we really are consumers, we are fairly inexpert ones. We buy them only seldom, and by the time we come to buy another, the market has changed so much that comparisons with previous experience are barely relevant. Although we talk about the rival merits of different models, and the newspapers provide some comment and criticism, we are none the less inadequately informed, and liable to be swayed by irrelevant considerations which the advertising media manipulate so as to have maximum psychological impact. Governments, like cars, involve a major commitment of resources, and we choose them too infrequently and under conditions too diverse to be able to make an informed choice. Elective autocracy credits us with being much more skilled consumers than we really are. It would be very difficult really to do a *Which?* guide to governments, and to disentangle which of its disasters each brought upon itself, and which were due to adventitious circumstances altogether beyond its control. Was it the Korean War or its own economic policies that blighted the prospects of Labour in 1951? Were Mr Heath's troubles in 1973-4 due to Sheikh Yamani and the miners, or to his own extravagance and abrasiveness? Although the newspapers carry a lot of comment and criticism about the performance of the government, we are still inadequately informed, and still liable to be swayed by irrelevant considerations. It is difficult for the electors to distinguish apparent euphoria for themselves from the real welfare of the nation. Whereas with small-scale decisions the facts are soon found out by those affected, to put a large question to a large number of people who cannot have direct acquaintance with most of the relevant details, is to put a premium on the phoney techniques of the P.R.O. man rather than on humble homespun truth. Each government approaching an election is tempted to inflate the economy in order to promote a temporary sense of prosperity to tide it over the election, and to leave it until after the people's verdict has been given to take unpopular remedial action, involving controls, freezes, high mortgage rates, credit restrictions, bankruptcies and unemployment. It is not clear that this temptation has always been resisted.

Although the government is properly concerned to promote the well-being both of individuals and of the country as a whole, it should not be regarded simply as a purveyor of prosperity. Nor is it. In so far as electors attribute their well-being or its absence to the government rather than the weather, they will do so in virtue of its policies and enactments. They may have only a hazy idea of what these are and how they work out. But although some voters vote out of habit or consideration of the rival leaders' sex-appeal, many are swayed by what they think the competing parties are likely to do, and, in as much as the consumer model is appropriate at all, they are consumers of policies rather than euphoria. Occasionally an election is fought on only one issue – the power of the House of Lords in 1910 – or gives a decisive answer as to what direction the country's future should take – in 1932 for America, in 1945 for Britain. Usually, however, each party programme is composed of many planks, and the relation between the elector's vote and the decisions either party would make if returned to power is complicated and unclear. One may think that the Conservatives stand for firmness with the foreigners or that the Labour Party will nationalize North Sea oil, and vote accordingly. Another may decide on the basis that the Tories will make the country more prosperous, or that Labour will do more for old-age pensioners. I may put problems of the environment first, while you are steamed up about the Third World, Mrs Robertson wants to re-introduce capital punishment, Adrian and Leslie are for gay liberation and legalizing pot, and the people in Acacia Avenue want to stop inflation and bring the trades unions to heel. So long as each party takes a different stand on every important issue, the elector who regards some one issue as all-important will be able to exercise his vote in a meaningful way. But unless the voter is single-minded to the exclusion of every other issue, he may find himself wanting to support one party on one issue and the other on another, and so unable to vote for either. As one non-voter put it in a letter to *The Times* (17 April 1973) after the first elections for the new regional authorities:

Sir, I do wish your correspondents would stop referring to those of us who choose not to vote as apathetic.

To cite my own example: I care very much indeed about the destruction of London which would result from the Ring Road proposals. Therefore I should have voted for Labour.

But, having taught in four of them, I am opposed to comprehensive schools being introduced at the cost of other forms of education. Therefore I should have voted Conservative.

Fundamentally, then, I must conclude that I disagree with the party system which insists that having voted for one item of a platform I therefore also support the others. There is only one way open to me to demonstrate my disapproval, and that is by not voting. That is what I did. But I am *not* apathetic. Nor, I do believe, am I alone.

WILLIAM EMMS
1a Carlingford Road, Hampstead, NW3.

The procedure of democratic voting results in our choices being very highly packaged. If everyone is to have a choice, it must be so much wrapped up that many will be misled by some of the wrappings, and some altogether put off by them.

It could be argued that we should not be too sorry for Mr Emms. After all, we are constantly having to choose between courses of action, each affording some advantages and disadvantages, without being able to pick and choose the advantageous aspects from both. Moreover, although in theory any variety of disparate items might be wrapped up in a package deal, in practice they are not. There is an underlying philosophy in each party which gives the separate planks of their platform an inner coherence; and a large part of the electorate will share the presuppositions of one or the other parties, and find the combination of policies offered intelligible and acceptable. Furthermore, it is argued that competition will ensure that the electors are offered what they collectively want. Each side is wanting to win, and therefore no substantial body of votes will go unwooed for long. If most voters who are against destroying London are also against comprehensive schools, then either the Conservative Party will seek to win their votes and will drop its plans for destroying London or the Labour Party will seek their votes at the cost of having to allow non-comprehensive education to continue. If a majority of opinion favours a certain course of action, then both parties will be inclined, other things being equal, to support that course of action, even if earlier they had been opposed to it. Many are the occasions that the Whigs have had their clothes stolen by their opponents just as they were coming into fashion. This is the reason why so often the parties seem to be becoming as indistinguishable as different brands of petrol or toothpaste. Policies, even more than petrol or toothpaste, are products for mass-consumption, and therefore tailored to suit a mass-market, and for that reason tend to mutual indistinguishability. But this, again, is often a cause for dissatisfaction. The voter feels he is being offered only a Hobson's choice – How should an anti-Marketeer have voted in 1970? In so far as the metaphors of the market-place apply in the arena of politics, the competition between the parties must be regarded as an oligopoly, since, for reasons that will emerge in the next chapter, there cannot be many contenders for power. One of the troubles with oligopoly is that it creates a symbiotic relationship between the few remaining rivals in which each is more concerned to capitalize on the defects of the others than to satisfy the real requirements of the consumer, and is impelled to market an identical product under an artificially differentiated brand-image, soliciting our custom not for what it is, but for what it is not. Just as advertisers spend millions telling us to buy petrol that is different, so politicians depend more on their rivals' tarnished images than their own merits when they seek our suffrages. Mr Heath's best friend is Mr Wilson, for no matter how badly he fared, he could always appeal to a widespread unwillingness to turn him out and put Mr Wilson on the throne. And the friendship is reciprocal. Mr Wilson would have had no hope of being returned to office in 1974 on the strength of his record or anything else but the one overriding consideration, that at least he was not Mr Heath. Oligopoly, in politics as in economics, makes for indistinguishable mass products and the elimination of individual choice, and is always liable to collapse, one way or another, into monopoly.

Occasionally, however, electoral competition may result in minorities being offered meaningful choices. Where important interests are involved it may pay a party to take account not only of the spread of opinion but its intensity also. If the government refuses to put up bilingual signs in Wales, it will save some money, and the majority of voters, who neither know nor revere the Welsh language, will be perfectly content. But their preference for a marginal saving of money is a weak one, whereas the people who want bilingual road-signs want them very much. If a party goes against the majority's wish, very few of them will mind and hardly any will switch their allegiance to another party on that account, whereas those who care a lot will come over *en bloc*. Of course, they are only a minority. But many minorities can make a majority. A coalition of minority interests – bilingualism, abortion-law reform, co-ownership of industrial concerns, cheaper mortgages for the newly-wed, penal reform and the provision of nursery schools – may constitute a winning combination, just because members of each minority care so much for one part of the party programme that they will put up with what in their eyes are the minor disadvantages of the rest. The recent history of the Liberal party may be seen as an attempt to use this strategy to break into the arena of serious politics. But it is a strategy from a position of weakness. A coalition lacks the inner coherence of a major party, and is always in danger of having some of its supporters suborned by one of the other parties. The fact that a coalition of minorities could be formed and could conceivably win is important in keeping the major parties from being too ready to trample on their rights and giving them some hope that some day their cause will prevail. But the general effect of electoral competition in a mass-electorate is, none the less, to limit rather than to widen the range of alternatives available to the individual elector.

Oligopoly often turns into monopoly, and electoral autocracy is similarly unstable. In much the same way as the logic of the vote eroded representative government and reduced it to electoral autocracy, so the logic of delegation is liable to erode electoral autocracy and reduce it to Platonic professionalism. As we saw in chapter five, the control of delegated power takes one of two forms: the choice of outline alternatives or the retention of the dormant veto. As we have described it, elective autocracy is an instance of the former. There are some pressures at work that make for an alternation of parties on the 'Swing of the Pendulum' principle, and in some countries and at some times the choice appears to be genuinely open. In others, however, there are periods during which one party seems to be an opposition party, only brought into power occasionally, when the predominant party is thought to have governed unusually badly. Once the alternation between parties has been broken, it becomes difficult to re-establish it, because after a few terms in opposition a party will have no leaders with any experience of power, and will cease to be a credible alternative in the eyes of the electorate. Elections will settle down to playing the role of a safety-valve; and over the course of years it will be increasingly felt to be irresponsible to throw the government out. Young men with serious ambitions will join the dominant party, and work their way up the party machine, and the opposition will become factious, the recipient of the protest vote rather than a serious rival for responsibility and power. The democratic aspect of government will be more and more attenuated, a safety-valve becoming ever less usable with disuse. In the tug-of-war between the government and the governed, the government has immense advantages, in knowledge, in professional experience, in confidence. It is difficult to mount a credible challenge. So long as the alternative government shows that it can govern by having in fact done so in the past, it constitutes a real alternative, which the voters can prefer. But it is a delicate situation. Rival rulers are not naturally or readily available. And if the only question put to the ordinary voter is *Who shall rule?* he will find it difficult to feel that he knows enough about the art of ruling to warrant voting for a change.

There are, however, some countervailing pressures, which may prevent the alternation of governments breaking down, and the voters' choice being reduced to a dormant veto. Our dislikes are much stronger than our likes. Decisions taken by the government are on average more likely to cost it votes than win them. Balfour once said that he had spent his majority like a gentleman, and every government is likely to suffer from attrition of its support, because people will blame it for what it does wrong, and remember that at the time of reckoning, while they will take its successes for granted and soon forget them. Nor is it only ingratitude. The very success of a government prepares the soil for the seeds of discord and loss of support. While a party is not in power it can seek support by concentrating on the points where the government is obviously wrong; but when the opposition comes into power itself, it will be able to remedy these, and then they will cease to be such important issues, and people will be less inclined to sink their differences in order to concentrate on righting them. The Labour Party in 1945 could achieve a high degree of unity on the programme of nationalizing coal, power and transport; but these once nationalized, the question of what to nationalize next became more relevant, and people who had been in harmony about coal fell to quarrelling over the merits of sugar, water and cement. The inevitable price of success is to move the divisive issues into one's own territory, and to start alienating some of one's own support. Clever politicians try hard to avoid it, and seek new issues which will not divide the nation against them, and sometimes succeed over one or two elections. But it is not altogether within the government's control to lay down what issues shall attract the attention of the electorate, and often the course of events will of itself raise issues on which, whatever the government decides, it will lose support. The swing of the pendulum is not an entirely idle metaphor.

But even if the pendulum swings, does it really signify? The picture that elective autocracy draws is one in which every five years we choose a prime minister, who, with the aid of a well-whipped majority in the House of Commons, can pass what laws and adopt what policies he thinks fit. But is this caricature correct? Does it really matter who is prime minister? Once, when the king died, it marked the end of an era in public affairs, and the death of King Henry V made a momentous difference in English history; but now the death of a monarch is a matter of symbolic rather than serious concern: since Queen Victoria's reign, the new monarch does not even have a new Parliament to give fresh counsel and advice. Should we not say the same about the occupant of 10 Downing Street? It is a matter for press photographers to record Mr Heath or Mr Wilson taking up residence there, but whether it is King Edward or King Harold who is nominally at the head of affairs, the measures seem much the same. The decision to join the Common Market was taken by the Civil Service around 1960. In the early 1960s and 1970s the Labour Party was strongly against it. But it was a Labour government which made the successful application to join. The Conservatives were elected in 1970 to fight inflation, and to stop subsidizing lame duck industries and trying to control prices and incomes by law; and duly stoked the fires of inflation, baled out Rolls-Royce, and tried to enforce a statutory wages and prices policy. As a rough guide, it takes about two years to bring a new government to heel, although some departments can digest a minister overnight. We should not be surprised, not unduly cynical. Most of the questions governments have to decide are posed not by the governments themselves but by the pressure of events; and the course of events does not divide up neatly into four-year or five-year periods. Moreover, many policies are long-term, and cannot be reappraised half-way through without severe loss. Once the Concorde project had been started, each successive government found that to cancel would mean writing off such huge expenditures that it seemed less costly in the long run to go on. Once one government has put its hand to the plough, the furrow is so long that there is no turning back for several succeeding administrations. Contractors come to have a vested interest in keeping the rolling programmes rolling and in structuring the official mind to prevent dangerous thoughts of reappraisal from being entertained. Even apart from considerations of continuity, the sheer size of modern governments makes it impossible for ministers to control more than a small proportion of the decisions being taken. It is a familiar story with autocracies all over the world, that the autocrat issues his ukase, but his servants, the *apparatchiks*, see to it that his intentions are not really carried out. In the British system, each department of state is nominally under the control of a minister, but the minister's writ does not run very far. He cannot know all that is going on in his department except what his advisers tell him about; and although we are very fortunate in having civil servants who not only are honest and competent, but try hard to keep the minister informed and to reserve the most important decisions to him, they have to use their own standards of what is important, and often find themselves having to make his mind up for him, because he is both too busy and insufficiently familiar with the issue to be able to think it through himself. To a very large extent, our system of government is a Platonic meritocracy, presided over by an outsider, a Tribune of Plebs appointed by a form of popular election, to whose views some consideration is shown. But the pressure of day-to-day business is always edging the control of affairs away from the nominal head and into the hands of the permanent under-secretaries. Some safeguard is provided by Parliament, and especially the parliamentary question, but a decreasingly effective one. It may seem a paradoxical conclusion, since the history of the constitution is all about how Parliament's powers have been first claimed, then asserted, then fought for and finally established, over a wider and wider front. But partly on account of the doctrine of the mandate and partly for personal and social reasons, each Parliament finds itself increasingly unwilling to force any issue against the government of the day; and since the government is normally formed from that party which has an overall majority in the House of Commons, it follows that the administration always has a majority, and never is in serious jeopardy in Parliament; and that therefore criticisms by back-bench M.P.s are unlikely to be able to make a department change its mind.

Although formally and according to the history books there has been a successful take-over bid of the Crown by Parliament, if we look beneath the surface we discern that what has really occurred has been a reverse take-over of Westminster by Whitehall.

Of course, it is not a complete take-over. Myths are potent. Civil servants continue to respect parliamentary forms in spite of the realities of the situation. Even manifestly incompetent ministers are treated with great deference. Though permanent under-secretaries may sometimes secretly despise their parliamentary masters, still they feel they need them, to shield them from seeming to claim Platonic powers. The doctrine of ministerial responsibility may be a lie, but it is, from the Civil Service point of view, a noble lie, enabling unpopular decisions to be taken and ensuring that there always is a suitable politician available to carry the can. Civil servants are aware of their own limitations, and of the inadequacies of any system founded on Platonic pretensions, and insist that they are but servants, and only carry out the orders given them by their superiors. And although it is built into any large-scale autocracy that most of the decisions are taken by the *apparatchiks*, it equally is built into it that the most important ones will come at least to the attention of the autocrat; if he is democratically elected, some element of electoral choice is preserved. But not enough. Even on the consumer model, elective autocracy is inadequate. Even if politicians were simply marketing rival brands of government, they would need to do market research, and would need more information than the ballot-box provides about the consumer reaction to different aspects of their product. They need feed-back, but stifle it. For there are costs not only in getting information but in giving it. Making up my mind about what I want is like making decisions – it takes time and energy I can ill afford, unless it is going to be some use. If I am merely asked my opinion by a pollster, I shall say whatever comes into my head, and no amount of statistical analysis can abstract from a number of ill-considered opinions anything but an unreliable guide to what people really want or will do. It is only if I have some prospect of what I say actually affecting the outcome – only if I am really participating – that I shall take the trouble to articulate my own opinion. Only a participatory system will elicit the information which even Platonic professionals need if they are to do their job properly. The motor manufacturers used to claim that they were highly responsive to the consumers' needs, that usually they anticipated them before they had ever been articulated, and that the volume of complaints was very low. All this was true, but missed the point that the volume of complaints was low precisely because complainants never got anywhere, and soon tired of grousing and just shut up. The Civil Service can likewise pride itself on taking considerable note of what the public wants, and often catering for new-felt wants long before Parliament has even become aware of them; and can similarly point to a general absence of specific complaint, without realizing that this may largely be due to their inflexible determination never to budge once their minds are made up. Few people enjoy battering their heads against a brick wall. It is a waste of time trying to fight a department. Even if you expose their errors in full Parliamentary debate, they will still win the division. If you cannot beat them, pipe down and save your breath. Elective autocracy discourages the generation of information and chokes its flow. Whereas representative government seeks information and provides fairly capacious channels for communication between constituent and government, elective autocracy is based on a principle of minimum communication. The electors are asked only one question every four or five years, and apart from the verdict of a general election, the government is in the dark about how it is faring and what alterations of policy are needed. It would be better if there were more moments of truth, and if, even at the cost of having its plans checked, the government were sometimes forced to reappraise its policies before they were pushed through to their disastrous conclusions. Manufacturers who brush off complaints save themselves trouble, but lose out in the long run; governments who share power with the people are sometimes crossed and have to abandon pet projects, but they learn far better what they should be trying to do, and often also earn the active cooperation, rather than bare acquiescence, of those they are trying to govern.

Our fundamental attitude to government should be that of potential cooperators rather than potential consumers. Not only is the consumer model basically inadequate, as we saw in chapter five, but if we take a purely economic external view of government we shall engender an equally external attitude on its part towards us. If we ask only what the government will do for us, we soon shall have cause to complain of what it is doing to us. We therefore should regard government as an activity of *our* community which *we* can to some extent identify with and can on occasion take part in. Seen in this light, elective autocracy shows up badly. Democratic in one sense it may be, but in others it is highly undemocratic. Although everybody has the vote, the vote does not give anyone any significant say. Even if the choice reserved to the electorate every four or five years is significant, it is only one, and the business of government involves many, many choices not all of which are of no concern to anyone but professional politicians and civil servants. Elective autocracy reserves all decisions except one to the autocrat and his *aides*, and in lieu of allowing anyone any say on any specific issue, fobs him off with the question whether he would prefer TweedleTed or TweedleHarold to take no notice of his views. It is like the American couple where the wife was unwilling to allow her husband to take all the decisions, and so they agreed that he was to take all the important decisions and she all the unimportant ones; pressed to reveal the distinction between the two categories, she explained that she decided what clothes the children were to wear, where they were to go to school, what new automobile to purchase, what neighbourhood to reside in, and what employment to take, whereas her husband decided whether the United States should recognize Red China and whether the Supreme Court was acting unconstitutionally. So too the voter may feel that the final arbitrament vested in his hands is too great for him, and that more valuable than having a small say in such high matters of statecraft would be to have an effective say in the things that he really is concerned about.

Although elective autocracy has its democratic aspect, it is deeply undemocratic as regards the way and the spirit in which decisions are taken, and has a built-in bias against freedom and justice. It is non-participatory. Apart from the minimal participation of casting a vote at election time, it gives would-be participators no part in the decision-making process. Decisions are not reached openly, after discussion with affected parties, but secretly by civil servants who are responsible only to the government and need not consult with anyone, nor are obliged to expose their real reasons to public scrutiny. We are baffled by the unfrankness of the bureaucracy and infuriated by its dismissive insensitivity to our views. Although most of us are usually not very active in politics, sometimes we have occasion to make a suggestion or register a protest, and want some sort of assured access to decision-makers, some way of making them give our arguments reasonable consideration. It was one merit of the vote under the theory of representative government that it constituted a lever which a man could use to press people to take proper notice of his views; under elective autocracy, however, its leverage is reduced to a minimum. The very fact that the government has won the last general election gives it a claim to legitimacy which often is taken to authorize neglect of individual initiatives and gross invasion of individual rights. Because those who exercise power exercise it in the name of the people, and are genuinely trying to promote the public interest as they see it, their moral perceptions are blunted by the magnificence of the commission they have undertaken, and they overlook the contrary interests of minorities and especially individuals. If we value political liberty, we must devise means whereby individual initiatives are fostered rather than politely ignored, and encourage people, not themselves full-time permanent administrators, to make their contribution to the life of the community. Equally, if we value justice, we cannot be content with elective autocracy, again on account of its unresponsiveness to the individual, who can neither move the autocrat nor gain the attention of the electorate. Without the help of special procedures and special obligations on decision-makers to pay attention to the justice of his case, an individual cannot make much impression on any government, and none on a monolithic one. His one vote is not only ineffective as a lever but inadequate as a shield – what is one among so many? Nor can he expect the electorate to bring the government to account for the injustices of its administration. It is not feasible to apprise a large number of electors of the circumstances of each individual case. Besides, the majority could be very uncaring about the ill-used or the less fortunate. Many take an *I'm all right Jack* attitude and do not want to know of the injuries and sufferings of others. If the fate of the man who fell among thieves had depended on a democratic vote, there would have been a two-to-one majority in favour of passing by on the other side. And so it is with us.

For every Crichel Down that comes to the ears of the public there are literally thousands that are buried in the archives of Whitehall and in the hearts of the people. Every M.P. and social worker knows of men and women who are living with a sense of grievance at the hand of authority, some of whom have had their lives ruined by persecution complexes.*

Elective autocracy, although necessarily not the worst form of government, is not good enough. It is a guarantee against bloody revolution and effective in preventing the government from systematically ignoring the interests or flouting the wishes of the governed. It avoids the worst abuses and makes the government responsive to large shifts of public opinion. But it cannot discriminate finely enough to take account of the individual, to remedy his grievances or carry out his ideas. It is difficult to say what is wrong, because it is not so much some major errors of policy as innumerable individual frustrations and injustices, each by itself too insignificant to attract notice but enough to make some individual miserable and prevent him from identifying with the public authorities. And so we have a situation in which there are few specific complaints but a general unease, few scandals but a general sense of alienation, few grievances ventilated but a claustrophobic sense of all the decisions that affect our lives being in the hands of 'them', who mean us no ill but are quite prepared to ride rough-shod over us, ignoring all our entreaties, disrupting all our plans and stifling all our aspirations, if, in their opinion, the public interest so requires.

* Reginald Bevins, *The Greasy Pole*, London, 1965, page 66; quoted by A. H. Birch, *The British System of Government*, London, 1967, page 259.

11 The Road from Wales to Westminster

The disadvantages of the existing party system are so manifest that people are often tempted to found a new party. Indeed, if the existing parties are all agreed on some issue, the only recourse for citizens who take the other view is to band together and present the electors with the opportunity of voting for a candidate of their own way of thinking. But there are difficulties. These depend on the nature of politics and government, and can be illustrated by considering the prospects for some single-plank party which could hope to win some seats and then set out to storm the citadels of power and put the government right on some specific issue. They turn on the practicalities of political activity and the peculiar position and special problems of the government, and give us some idea of what needs to be done if our system is not to be one that is only nominally democratic and minimally participatory.

It is difficult to get a new party going. Many voters inherit their party loyalties, like their names, from their fathers. A new party has no hope with them unless some sixty years before it came into existence it succeeded in converting their grandfathers to its way of thinking. The hereditary system is usually supposed to be a hangover from feudal times, and modern political scientists avert their eyes from the fact that modern political parties, Labour and Liberal as much as Conservative, depend on it for a large part of their electoral support and are often guided by it in their selection and promotion of M.P.s. But it is perfectly natural, and follows from the games-theoretical rationale of the state given in chapter four. Just as we need authority because otherwise we do not know where we are and cannot cooperate with one another, so because we realize we cannot individually and separately concert our political efforts, we are predisposed

to be guided by anything we think others will be guided by too.
You may be unenamoured of the Labour Party lefties, and much
better suited by a new centre grouping, but the Labour Party is
there, and therefore you vote for it, just as your father did, as
the only way of keeping the businessmen from muscling in on
the country. Simply because it is largely a matter of convention
whose validity depends on its being concurrently accepted by a
large number of people at once, political allegiance tends to be
handed down in families as part of the family tradition. In a
much more obvious way, the hereditary principle works in the
selection of leaders. For what makes a man a leader is being accepted as such; and though some gifts of personality and intel-
lect are necessary and a few people are so forceful that they could
establish themselves in any society, there are many men who, if
they were looked up to, would give a satisfactory lead, but are
not on their own account looked up to by a sufficient number
of people to be already established as leaders. In such a situation,
any adventitious advantage is enormous. To have run the four-
minute mile or sailed round the world single-handed or climbed
Mount Everest would do, but to bear a well-known name and be
the son of a man already famous is a more commonly possessed
attribute and gives just the edge required for success early on. If
I am to be effective in politics, I must be known. I must be a
celebrity – that is, a man who is famous simply for being famous.
But it is very difficult to arrive at that state, and will take most
people a long time. A democracy, as de Tocqueville observed,
tends to be a gerontocracy, and if we attempt to lay the accent
on youth, as modern political parties say they do, then we are
bound to give scope to the hereditary principle, since young men
have not had time to make a name for themselves or to have done
more than be their fathers' sons. The original sense of the word
'noble' is 'knowable'. And the fundamental need for knowability
on the part of any would-be politician in a large-scale society
explains how the hereditary principle, however often thrown out
of the window, still returns through the door. Cicero once com-
plained that while he had to work hard for his promotion, the
Roman nobles were promoted in their sleep. But that just is the
logic of large-scale leadership, and is one of the underlying

reasons why the going is so difficult either for a new man in ancient Rome or a new party in modern Britain.

Another difficulty is money. Contrary to received opinion, democratic institutions both favour and need the very rich. If we give everyone the vote, then there are very many decision-makers to whom a new party must address itself. Moreover, if many of the voters are only minimal participants, anxious to keep the cost of informing themselves as low as possible, all the expense of telling them about the new party will have to be met by others. Newspapers and broadcasts provide some coverage, but not repetitiously enough to make an effective impression on the awareness of the minimally interested; there will be a premium on more direct, and therefore more costly, approaches. It is an instance of the principle we formulated in chapter eight, that the greater the number of decision-makers, the harder it is to address them all, and the fewer the opportunities for getting new ideas across to them. In a small society the unostentatious man without great wealth will none the less be known and valued; the more voters there are, however, the greater will be the proportion who will not know of him unless they are specially told of him, and therefore the greater the premium on self-advertisement and wealth. It is no accident that the century of the common man is the one that has favoured millionaires as candidates for the presidency of the United States. We should not be surprised at this fact, nor should we deplore it. Rich men at least can afford to be honest: Kennedy had no need to cheat the income tax. Better have some rich men running for office than all the candidates financed by campaign contributions from sources that may expect some return for their outlay. It is an unwelcome conclusion for many modern-minded democrats, who believe that democracy requires strict economic equality, but one which must nevertheless be faced; it is very difficult in an egalitarian society either to oppose the central government or to launch new ideas. Equality favours the existing establishment. It is inherently costly to communicate with myriads of decision-makers, and therefore expensive to break into a mass-market in politics, just as it is in economics. In particular, our present electoral system, with constituencies each returning that one candidate who gets more votes than any other, makes it difficult for a party to attract votes unless it already seems to have a fair chance of winning, and thus sets the threshold of viability especially high. Later we shall need to consider further how innovation can avoid being stifled by the need to operate immediately on a large scale if it is to operate effectively at all. But if there is to be a traditional democratic part of the decision-procedure, involving a mass-electorate, and if we do not wish to confer a vested interest on the existing major parties, there must be sufficient concentrations of economic resources, distributed up and down the country and outside the control of the government, for new parties to have some hope of attracting adequate finance.

These difficulties are already formidable, but not yet insurmountable. New parties sometimes find sufficient financial backing and popular support to get off the ground. In present-day Britain, the best examples are the various nationalist parties of Wales and Scotland. Because of the geographical nature of their appeal, they are not hamstrung, but positively helped, by constituencies being drawn up on a geographical basis. And although the number of seats they have won is small, they often reach second place in elections and could, without too great a strain on the imagination, be supposed to have won most of the seats in Wales or Scotland. But what then? The strength of their appeal lies in its simplicity, and government is a complicated business. So long as I stand for home rule for Wales, or for a larger proportion of the oil revenue to be devoted to Scotland, I shall find many supporters. And so long as I am not in power, I can continue to plug this same safe line, and give my supporters complete satisfaction that I am representing their views. But if I form, or even join, the government, the case is very different. For then I am constantly having to decide all sorts of questions, which are never discussed at Plaid Cymru conferences at Llandrindod Wells and on which no bard at any Eisteddfod has given prophetic guidance. I shall have to decide about the composition of Regional Health Boards, and the provision of nursery schools, and how much more money to spend on Concorde, and how to try to stop East African potentates being nasty to Indians and Indians from being nasty to Pakistanis, and ... and .. and. The state, as we saw in chapter five, because it is an unselective community, has to be omnicompetent, and governments have to hold themselves in readiness to decide any question that crops up. Hence, not only governments, but would-be governments, must have views on a large number of questions that are likely to arise. So long as I am a private individual, or even if I am a zealot for Welsh Nationalism, I can brush off awkward questions by confessing my ignorance and unconcern. But if I am seriously asking people to put me into power, I expose myself to their questions, 'What would you do about ...?' And unless I have some clue as to what I should do about the burning issues of the day, people are unlikely to want to put me in a position to do anything about them. We want to know what the Liberal line is on the Third World, local government, value-added tax, or pollution, or what the Conservatives are going to do to maintain law and order, or to help the pensioner or restore the railways. Of course, one cannot anticipate every eventuality and on occasion it is acceptable to reserve one's position and say, 'We will cross that bridge when we come to it.' But people are rightly suspicious of a politician who plays all his cards very close to his chest. He is asking for *carte blanche* without giving us any reason why he should have it. We want to enter into some sort of dialogue with him about some of the things he would do if he could, and this dialogue inevitably blurs the stark simplicity of the single-plank platform.

As a party becomes more powerful, it is more capable of exerting some influence on the course of events, and will be under pressure to exercise that power responsibly. Up to a point it can discharge its responsibility by bargaining. The party will give its support to any government on the one condition that the government in its turn secures that the party's one aim is achieved. It is an effective tactic. Most governments are very keen to obtain and keep power, and are seldom going to be so anxious that the single-plank party's one aim should not be realized that they will sacrifice the possibility of power for the sake of frustrating it. In Israel, the Strict Orthodox Party, the N.R.P., has supported every government, and has been highly successful in securing that Rabbinical laws are still upheld by the secular State of Israel and that only kosher food is served in government hotels

and airlines. But although bargaining is very likely to be successful, it always may fail, and even when successful exacts a price.
If the Welsh Nationalists demand too much, no other party will
be able to meet that demand without forfeiting support from the
rest of the electorate. Moreover, if one party is bargaining, the
other may be able to drive a fairly hard bargain. The Ulster
Unionists did not like the Conservative government's policy in
Northern Ireland, but could not hope to do better with the
Socialists. Even if bargaining succeeds in its immediate aim, it
does so at the price of having to give the government some support in return and taking its side on some of the very different
questions that it will have to face. And since these are sometimes
divisive issues, there will be some supporters of the party who will
dissent from the policies that the party is having to support.
Some Welsh Nationalists will be in favour of comprehensive
schools, others will cherish the traditional grammar school. So
long as their M.P. is a voice crying in the wilderness about the
iniquitous exploitation of Wales by English industrialists and
Midland water boards, they can all unite in supporting him. But
once he starts taking a stand on divisive issues, they will be
divided. They may still support him, reckoning the cause of
Welsh Nationalism to outweigh all more mundane considerations, but their case then will resemble the normal one of the
elector voting for one of the major parties with considerable reluctance, weighing the unattractiveness of some planks of its
platform against the attractiveness of others. The single-plank
party answers the needs of those who care about only one question of public policy, or care about it incommensurably more
than about any other question. But the logic of government is
to be concerned with many questions, and as the single-plank
party approaches the centres of power, it is inevitably caught by
the logic of the position it is seeking to occupy.

Power, like gravitation in the general theory of relativity, imposes curious curvatures on the conceptual space of politics, and
makes the road from Wales to Westminster a long and winding
one, with many diversions and many pitfalls. It is often argued
that nobody, certainly no party, can traverse it, and that therefore
between Wales and Westminster there must be a great gulf fixed,

so that while Westminster may send down to Wales its decisions on road-signs or reservoirs, Wales can never exert any effective pressure on Westminster. Our present institutions give substance to this argument, and engender alienation and violence in the body politic. It is, of course, true that a single-plank party is, in most circumstances, an implausible candidate for power, and that most people do not attach such overriding importance to one aim that they are supposed to forgo their say on all others in order the more effectively to say just one thing. But some people do. They may be a minority, but they care passionately. And the fact that their feeling, or at least their intensity of feeling, is not shared by the majority of voters is not sufficient to disqualify them from all consideration. What has been happening in recent years is that minorities, bound together by strongly-held values, have not been able to get themselves heard by those in power. They feel themselves ignored and suffocated. They turn to violence both as a natural response to being ignored and as apparently the one effective tactic open to them. Violence not only relieves the feelings but attracts attention. Instead of being reported merely on the inside pages of the *Aberystwyth Advertiser*, a Welsh Nationalist by the use of a little gelignite can get on to the front page of the *Daily Express*; and whereas civil servants are very good at thinking up reasons why the serious arguments adduced by a nationalist should not, or better, could not, be acted on, they are frightened by violence and rapidly moved to adopt a more conciliatory posture. Violence should, however, be seen more as a symptom of, than a remedy for, the ills of the body politic. We can understand why people resort to violence without encouraging them to do so. Its effectiveness is necessarily limited. Only so long as it is exceptional will it attract publicity or induce civil servants to avoid provoking it. Once it becomes the rule, it will be ignored. After all, far more people are killed each year by the motor-car than by the I.R.A., but no newspaper takes much notice. Demonstrations will become another hazard of life – like strikes, just one of those things. Moreover, violence can be counter-productive, as the students have discovered to their cost. Furthermore, it is all right only so long as the other side is not violent too. But if minorities can resort to violence, so can majorities. And whereas a minority can often win the argument, in a real fight the weight of numbers is likely to prove irresistible.

For these and many other reasons, the resort to violence is no remedy for the frustrations which minorities feel. But it is not enough to deplore. Something has gone wrong. The way we are spelling out democracy is failing to accord with the natural and reasonable desires of many people, who, although they are given the vote – almost because they are given the vote – are denied any effective voice in the decisions that concern them most. We have failed to discriminate between the many things on which many people have weak preferences and the few things on which a few people have deep concern, and have effectively diluted the latter by counting it in with the former. It is, as we have seen, a natural tendency of a voting system, but it is a defect none the less. It is also the consequence of the way our constitution has developed in response to political theory. When kings really ruled England, the House of Commons really did represent the limited local interests of communities up and down the country. Members of Parliament could be spokesmen of particular interests, because they did not have to assume the day-to-day responsibility for all the decisions taken by the government. Rather, there was a contrast between the ordinary business of government and extraordinary decisions, for which the king would seek parliamentary approval, and might need to make concessions and compromises in order to obtain it. The contrast preserved the freedom of the individual Member to represent those matters which interested his shire or borough without having to take up a position on all the other questions that the government had to decide. In the American Constitution – which is often an illuminating guide to what the Founding Fathers thought the British Constitution should have been – the members of Congress have this role much more clearly, and still act very largely as agents bargaining with the central government on behalf of their own localities. But in Britain, as Parliament took over the powers of the monarch it lost its distinctive role as the fortress of particular interests. The comparison made in the previous chapter with the Electoral College of the United States is exaggerated but has point; it goes far to explain why the House of Commons, having become in effect our king-maker, can no longer discharge the incompatible function of representing the different interests of the different constituencies of the realm, and trying to secure that the government's policy, if not ideal, at least should be reasonably acceptable to all concerned. The road from Wales to Westminster has been diverted to Whitehall.

It is easier to diagnose than to prescribe. Many remedies have been canvassed. Parliament should be resuscitated. We should have a written constitution incorporating a Bill of Rights, which the courts should be able to enforce against the government. We should adopt the French *Conseil d'État* to compel the bureaucrats to behave, or the Scandinavian *Ombudsman* to shame them into repentance for their grosser misdemeanours. There is merit in all these suggestions, and some are worth elaborating further, but not in very much detail, because the effectiveness of institutions and the practicability of proposals depends on the circumstances obtaining at the time, and we do not know what they will be. What we can do now, and need to do if any remedies are to work, is to examine the logical geography of politics and see more clearly the lie of the land. We are led astray, and our efforts to return into more advantageous courses go awry, because we are in thrall to distorted concepts, which make us see necessities where none exist, and overlook possibilities that might well prove beneficial if only we would explore them. We have certain slogans, such as the separation of powers and ministerial responsibility, which prevent us from understanding what is going on in the places of power. Power itself has been wrongly understood, and supposed, on account of an equivocation in the word 'sovereign', to be necessarily unshareable. The attitude of mind of those who exercise power has been corrupted, in part by the *amour propre* that is the inheritance of all the sons of Adam, in part by a high-minded determination to serve the public interest with their utmost zeal. The countervailing power of Parliament has been eroded, in part by deficiencies of procedure, but more insidiously because back-benchers lack both the means and the will to exercise it, and are generally confused about their role as representatives. If representative government is to be restored, we need a deeper understanding of why representation is needed and how it is possible, as well as institutional changes to enable relevant representations to be brought to bear on the centres of power.

The concept of sovereignty has been responsible for much spilling of ink and occasionally the sadder shedding of blood. The conflict between king and Parliament was not a gratuitous one. Each claimed the final say, and the logic of Leviathan will not let us serve two masters and stay one state. But the final say is not the same as the initial say. Although it is a requirement of logic that a state should have only one ultimate decision-proce-dure, it is also required of any state which is going to survive that its authorities shall be able to resolve most disputes expedi-tiously and inexpensively. That is why, as we saw in chapter five, we have to have some professionals giving continual attention to the affairs of state. These will naturally have first say, which must in most cases be *the* say, but not necessarily always. We need to differentiate the two functions, one traditionally discharged by the king, the other by the king-in-Parliament. Both have been called sovereign. But a real conflict over the ultimate decision-procedure obscured an equally important separation of roles, which, whoever occupies them, it is vital to keep distinct, be-cause otherwise the professional point of view will override all others in the name of firm government. There are occasions when firm decisions have to be taken by whatever procedure is recog-nized as ultimately authoritative, but this need for ultimate firm-ness is often misconstrued in British constitutional practice as justifying ministers in pushing their measures through Parlia-ment, whatever the opposition and however good its arguments. We need to distinguish the first say from the last say. The first say is for the professionals. Only they are on the job full-time, and only they can give the snap answers to all the questions as they arise. Often this is enough. But some questions are of deep concern to non-professionals, and the fact that it is inherent in the nature of the state that a citizen's views may be ultimately overridden is no reason whatever for excluding all non-profes-sionals from having any effective say in the decision-taking of their society.

But there are difficulties in making the government have second thoughts. Some are purely human. Men dislike making concessions. Governments in particular have a deep-seated urge to get their own way. It does not much matter what that way is, concession – particularly concession in the party atmosphere of Parliament – seems to be a sign of weakness, and ministers prefer to manifest their virility by obstinately obstructing every attempt to persuade them to alter their minds, sometimes even maintaining, as Sir Robert Peel did, that people like it that way. Of course, people like strong-mindedness. But obstinacy is normally characteristic of the weak rather than the strong. The extreme reluctance of departments and their ministers ever to give way is understandable but unpardonable. It makes government not a matter of reason but of force, and encourages the governed to regard it not as an authority whose lead is readily followed, but as a power which may have to be obeyed on occasion but is to be circumvented or resisted whenever possible. The practice has grown up whereby grievances are ignored as long as possible, and only if there is a major row will the government alter its course at all, and then only by changing its policy for the future rather than putting right the original grievance. It should be the other way about. A government should take pride in seeking out complaints and remedying them, and in accepting criticism and acting on it whenever it can be constructively incorporated in the policy finally adopted. There will still be plenty of occasions for firmness. Greatness of mind is shown not by a ruler's insisting on his own way against the opposition of those who are in a weaker position, but in being able to include them in by reason of the breadth of his vision and the largeness of his purposes.

The public interest is often invoked by the government as a reason for not giving way. But it is a confusion, as we saw in chapter six, to think that there is a single concept of the public interest, and the question is not whether the public interest should give way to some sectional interest represented in Parliament, but rather how a balance should be struck between different aspects of the public interest. And in deciding this, one consideration is often of preponderating importance – that it is very greatly in the public interest to achieve a consensus. We need not merely to decide on policies, but to be able to carry them out; and if we are to be able to do that, we need to be able to carry people, even those originally hostile, with us. We may not always win their agreement, but need to disarm their vehement dissent as much as we can. Elective autocracy suffers from its enabling the successful contender for power to push through Parliament a party-political programme without any need to conciliate the opposition as much as possible. The public interest required an Industrial Relations Act, and since Mr Wilson abandoned his, Mr Heath was right to enact one in his Parliament; but most of the benefit was lost because it was too abrasively enacted to secure the cooperation of the trades unions. A less ambitious act might have been technically less good. But a less good act that worked would have been better than a better one that did not. So, too, more generally, when a government proposal is resisted by the representatives of a particular interest, not only is it possible that the government's initial proposals were wrong on any count, but often it would be better for the country to pursue a sub-optimal policy and preserve national unity than to be directed towards one that the Civil Service correctly believes to be best, but at a cost of dissension and non-cooperation on the part of an informed and concerned minority. The minimax principle we invoked in the previous chapter applies not only to governments but to policies. Rather than aim to achieve the best, we should endeavour to avoid the worst, and reckon that an adequate measure that is acceptable is better than an ideal one that is divisive.

Governments have been loth to allow their measures to be assessed individually, and have claimed that they form an integrated package and the country must take it or leave it as a whole. The argument from coordination, as we saw in chapter five, carries some weight, but not all that much. Some combinations of policies would be incoherent, and the government would be entitled to say that it should not be asked to carry any such combination into effect. But far more combinations are feasible and there is much more latitude for concessions than is admitted. The edifice of governmental policies is pretty ramshackle anyhow, and it is almost always implausible to maintain that no alteration may be made on pain of bringing the whole structure crashing in ruins to the ground. It is also argued, as in the previous chapter, that only by giving the government complete power can we hold it completely accountable at the end of its term of office for whatever happened during it. But that argument we saw to be invalid. No government is all-powerful. Most of the factors that influence what actually happens are beyond its control. The need to make concessions to secure consent or conciliate the opposition is only one among many factors which prevent the government from being able to do what it likes or achieve all its aims. In so far as electors attribute their well-being or its absence to the government rather than the weather, they will do so in virtue of its policies and enactments, and the more acceptable these are, the more readily they will return the government again to power; or rather, what really loses a government votes is being associated with a measure voters strongly dislike. The electorate is not the amorphous lump that advocates of elective autocracy assume, but a heterogeneous collection of individuals many of whom are capable of discriminating between different measures. Many of them are moderately apathetic and opposition is therefore fairly easily disarmed. But the modern practice of pushing policies through with no concessions at all inevitably antagonizes some voters, and helps to bring about electoral defeat, and ultimately disenchantment with the system.

The doctrines of ministerial responsibility and the separation of powers have greatly distorted Whitehall's own understanding of itself. Together they exclude almost all non-professionals from almost all important decisions. The separation of power is invoked to exclude almost all those who are Members of Parliament and ministerial responsibility to Parliament is invoked to exclude those who are not. According to the separation of powers we should distinguish three functions of government, the legislative, the judicial and the executive, and have these functions discharged by separate organs. It never was an apt description of British practice, and even in the United States, where the constitution was based on this doctrine, it has become increasingly inaccurate with the passage of years. Not only has the Supreme Court in recent years become the most important legislative organ, but, more significantly still, the enormous growth of the executive has shown how inadequate the classification of functions was. In Britain, too, more and more regulations of general application stem from civil servants who nominally are merely carrying out the instructions of others: more and more adjudications of conflicting interests are made by civil servants whose only legal status is that of *aides* to ministers. A long time ago, when departments were very small, it was quite reasonable for civil servants to be regarded as personal assistants to their minister, and to have their loyalties exclusively directed towards him. A very important man needs personal assistants, to carry his briefcase, write his speeches, answer his invitations, and generally to help him along; and in a personal staff total personal loyalty is seemly. But a department of state is not like that. It is very large. It serves not one man personally, but a succession of holders of the office. If civil servants make a boob, dismissing the minister will not get rid of them: they are not appointed by the minister, and cannot be dismissed by the minister; and to view them as being simply the minister's personal staff responsible solely to him, with the minister alone responsible for them, is a fiction that has now outlived its usefulness. It was originally a good principle. Irresponsibility is bad. Parliament, by calling all the king's ministers to account, secured us against the despotism of the *ancien régime*. But always it recognized that it could not call the judges to account, and now it should recognize that since, for reasons of time and complexity, it cannot effectively question all the bad decisions made by civil servants, it should establish other institutions for controlling them; otherwise they will be effectively uncontrolled, being in theory answerable only to a minister who in fact is quite unable to call them to account. Instead of seeing themselves as secretive secretaries whose sole function is to support one man and enable him to carry out the duties of his office, they should see themselves as open legislators and responsible judges. Their jobs confer security of tenure in practice almost like that of the judges, and should, like judicial office, impose a personal responsibility to uphold certain standards of fairness, impartiality and integrity even to the disadvantage of the Crown. Instead of cloaking their decisions with the authority of a minister who nominally takes them but hardly ever really has any say in them, they should see themselves as performing functions comparable to those of legislators and judges, requiring analogous attitudes of mind, and subject to similar controls. They often make general decisions affecting the rights and interests of citizens at large, and therefore should discuss their proposals not only confidentially with interested parties invited by the department, but openly with representatives of the public at large – in some cases, Members of Parliament, whose frustration at present is partly due to their being excluded, because of the doctrine of the separation of powers, from all part in the initial, and effective, stages of deciding what form new laws and new regulations shall take. Judges too have been inhibited from reviewing any question that could be deemed a question of policy, and in deference to Dicey's disastrous distaste for *droit administratif* give Britons far less protection against well-administered wrong than Frenchmen or Americans enjoy. Civil servants also have been led to believe that, as administrators, they are not supposed to approach questions in a judicial frame of mind. But they are in effect exercising the power of the state, often potentially to the disadvantage of the individual, and are for that reason responsible for their decisions, and under a duty to be moved not by reasons of state alone but especially by consideration for the rights of the individual. They can be responsible without being responsible *to* anyone. Judges may not decide arbitrarily, but must give reasons for their decisions; only, instead of reporting quietly to the Minister of the Interior, they give their reasons in open court, and any member of the public can hear them and assess them, and badly grounded decisions are subject to appeal. We have to have judges of very high calibre, but many civil servants are intellectually and morally responsible enough to be vested with something of the same authority, and although sometimes procedures would be more cumbersome and principles more difficult to articulate, the gain in public confidence and co-operation would outweigh the loss of administrative clarity and convenience.

With these changes of perspective, Whitehall would see itself and be seen as much more flexible and less obdurate than now. It could be less secretive than it has to be if it is supposed to be merely briefing the minister before he makes up his mind. There could be more realistic, and therefore more effective, assignments of responsibility. There would be more channels of communication, especially between the Civil Service and Members of Parliament, instead of routeing them all through a few overworked ministers.

Members of Parliament are quick to attribute their frustrations to the civil servants' determination to keep all decisions in their own hands, but slow to acknowledge that they themselves are also largely to blame. They allow themselves to be too well whipped; indeed, take almost a masochistic pleasure in the experience. Although it is right and proper to be guided on many matters by the opinion of one's leaders, it is neither necessary nor desirable to troop through the division-lobbies in order to ensure that the departmental view of the matter should triumph over that of its critics. It is reasonable to expect a Labour M.P. to be ready to vote for some measure of nationalization or a Conservative M.P. for an Industrial Relations Act – if an M.P. does not feel happy voting for these, he is in the wrong party. But many bills before Parliament come from the departments, not the party manifestos. When the Burmah Oil Company won a lawsuit against the Crown, the Treasury decided, as it had earlier warned them it would, to pass a special Act of Parliament changing the law retrospectively. In the course of doing so, there was a general election, and a change of government; but the bill went through just the same, with the opposition spokesmen arguing against the bill which they had themselves promoted, and the government spokesmen urging a measure they had previously condemned. In such circumstances party discipline becomes absurd. Party leaders need to be able to rely on their followers for support over the major items of their programme, and are entitled to expect a sympathetic hearing over the humdrum items of government business; but it is absurd to make out that a defeat in a clause of the Trades Descriptions Bill should be taken as a vote of no confidence in the government of the day.

The threat of dissolution has greatly weakened the backbenchers' position. By a historical accident the prime minister has come to possess the power to dissolve Parliament and appeal to the country, and therefore can threaten his own dissident supporters that if the government is defeated on the issue they are pressing, he will dissolve Parliament, and in the resulting general election they will find that 'their dog-licences have not been renewed'. If people are elected to Parliament on the strength of a party ticket rather than by virtue of any merits of their own, then they are not going to feel able to vote according to their own judgement rather than that of the party whips. It was considered an act of quite exceptional courage for Mr Taverne to resign his seat at Lincoln, which he had held as a Labour M.P., and fight it again under his own colours, even though his offence in the eyes of the Labour Party was simply that he had continued to vote for what had been his party's policy after the party had decided to change sides. If even on such a clear case as this it is thought to be tantamount to committing political suicide to vote against the Whips' orders, it is clear that it is very unlikely indeed that a Member of Parliament will press any minor issue to the point of bringing the government down. It would be much easier for backbenchers to teach the front bench a lesson if the right to dissolve really was reserved to the Queen, as it is in theory; or, were that felt too invidious a decision for a hereditary monarch to make in a democratic age, if it were understood that the queen should grant a dissolution before the normal time only if the advice was tendered by the prime minister in conjunction with the leader of the Opposition, or was supported by an affirmative resolution in both Houses.

The economic and social position of M.P.s is weak. Few have independent means, and it would be undesirable to restrict membership of the House of Commons to those who had acquired a substantial fortune. If a Member of Parliament gives himself full-time to Parliamentary affairs, he cannot afford to fall out with his party, or he will be out of a job; and an ex-M.P. is often unemployable. Moreover, even if he takes his full share of committee work, he still will find it difficult to exercise a proper surveillance of the administration. Parliament has no independent information service. The administration does not allow Parliament or parliamentary committees to find out the facts for themselves, but insists that they rely on the facts provided by the administration itself. These are not deliberately doctored or distorted, but inevitably a department tends to discover and present facts which fit in with its own departmental philosophy, and therefore parliamentary criticism will appear either amateur and ill-informed or else otiose. In its origins Parliament was very much a part-time body, and it still retains its part-time amateur ethos. A Member of Parliament is much less professional, and much less well-supported by professional services, than a senator in the United States. There are virtues in this, but we need to be clear-sighted about what we want and what we are having. If Parliament is to retain its amateur status, then we cannot expect it to control the Civil Service, and we must devise other institutions to undertake that task. Parliament could debate general matters, and give a second reading to a bill, but could not be expected to masticate and digest all the legislation now presented to it. If, on the other hand, we want Parliament to exercise detailed control of the government's policies and enactments, then it will have to be largely composed of professional politicians who will need some cushion against financial and occupational insecurity.

More insidious is the inner motivation of most M.P.s. They want to succeed. And success, for them, is appointment to office. Since the power of appointment has come to be exclusively in the prime minister's hands, to criticize one's own leader is effectively to lose all hope of promotion, and therefore the only M.P.s with the courage of their convictions are those on the way out, who for that reason do not command much of a following. It is unhealthy to have the House of Commons inhabited by people hoping some day somehow to be prime minister, just as it would be unhealthy if every member of the royal family regarded it as his *raison d'être* ultimately to ascend the throne, and his life otherwise a failure. Most members of the royal family will not succeed to the throne, and are more than reconciled to the fact. It would be well if the ambitions of most members of the House of Commons were similarly moderated, so as to leave members less vulnerable to the disapproval of their party leader, and readier to back their own judgement against his.

Complaints are often made about the calibre of M.P.s. It is difficult to evaluate them. Complaints are often made about the calibre of men in many other walks of life – doctors, dons, clergy-men, schoolmasters, naval officers, undergraduates and school-boys. After all, in any society there are bound to be men who knew the heroes of yesterday well, and are not in a position to notice the merits of those who have yet to make their mark; and they may naturally conclude that the old place is going to the dogs. So far as the House of Commons goes, all we can say is that we get better M.P.s than we deserve. The 'career structure' for an aspiring candidate is daunting. If he is reasonably competent and conscientious he may become a junior minister for four or five years before being relegated to the back benches. Even if he becomes a minister of the Crown, he will find the reality of power much less than the semblance, and will often have to defend in public decisions which he never took or always disapproved of. Parliamentary work is seldom very rewarding and often down-right boring. It is not to be wondered at that most young men who wish to devote their life to public affairs go into the Civil Service, where merit is more likely to be recognized, rather than Parliament, where frustration is built into the system. Neverthe-less, it is a matter for regret. We need good M.P.s, even if we do not deserve them. And the fate of other countries should be a continual warning of what could befall us too if we allowed poli-tics to be a career monopolized by the dishonest and the incompe-tent.

If politics is to be more attractive to the able and the high minded, it must offer greater opportunities of achievement. The top of the greasy pole is, in the nature of things, beyond most politicians' reach, but lesser satisfactions should be more readily available. Some people have suggested that Parliament should be more like Congress, with more committees investigating more things. What is needed, however, is not so much more commit-tees as more effective ones. The complaint of back-benchers is not that they do not have enough to do – most M.P.s are kept very busy – but that they are not able to get anything done. It is not a sense of busyness but of achievement that they lack. The gibe that they are the best trained chorus of male sopranos in Europe cuts deep. Rather than spend all their time on the rituals of party warfare, they would like occasionally to be in on actual decision-making. As we have seen, this would sometimes blur the distinction between Members of Parliament and civil servants by involving Members of Parliament at the outset of the decision-making process when proposals were being first formulated and tentatively canvassed, greener than any green paper; at other times the distinction would remain, and it would remain the role of the department to make the initial proposals, but it would be Parliament's function to be an effective critic, representing interests that the department had not thought of consulting and deploying information that the department had never heard about.

Members of Parliament are uncertain what their function is. They are representatives, but of whom or of what, and for what purpose? As we saw in the previous chapter, the concept of political representation is woven of many strands, and cannot be explicated in terms of any single one. Perhaps now a Member of Parliament is, first and foremost, a representative of a political party, but he also represents his constituents – else there would be no point in having separate constituencies, with all the electoral anomalies that ensue, and we should do better to elect from party lists on the basis of a nation-wide poll. It is a further grace mark of the actual composition of the House in this century that many non-geographical interests find some M.P. ready to represent their views. My own M.P. is not keen on the environment and puts on a patient look when I go on at him about reservoirs or motorways, but other M.P.s have the right ideas and listen to my arguments with enthusiasm and use them on their colleagues in the House; if, however, you are steamed up about Greece or the United Nations you may find my M.P. much more responsive to your enthusiasms than your own. In this way the House of Commons achieves a measure of typical representation which is important for two reasons. First it enables members of the general public to participate in one of the senses we distinguished in chapter eight: they not only learn the reasons for the decision, but hear their own arguments, for or against, put forward, often better than they could have put them themselves had they been present. Even when I am present at a meeting, I do not insist on speaking myself but am content provided others bring forward the points I would myself have made. And if you are in Parliament and adduce the arguments I consider cogent, I shall feel that you have spoken for me and put forward my reasons, and that therefore my reasons, and thus I myself, have had a part in reaching the decision. Typical representation is important, secondly, in enabling the House to be relatively well-informed in its deliberations, especially on the crucial matter of what various classes of people actually want or think. But information is not enough. There is some element of commitment in the concept of political representation. A political representative does not merely state his clients' case but bargains and compromises on their behalf. He will agree to some things they do not like – in the original Parliaments, taxation – in return for the government's meeting them on other points – redressing their grievances. But it is seldom a pure bargain. A pure bargain, as we saw in chapter two, is the limiting case of a compromise in which there is no attempt to see the other's point of view, and his scale of values is seen as being entirely external. Even in the world of business, operating under the market economy, there is some need to accommodate other parties, and not merely drive hard bargains with them, if only to establish a *modus vivendi* for the future; and for making collective decisions pure bargaining procedures are highly inappropriate, and likely, as we saw in chapter three, to result in outcomes that are both inequitable and against everybody's interests. Although there may be some element of bargaining in reaching a communal decision, it must be much more a compromise if the community is to continue as a coherent whole. The representative does not just represent his constituency and do the best he can for it, but sees himself as a member of a larger community too, with a corresponding willingness to see things from the standpoint of the larger community as well as his particular part of it. It was a common theme in the seventeenth and eighteenth centuries that Members of Parliament were not elected to serve their own constituencies, Kent or Sussex, Lewes or Maidstone, but the whole nation, and that the House of Commons was not a congress of ambassadors from different hostile interests, but the deliberative assembly of one nation. The negative point is well taken, but the positive one was made too much of. Parliamentary proceedings, like every form of consensual decision-making, depend on a willingness to modify one's view in the light of arguments adduced by others and to take into account considerations not based on one's own self-interest. A man of Kent has much in common with a man of Sussex, and were this not so, and were there not some give and take between them, they could not make common cause or acknowledge each other as fellow Englishmen. But from the fact that they have much in common it does not follow that they are of the same mind on every question, and from the fact that their representatives are members of the same Parliament it does not follow that they ought not to represent different interests. If the oneness of the nation is the sole significant fact, the appropriate form of government is not parliamentary but monarchical. The whole point of having a deliberative assembly is that there are many views of what had best be done, and that a common mind must emerge from these by discussion and debate. And if the deliberative assembly is not to be just a debating society, but the grand inquest of the nation, it is needful that its members should not speak for themselves alone, but, because they speak for their constituencies, should carry their constituencies with them when they concede, conciliate or compromise on their behalf. True, M.P.s are not just delegates – if they were, they would not have sufficient freedom of manoeuvre to accomplish anything. A political representative needs a lot of latitude, because he is constantly having to make up his mind on general and often unforeseen questions which his constituents cannot have adequately thought about. He must exercise his own judgement, not follow what he takes to be their opinions, about what points to press for and what issues to give way on, and must be prepared on occasion, as they would, to sacrifice their interests to the public interest of the country as a whole. But to be willing to give way some of the time does not mean that he should treat their interests always with a high-minded disdain. Unless he is fairly vigorous in their defence, he cannot carry his electors with him on those few occasions when he has reckoned that the national interest ought to override those of his constituents, or the many more when he has settled for less than they had been demanding.

Like the parochial system of the Church of England, the geographical basis of parliamentary representation is a survival from an earlier age, which still has some merits as well as obvious demerits. It provides every man with an M.P. to whom he can turn, and every M.P. with a field of responsibility that is peculiarly his own. Moreover, even now communications are not that good, and many men and even more women live most of their lives in a very local setting. Even the charge, which is substantially true in many cases, that the parliamentary constituency does not constitute a real community with any identifiable common interest, can be turned into an advantage as reflecting the unselective character of the state. The state is essentially not a gathered community of like-minded souls, but contains anyone who happens to be within its borders, and it is congruent with this characteristic of the state that the way in which the supreme king-making body is chosen should also be based not on various voluntary and selective principles, such as a man's vocation or religious affiliation, but on the bare fact of residence in a particular district. Nevertheless, the disadvantages are great. If representation is to be real, there must be a bond of common interest between those represented which the representative can understand and argue for; and if representative government is to work and is to conciliate the various interests inadequately catered for at present, we need to identify those who share a common interest and find people to speak for them. In some American cities after the race riots, peace was restored by the mayor calling together the leaders of the black community, the business community, the suburban whites, the police, the churches and the social workers, discovering what the real grievances were and thrashing out a solution. The trouble with having political representatives elected by geographical constituencies is that they are seldom really spokesmen for any community and certainly not for the significant ones, just because geographical constituencies seldom constitute real communities, and most M.P.s, being full-time politicians, cannot also be the real leaders of real communities. And therefore they both fail to represent important interests and are unable to bargain and make concessions on their behalf. We need a two-way communication. If black people feel they are being discriminated against by employers, and employers feel that blacks are less responsible than whites as workers, both of these things need to be said and if some agreement is reached – employers will take more black employees for an experimental period, but these must not fail to turn up for work without giving proper notice – then the agreement needs to be mediated back through the leaders to the members of their respective communities as an agreement they must honour. One of the best arguments for political obedience is the argument from consultation and consent; but it can work only if the consultation is between the interests involved and the consent made by real, and not merely putative, representatives. The representatives need to be fairly closely identified with their constituents; then, having their interests, duly subordinated to other aspects of the public interest if need be, close to their hearts, they can bring into the assembly the various conflicts of interest existing in the country, and settle them there by discussion, compromise and bargain. Divisions of many different sorts would often run deep in the assembly, but its deliberations would reflect the division of opinion in the country, and many citizens would, through their representative, have a real sense of participating in its debates. If their representative made a concession, they would feel committed to it too, because he was generally identified with their interests. Such an assembly would be less homogeneous than the present House of Commons, and much more unmanageable; but would command greater support in the country. In the House of Commons I know pretty well how my member will vote, and the fact that he votes the way the Whips tell him does not much incline me to go along with him. The result is that the House of Commons is highly predictable in what it says and does, but out of touch with many of the communal interests that go to make up our national life, and, because it is unresponsive to them, unable to accommodate them to one another, to arbitrate between them, or secure their allegiance to the difficult decisions that have to be taken in the course of our common life.

The House of Commons was once a house of communes, but no longer is, nor can be so long as it fulfils its other function of being either itself sovereign or – on the theory of elective autocracy – part of the sovereign-making process. The House of Lords has always contained the leaders of one nation-wide community in the bishops: in recent years they have been reinforced, but only on a personal and *ad hoc* basis, by trades-union leaders, vice-chancellors, leading doctors and businessmen. It would be better if their presence in the peerage could be formalized, so that instead of depending on life-peerages conferred *ad personam* at the discretion of the prime minister, they were summoned by virtue of their office and only while they held it. The temporal peers should be like their spiritual brethren, and like them, not only temporary, but part-timers too. Their value when they attend the House lies in the attention they give most of the time to their other duties, which not only enables them to speak with first-hand authority about their diocese, trades union or university, but carry these institutions with them when an agreement has been reached. The part-time character of the Upper House is, like its limited authority, essential to the role it is now beginning to fulfil. If the crunch comes, the Lower House now, like the monarch in the Middle Ages, must be able to get its way, for this is the logic of sovereignty. But crunches are costly to rulers as well as to ruled. Although it is in the nature of an unselective community that its decisions may have to be enforced on those who will not agree with them, it is also in the nature of the state, as of all communities, that without a large measure of agreement, or at least acquiescence, in most of its decisions, they will be ineffective and it will become increasingly impotent. Sovereigns need to be sensitive to the interests of their subjects, both individually and collectively. Consideration needs to be built into our treatment of minorities. We must make sure that they shall be heard, and so far as possible heeded. There must be a receiving station in Westminster ready to pick up messages from Wales or some non-territorial principality. And if it is difficult to accommodate such representation in the House of Commons, then it should find a lodgement in the House of Lords.

12 Participatory Practices and Their Price

In the Middle Ages governments were often bad, and people groaning under great grievances prayed that a just king might ascend the throne, and give the poor their right and restore peace to the realm. So, too, men now, knowing that the present political parties and parliamentary procedures have let them down, put their trust in a new political grouping or a reform of Parliament to alleviate our sense of alienation and to procure a proper degree of participation in the processes of government. But just kings, although far, far better than unjust kings, did not, and could not, set the world altogether to rights, and a new party or a restored Parliament will not be a panacea for all the problems of government. Although bad decision-making at the centre of power has greatly debilitated Britain, the number of decisions which have to be taken is so large that Parliament, whatever its party complexion, could not possibly supervise them closely or provide for them any tincture of participation. However necessary, parliamentary reform by itself cannot be enough. If we try to channel all information through Parliament, there will be overloading and many messages will not get through. We need a greater devolution of power, allowing many more channels and much shorter ones, enabling many more people to join in, and to have much more direct access to, the processes of decision-making.

Much of our disenchantment is due to Rousseau. His style of democracy has proved too totalitarian. Valuable as the vote is, it does not guarantee either justice or freedom. If they are to be adequately established, we should look instead to Locke and the exemplification of his thought in American practice. The simple paradigm of chapter three will not do. Rather we should distinguish two different demands, one of security, the other of liberty. We need security against Leviathan. Individuals and minorities generally are in danger of being trampled on by the democratic state. Having the vote is no safeguard. As we saw in chapter ten, a democratic government cannot ride roughshod over everybody's interests all the time – and this is something to be thankful for – but being able to cast one vote, among many millions, for a different government once every four or five years does not give individuals or minorities any effective power to divert the bureaucratic juggernaut from bulldozing its way through their lives. If we are to live safely with Leviathan, we must be able to force him to think again when, by oversight or ill will, he sets out to obliterate us; we need some sort of veto to ensure that highly injurious decisions will be at least reconsidered and in general reversed. But a simple veto is the wrong remedy. We want a qualified veto, which will not give us the right – a right we neither want for ourselves nor are willing to confer on others – of preventing every sort of public decision-making we happen to dislike. It is in the nature of politics that a good many of the decisions reached will be ones we have argued against. It is only a few, against which we are vehemently and justifiably opposed, that we want to be able to forbid. In so far as we have any veto, it must be one which it is difficult and costly for us to exercise, so that we shall not use it wantonly or in order to further some ulterior interest of ours. Ideally also there should be some way of distinguishing between justified and unjustified uses. It is one thing for Naboth to refuse to sell his vineyard to Ahab because it is his patrimony, and he will be breaking faith with his fathers and abandoning his family traditions if he parts with it. It is quite another thing for Naboth Holdings Inc. to refuse to sell one of their properties to the Ahab Education Authority because they are holding out for a higher price. Naboth's right to retain his ancestral acres ought not to become the means whereby big business can profiteer at the expense of the community.

Liberty leads to quite different demands. We do not wish to be entitled on a few issues to say No, but would rather be able on lots to say Let's. A man has ideas about possible communal action, and wants to have the opportunity of putting these ideas into practice. In the nature of the case he can achieve what he

wants only if he can gain the cooperation of others, and therefore
it is built into the situation that other people may be altogether
unwilling, and the project founder on their refusal to cooperate.
Even if I could boss everybody else about, it would not really
satisfy me. I want their approbation, not merely their grudging
acquiescence. I do not demand, therefore, as part of my political
liberty that I should have sole say on what we should do, but only
that I should be able to take the initiative, and not be needlessly
frustrated by procedural difficulties or adventitious impediments.
If, after I have made my proposal, those who would have to carry
it out find it unacceptable, I shall – or at least I should – accept
their refusal with a good grace. I do not expect to have everything
my own way. All I can reasonably demand is to have some attention paid to my suggestion. I should not be denied a hearing or
have all my proposals automatically dismissed, or I shall feel I am
a nobody, who does not matter and has nothing to contribute.
Being a rational agent, I want to do something, and therefore as a
member of the community I want to make my mark in communal decision-making. But there are many *me* s. We cannot
all be getting everybody else to dance to each one of our tunes.
The inertia of large-scale communal action is enormous. If initiatives are not to be nearly all necessarily unsuccessful, they must be
modest. I cannot hope to have much impact on the public life of
the British nation as a whole. If I want to fulfil myself as a political being, in a way that shall be open not to me only but to as
many of my countrymen as would like to too, I must set my
sights lower. I can hope to get some of my ideas adopted by the
City of Oxford, or the University of Oxford, or at least Merton
College or St Thomas' Rural District Council. Individual initiatives can overcome inertia only if the mass that has to be moved
is relatively small. If we value political liberty, therefore, we must
decentralize, so that everyone who wants to can have some chance
of priming his own parish pump.

We can thus decentralize in two ways. To borrow an analogy
from the electricians, we can arrange switches either in parallel
or in series. We can arrange them in parallel when we want to
make it easy to initiate action, in series when we want to make it
easy to stop it. There are many newspapers that people can

write letters to, many hospitals that consultants can try out new treatments in, many universities and colleges where dons can experiment with the syllabus, many local authorities operating many different housing schemes. It is relatively easy to take the first steps, and to put up a trial balloon. If the idea is a good one and works well in practice, it may well be taken up elsewhere, and may be adopted generally. But, of course, very often schemes will be adopted in some places but not in others, and the would-be reformer will often have to content himself with only forty-five per cent success. The administrator also will find grounds for discontent, since anomalies will abound, and different authorities will do things differently for no better reason than that different enthusiasts succeeded in persuading them to adopt different pet schemes. Nevertheless out of this variety excellence may emerge, and even if it does not, innumerable innovators will feel some satisfaction at having their own proposals put into practice in their own circles.

As in electrical circuitry, switches in parallel can be equivalent to switches of the opposite sort in series. If my object is to establish comprehensive education everywhere in Britain, I can achieve it only if every education authority agrees. Many uniformities of practice are a similar case, and cannot be established if there are a substantial number of dissentients. In other kinds of decision we may, of set purpose, require the agreement of various bodies. In the traditional British Constitution, a parliamentary bill could become law only if it had been passed three times in each House and also was assented to by the monarch. An amendment to the American Constitution needs to be passed by a two-third majority in each House of Congress and by the legislatures of three-quarters of the states. This makes it more difficult to pass laws or constitutional amendments than to prevent them being passed. If any constitutional amendment seems to invade the rights of a minority of the citizens of the United States, they may well be able to veto it, even though the majority want it passed.

The United States is decentralized in both respects. Most questions are left to the separate states to decide, and it is quite possible to bring about a significant change in Massachusetts without having to persuade people in Wyoming of its merits. On Federal issues, however, the switches are in series, and it is necessary to persuade many people of the virtues of a measure before it can be passed. The United States is the best exemplification the world has yet seen of the ideals of Locke, not only in its federal and well-balanced constitution, but in resolving many important questions by adjudication rather than politicking. The strength of one's veto depends on the merits of one's case, and individuals or states can rely on the Supreme Court's upholding justified resistance to any invasion of their constitutional rights, while not being ready to defend its use merely as a bargaining counter. Many recent writers, however, have criticized the United States for the way in which effective power is diffused widely and shared by many different people, and have maintained that the Americans ought to copy the British and concentrate power in one position, because, they say, a decentralized system is inherently inegalitarian in that only 'the good, the wise and the rich' have sufficient drive, intelligence and time to find out who actually are in positions of power, and persuade them of the advantages of their proposals. There is truth in this contention, but it does not constitute a valid criticism. Elective autocracy – the model of a power-concentrating system – admittedly makes fewer demands on the energy, intelligence or finances of the voter, but at the cost of giving him an almost infinitesimal say in the course of events. Any system that caters for more than minimal participation will favour the active over the apathetic and the rich over the poor – it is a great advantage in running a crusade to enlist someone who has access to a duplicator, or on a grander scale to have funds to finance a full-time organizer, or an adequate research team. It is the Kennedy effect on a smaller scale. Participation is inegalitarian. It both requires and creates a certain degree of inequality. It requires that there should be some concentrations of economic power outside the control of the state and will benefit those with access to them more than anybody else. But this is no argument against participation. Better that some should be able to participate than that none should. Indeed, we all benefit from the initiatives of the fortunate few. It was only because Commander Marten was well-heeled and well-connected that he was able to fight the Ministry of Agriculture over Crichel Down; but we all benefited from his success. We should not admit it as an objection, but must acknowledge it as a fact, that participation, like freedom, is inherently unequal. If all participants are to have an equal say, then it will be a minimal say, and we shall have the frustrations and injustices that elective autocracy engenders. And we still shall not have equality. For while all outsiders will be on a level, the autocrat himself, together with his *apparatchiks* and his party acolytes, will be in a position of incomparably greater power. If it be taken as a criticism of participatory systems that they are inherently inegalitarian, exactly the same criticism can be made of non-participatory systems too. Even in an autocracy, those who are well-off and well-placed and energetic are more likely to catch the ear of the autocrat than those who are not: some pressure groups have been singularly successful in capturing the Civil Service; the British Road Federation has done as well by persuading officials that tarmac beautifies Britain as the American oil lobby has by cultivating members of Congress.* Whatever form of government we have, there will be an inequality between insiders and outsiders. Elective autocracy, far from obliterating the distinction, only makes it more difficult for an outsider openly to penetrate the corridors of power. It has one merit, which we should preserve – it gives even the apathetic the opportunity of having some say, albeit a minimal say, in the running of their country. But that is catered for, in American constitutional practice as it has developed, in the presidential election. The choice of president is as meaningful a choice as a minimal participant can hope to take part in. The ungood, the unwise and the unrich are not excluded, and every citizen can feel he has a share in the American Constitution.

Criticism of the United States is fashionable, but often unfair.

* See, in general, S. E. Finer, *Anonymous Empire*, Pall Mall Press, London, 1966, and, in particular, compare over a period of sixteen years, S. E. Finer, 'Transport Interests and the Roads Lobby', *Political Quarterly*, 29, 1958, pp. 47–58, and Mick Hamer, *Wheels within Wheels*, Friends of the Earth, 9 Poland St, London, 1974.

Not that there is nothing to criticize in American institutions; but the criticisms arise not from a comparison between the American and British way of doing things, which is equally open to criticism though on different scores, but from resentment of American arrogance in years gone by. We slate the Americans in the seventies because they were too full of themselves in the fifties; having been lectured at by John Foster Dulles, we are still anxious to prove that the American way of life is not all it was cracked up to be, and cite the sinister influence of the lobbies on Congress to make up for the humiliation of Suez. But we have a lot to learn from the Americans. Although sometimes their system has worked to the advantage of privileged minorities and sinister interests, it has also enabled many other minorities to find a place in the sun, and protected many legitimate interests and assuaged many communal fears. The Irish have fared far better in the United States than in the United Kingdom. Doubtless, decentralization has its disadvantages; but it offers so many more opportunities for participation and so much greater security against tyranny that we ought not to reject it out of prejudice as an American-fangled invention.

Locke's formula for decentralizing was too simple. We cannot divide up decision-taking into neat areas and parcel them out as the private possessions of their owners. Spheres of influence are not territorial domains under the exclusive sway of one landlord. The whole concept of property, which Locke takes as basic, should, rather, be seen as derivative, and instead of starting from the principle that a man has a right to do as he will with his own, our first difficulty is to devise ways of identifying the people who want to, and ought to be allowed to, have some say in a decision. Each man is apathetic on some issues, concerned on others. But the issues are not the same for all. Some things I do not mind about, but you do; others I care passionately about, while to you they are a matter of indifference. The customary distinction between the concerned activist and the uncaring mass is too crude, and should be replaced by a multitude of distinctions between different, overlapping élites. For every man there are some issues on which he is an expert, he is an authority, and about which he is concerned – he is an expert on his own home, he is an authority on what he wants, and he is deeply concerned about his health, his future and his family. In many cases his interests extend far further afield. But no finite being can care for everything: each of us has some things he could not care less about. We are all of us ready to opt out of some decision-making, but not out of all. Often opting out, we need to keep open an option to come in on those questions that are of interest to us. Our difficulty is to create institutions to achieve this without either diluting the decision-takers with a large number of people unconcerned with the question at issue or excluding those who feel seriously concerned.

Considerations of justice often enable us to identify those who ought to be allowed to participate. We can tell more or less what the effects of a proposed decision will be, and the interests affected; and where these interests are exclusive interests, the people whose interests they are have a *prima facie* claim to participate in some suitable, sub-maximal, way. With shareable interests the problem of identification is more acute. We cannot assign them to individuals without consultation. Interested parties have to declare themselves, and although it is incumbent on us, in accordance with the canons of freedom, to allow people to sound off about public affairs, it is difficult to devise institutions that will filter out the relevant signals from the background noise. The trouble with procedures that are democratic in the sense of everybody's having a vote is, as we saw in the previous chapter, that one has to shout to make oneself heard. Most people have neither very loud voices nor easy access to megaphones. We would like to place on decision-makers a duty to listen to whispers, but can do so only if we can indicate to them in advance whose whispers they are to listen to. Often this can be done, not only where considerations of justice indicate who ought to be heard but where some interest group has already established a right to be consulted on certain matters. But there are many residual cases which are not justiciable and where either no organizations have yet established themselves or existing organizations are inadequate. These cases are important because they are new and likely to give rise to valuable innovation. What we need are amplifying systems, which will pick out those messages that are important even if they are uttered very quietly at first, and amplify them until they are loud enough to reach the ears of the decision-makers above the din of day-to-day business.

I have many ideas, most of them bad. As an isolated individual I lack both the information and the ingenuity to pick out the few good ones from among them. But what I lack, others can supply. If I can talk over my ideas with friends and acquaintances, I can discover which of my opinions are open to grave objection, and which make sense to others. If I can ventilate my views in the workshop or the canteen, my foolish fancies will evaporate into harmless hot air in the warmth of friendly argument and laughter, and what is left will be a judgement which is both more substantial and more widely shared. We need not only places where we can meet our friends, but means whereby we can discover who our friends are. It is a function which local newspapers discharge well. Their correspondence columns give publicity to individual views, and their reports of meetings enable groups to canvass further support for their opinions and policies. We should not take them too much for granted. Once, when circulations were small and several papers could co-exist in the same locality, we could rely on competition to ensure that no shade of opinion was silently suppressed. Mass-communications, however, mean fewer outlets. Wireless, like water and gas, is a natural monopoly, and newspapers now have a manifest tendency towards oligopoly. Editors have endeavoured to be fair. But there is, potentially, a problem of access to the means of communication, and we should not assume that a free press is our only, or necessarily an adequate, resource. Before newspapers existed other institutions sometimes served the same purpose. In ancient Athens and Rome, the theatre enabled new opinions to be canvassed; in Christian societies often the sermon. But it is more difficult to preach a sermon than to write a letter to the paper; and very few of us can even write a play, let alone get it produced. Initiatives are difficult to take in any case, and easily stifled. No doubt some should be. But if we want to have a society in which people feel unstifled, then we need to make it easy to take the first steps

– to make suggestions, and canvass support for them, and bring them to the attention of those who have authority to decide.

The next stages are inevitably more difficult. Even if we could make the authorities listen, we would not want to be able always to make them agree, or they would be agreeing to all sorts of silly things that other people might suggest. We want them to discriminate. How are they to know which letters in the local paper express currents of responsible opinion that ought to be taken seriously and which are just the outpourings of the local lunatic? Or which pressure groups really represent a substantial body of citizens and which speak for nobody but themselves? A lot of guidance is given by the structure of society, which can generate not only opinion but informed opinion. I do not know much about medical matters, but I can fairly easily find out who does. A letter signed by several doctors criticizing the administration of a hospital deserves serious attention. Nor should we consider only letters to the papers. Social institutions can be even more influential. The annual dinner of the local medical association is an admirable occasion for putting the skids under a recalcitrant Executive Board, for it provides just the right sounding board to get through to the authorities the seriousness of what is being said. It has long been a virtue of English public life that it is organized on a collegiate system. Professional men constantly meet their colleagues, and establish and apply professional standards, and consequently produce professional opinions on all relevant topics. Inns of Court, universities, conferences of scientists and professional associations of every sort play a large part in distilling what is important from the general hum of conversation, and pressing the authorities to take notice. Many modern theories of the state discountenance these ways of channelling information and reaching decisions by making a sharp separation between organs of the state, whose authority ultimately derives from a democratic vote, and private associations which have no rights or responsibilities *vis-à-vis* the state. It is, as we saw in chapter four, an unworkable distinction. Often we should recognize the right of professional associations, trades unions or other bodies to be represented on a decision-making authority; and there are no grounds of principle for objecting to representatives of the public interest having a say in the decisions of the Law Society, the British Medical Association, trades unions or industrial firms. We want there to be effective channels of communication in both directions, and to have those channels both wide and selective, so that few sensible opinions are overlooked, and yet attention is not wasted on irrelevancies. On the whole, it is best to have the actual decision-making body small, with its members drawn from different spheres of activity and exposed to a range of social pressures. They will be able to go into each question thoroughly, be less subject to party feeling, and will be open to very diverse representations. A large body, as we noted in chapter eight, although nominally more participatory, is often in fact less so. It is more difficult to get hold of a sufficient number of its members to argue one's case with them, and they are more likely to be inattentive or bored, and vote along party lines. It is, fundamentally, a problem of information costs. The more people there are involved, the more communications are required in the course of reaching a decision, and communicating is difficult and imposes costs on both sender and recipient. It is difficult enough to address the inspector at a public inquiry; only a skilful public speaker will make much headway in an assembly of four hundred. Unless we keep the numbers down, we exclude all except the talented orators and determined spokesmen; and equally, a large body is much more likely to be taken in by specious show and self-advertisement, because it costs time and thought to see through appearances in the absence of continuing personal experience, which, in a large body, must often be lacking in most of its members. Unless we take steps to prevent it, only the pushing and self-opinionated will in fact participate, and participation will favour the manipulators rather than the unsophisticated exponents of honest truth. At present we tend to assume that only election by relatively large constituencies can confer political authority on would-be participators, but although this is one mode of selection which, inevitably, we must often resort to, we should do well to institute very small constituencies, and to select not only by election, but rotation, and sometimes, as for jury-service, by lot. Many people have a distaste for putting themselves forward, and would never stand for election, but would, if asked, take their turn as select man, clerk of the parish council or secretary of the W.I., and would have much to contribute and much to gain from the experience. A far smaller proportion of the electorate in Britain or America ever hold public office than did in ancient Athens, and although we should allow people to opt out, and often should aim to have only the reasonably competent chosen, we could do much to widen the effective opportunity to participate. Archaic institutions – whereby different wards or parishes or streets took it in turn to elect to different offices in different years – were often much more effective in involving more people in the life of their community than modern and supposedly more democratic institutions. Sometimes voluntary associations achieve a higher level of participation than those established by the state. But we cannot lay down a rigid rule. Different forms of participation are appropriate in view of the question at issue and the degree of concern felt about it. Most of them have some advantages and all have their demerits. They are all complicated, and lack the monolithic magnificence of monarchy. Decisions will take more time and effort to reach; some may be less satisfactory. A premium will be placed on skills and resources that only a few people possess, and although this by itself is not a fatal objection, there will be a danger, unless we guard against it, of their abusing their position to further selfish or unworthy ends. Means must be found of minimizing it, and we need to have some general grounds for believing that men's selfish moves will usually cancel one another out, but their good ideas will not.

Participation takes time. Unofficial participants are, by definition, not full-time. Most of their day is occupied with earning their living, and they have to wait until they have finished their work before turning to public business. It takes a long time to arrange a meeting of unofficial participants who cannot give it priority over their work-a-day commitments, and it takes them a long time to familiarize themselves with the facts and problems they have to face. Officials are naturally impatient, and because they understand the issues and have already made up their minds, find the snail's pace of participatory processes intolerably tedious and are always yearning to use 'accelerated procedures' which will allow them to cut corners. We can sympathize with them, but must not give way to them. To cut corners is to cut out the non-professional. It is an ineliminable feature of participation that it takes time. Often, in consequence, the decisions finally reached are themselves improved; but even if the ultimate outcome were the same, it would be worth the extra time taken to secure the public understanding and support they need if they are to be sustained as decisions of the whole community.

Participation takes up the time not only of the officials but of the unofficial participants, and costs them money and effort. In Britain there is great reluctance to make it easier or less costly for ordinary people to participate. Recently and welcomely, although with a lot of opposition, the principle has been accepted that local councillors should not be out of pocket. But objectors, unlike their counterparts in America, have to pay the full cost of being represented at public inquiries. The Americans reckon that objectors are performing a public service in raising their objections. Not only do they give the government the opportunity of avoiding costly and inequitable mistakes but they provide a source of information not otherwise available. Although much of it may be, as we noted in chapter eight, irrelevant, it has one great merit: it is not official. Officials have a natural tendency to rely on official information, and official information is the sort which officials think of gathering and which can easily be stored in files. Although officials try hard to be impartial and accurate, their vision is often limited and they tend to lose the personal element. They think of a bus service in terms of peak-hour passenger units and not of an old lady trying to bring back her week's shopping. Unofficial information, just because it is unofficial, can act as a corrective, and therefore, although often unwelcome to the official mind, is for that very reason valuable. It ought to be encouraged in Britain as elsewhere. We ought to help unofficial participators, not brush them off. As taxpayers, we have good cause to be grateful to those objectors who, at great cost to themselves, managed to prevent thousands of millions of pounds being squandered by the government's megalomania at Cublington or Maplin. Not only gratitude but expediency should lead us to foot the bill when people are trying to save us from the expensive proposals of a government department. Even if in some particular case the objectors be proved wrong, it still is valuable, in view of the propensity towards empire-building on the part of officials, that their proposals should be thoroughly scrutinized and adequately justified before going forward. For this reason alone we should reckon to bear objectors' costs at public inquiries. In addition, two other reasons, one of justice, the other of equity, should weigh with us. Objectors at public inquiries are not, as advocates of the proposals like to make out, merely selfish. Their interests are often legitimate ones, which it should be a public concern to protect, in the same way as we are concerned to protect the liberty of a man accused of serious crime from unjust imprisonment. All the arguments for legal aid apply. There is something amiss in a society which, while properly protective towards the wrong-doer, is quite unconcerned at the fate of the innocent whose only crime is that he happens to be in the way of the government's plans, and may be evicted on the say-so of a secretary of state. Considerations of equity argue the same way. Participation is inherently inegalitarian, but that is no reason for making it more so. Although at present it is true, as Mr Crosland points out, that objecting is a middle-class activity, it is not because working men do not want to object, but because they cannot. They cannot afford to, any more than they could afford to be Members of Parliament before Members of Parliament were paid. Rather than argue, as egalitarians do, that since not everybody can participate as much as everyone else, nobody should be allowed to participate at all, we should recognize that different people will be able to avail themselves differently of the opportunities offered by a participatory system, and seek to help those least able to help themselves, so that while some will benefit more than others, all shall benefit to some extent and nobody need be avoidably disadvantaged.

Financial obstacles are not the only ones. Some others – lack of know-how, inadequate access to expert information – could be obviated too, but participation is always going to be a tax on the time and energy of participators. It is not enough, in most cases, merely to blurt out that the Emperor has no clothes on; much more energy than that must be expended to hammer home a point and force decision-makers to think afresh. Although some people are moved by a general desire to join in the decision-making of their community, others are limited in their concern to highly specific issues, and will give their time and energy only if there is a reasonable chance of their efforts being rewarded with success. If, no matter what efforts they make, the decision will be the same, they will not make efforts. This was one of the troubles of elective autocracy as we saw in chapter ten. It breeds apathy. People find that they get nowhere with government departments, and give up the unequal struggle. If we are to have any form of participation, not only must we accept the fact that sometimes participators will get their own way, but we ought to regard it as positively desirable that they should. It is another ineliminable cost of participation. Not only will the decisions arrived at be often other than what an impartial spectator would approve, but each individual question will have to be approached separately and the government's freedom to reserve the final decision to itself will be fettered. Administrators find it galling. They feel themselves being driven off course by participatory pressures, and take it to be their duty to defend all the more tenaciously the public interest as they see it. If give way they must, rather than give way on this issue they will make some silent adjustment to their future course of decision-making, and claim that they have thereby shown themselves sufficiently responsive to public opinion, and that the participator ought to be grateful to them for that. But he is not. What he wants is not so much to modify public policy for the future as to obtain redress of *this* grievance, or ensure that *this* adverse decision be not taken. Just as if I am innocent, it is *this* verdict I am concerned about, much more than about verdicts in general, so it is *this* pension, *this* job, *this* licence that the participator is steamed up about. And although, clearly, we cannot guarantee that he will always be successful, there is an inherent thisness about much participation, which runs counter to the whole tenor of administrative thinking. The administrator is being pushed to give way on specific issues, and to substitute for his own considered decision some other which must in his opinion be regarded as less good. He is thus bound to find participatory procedures yielding results that are, in his judgement, contrary to the public interest. We should admit it, but deploy the arguments of chapter six to show that it is common form to have to sacrifice one aspect of the public interest for the sake of another. Often the disadvantages discerned by the professional administrator in a measure advocated by a participator are real disadvantages, and should be decisive in securing their rejection; but sometimes, too, they are a small price to pay for the greater flow of information stimulated by participatory procedures, the greater feeling of harmony when justice is being manifestly done, and the greater happiness that will ensue if many people find that they have been able to get some of the things they wanted and that they have made some contribution of their own to their community. We should not be afraid to compromise other aspects of the public interest for the sake of justice and freedom. On the contrary, just as we are ready in the criminal law to forgo other public objectives rather than contravene the canons of justice and freedom, so too we should lay on decision-makers generally a duty to accept results in other respects sub-optimal, rather than stifle freedom or deny justice. The country is better served by ministers gracefully giving way when participatory procedures go against them than by their insisting on their own view of the public interest without regard to the rights of participators or the requirements of justice. People felt it was unfair when the Secretary of State for the Environment, Mr Rippon, and the Secretary of State for Scotland, Mr Campbell, overruled the reports of public inquiries, and decided to go ahead with the M54 and the extension to Edinburgh Airport at Turnhouse. No doubt there were arguments in favour. And it is conceivable that the Secretary of State in each case was right in his view of what would be most in the public interest. But if the objectors, having won their case, were to be pipped at the post, they were not being given a fair run for their money. If the minister is playing 'Heads I win, tails you lose' with the objectors, he is showing, on behalf of the state, a cavalier unconcern for the aspirations and exertions of the objectors. Objectors are not just nuisances to be swept under the departmental carpet, but people. And the state fails to treat them as people or do them justice unless it is willing to play fair by them, and itself abide by an adverse result, even though it were to its own hindrance.

Participation makes life more complicated and arduous for everyone. It increases information costs. Under elective autocracy all I need know is the names of the would-be prime ministers or the parties competing to form the next government. In a decentralized system I should need also to know the names and merits of rival candidates for my parliamentary constituency, for the county or borough council, what they really stand for, and even how they have voted on particular issues. I shall need to find out – and it takes much time and effort to discover these things – whether Mr Smith is keen on education or comprehensive schools, whether Mr Robinson is pushing family planning or stonewalling on it, whether Mr Goldsmith supports the Jews or the Arabs. Unless I am already fairly well up in public affairs I shall not know, and often shall not know how to find out, the answers to these questions. Only if I have myself an axe to grind or know other people with axes to grind, shall I actually be able to make an informed choice. Uncle Tim, who is deputy head of St Magdalen Mead unmixed school for girls, will tell me who the goodies and baddies on the education committee are if I live in the same area and happen to see him, and Isaac Rothenstein who is a partner in a firm I do business with in the City may mention that Goldsmith's opponent is a rotter, and would mortgage British interests to Arab oil. Minorities with special interests will know how to vote and will urge others to vote similarly, but the apathetic majority will be to all intents and purposes disfranchised because it will be too much trouble to find out how to cast votes effectively.

Participation puts a premium on effort. If I do not like the way things are going under elective autocracy, all I can do is write a letter to my M.P., and if that does not do any good, vote against him at the next general election. Under a decentralized system, however, there is a lot else an energetic man can do. He can find out who is on the hospital board and telephone him and explain how difficult it is to visit his wife now that they are closing down cottage hospitals and sending all maternity cases to regional centres. He can go to a Parent–Teacher Association and speak about the devastating effect unstructured schooling is having on his younger son. He can organize a petition from all the parents in the neighbourhood that the pedestrian lights should not be switched off just as the children are making their way to and from school. We are in effect giving weight to intensity of feeling. Those who care a lot will have a much greater chance of achieving their aims than those who could hardly care less; and instead of being concerned only to promote a diffused sense of general well-being, the government will be pressed to give satisfaction on highly specific issues, and to placate very articulate interests. But this is no bad thing. Once we abandon a one-dimensional concept of the public interest of which the government is the best judge, it ceases to be obviously wrong to forgo measures which will be intensely disliked by some, even if they would be beneficial to, or marginally preferred by, most. Although utilitarians are prepared to do great injury to some so long as the total of human happiness is thereby increased, we for the most part believe that utilitarian prescriptions are not only unworkable but wrong; in so far as any analogous approach is applicable at all, it seems both more meaningful and more moral to pursue a policy of least unhappiness, of minimizing the greatest misery that could befall anyone. And this will be more likely to result from a decentralized system in which those who feel intensely are more likely to get things their own way than those who are only lukewarm.

However good it is that a system should be in general sensitive to intensity of interest, it is not always good. A system that favours Zionists and zealots favours also property developers and manufacturers' associations. They too have a fairly intense interest – not an idealistic one but a financial one – in a course of public action which most other people would suffer from, but not so much as to galvanize them into activity. In a decentralized system producers will be able to band together and push through high tariffs, while consumers will be too unorganized to protect their greater, but more diffuse, interests. Nor is it only the crude case of the estate agent getting the planning committee to decide that the town should expand on the side where his wife's uncle owns some land. More insidious is the corrupting effect of corporate self-interest, all the more so if we are relying on corporate bodies to relay relevant messages to the rulers. Professional associations in the present century, like the guilds at the end of the Middle Ages, are becoming closed shops, too much concerned with the provision of feathers for their own members' nests and not very ready to address themselves to questions of public policy or to give due weight to considerations of the public interest. We need to reinstate the principle of public responsibility and sometimes to re-establish the institution of lay control. Otherwise, lawyers may be able to frustrate measures to make them accountable to their clients for their dilatoriness and incompetence, university teachers may be able to make the possession of a degree a necessary qualification for employment in the public service, and doctors may forget that patients are people whose time also is valuable and whose convenience should sometimes be consulted.

It is a real problem. A decentralized system, just because it is sensitive to intensity of interest, is vulnerable to self-interested manoeuvres. If participators are to be able to turn the course of public decision-making towards their own vision of the public good, they can also, in the absence of further considerations, turn it towards their private advantage instead. Criticisms can properly be levelled at American practice on this score. But selfishness is a problem whatever political system we adopt, and we must not view a participatory system as being peculiarly prone to it. When we sought to protect individual interests by giving each man a veto, there was a danger of some, and soon all, men using their veto not to protect their rightful interests but to hold everybody else to ransom. And similarly, if we now have a system in which there are many switches and it is relatively costly to manipulate any of them, there will be a danger of manipulators muscling in and manipulating the controls not in legitimate self-defence but in order to annex to themselves an unfair share of the good things going. In each case a merely mechanical procedure can be used for bad ends as well as good. If adequate to secure sufficient protection for the individual's respectable interests, it can be manipulated to enable him to enrich himself at other people's expense. But decentralization is not merely a mechanical procedure. Although a decentralized system is more complicated than elective autocracy is supposed to be, and there-fore the energetic and competent will be at an advantage in it, energy and competence by themselves are far from being suffi-cient to win the day. What makes a system in which major deci-sions need the concurrence of several different bodies a good system is that people are to some extent rational, and therefore a number of different bodies are more likely to concur on a pro-posal for which good reasons may be advanced than on any other. If there is a public decision – say the grant of planning permission – which I very much want taken because it will bring me in lots of money, I may be able to nobble one or two decision-makers, but cannot hope that most men will agree to a proposal just because it will make me rich. The only thing that will move a number of different bodies, differently composed and differently situated, in the same direction is reason. Although for the pur-poses of elucidation we distinguished reason from authority in chapters two and four, in practice they are not normally opposed. I act partly because there are arguments in favour, partly because you are telling me to. I am much readier to accept your authority if it seems reasonable to me. Although the authority of the state ought on occasion to be accepted even against our own judge-ment, for the most part it should and will be accepted because its behests are congruous with our own reasoning. It guides rather than commands, and we agree to carry out its proposals not simply because we are told to, but because we also see some reasons why we should. The reasons may not be all that good – we are all subject to fads and fashions, and often are swayed by considerations which are subsequently seen to have no substance – but they cannot be all that bad. If I want to gain selfish ends in public affairs, I have to be a hypocrite. I have to cast a veil of specious reasoning over my proposals, dissembling my true motives, and making out that I am actuated only by altruistic considerations, and that the measures I suggest will work out for the public good. And the fact that I have to be at least a hypocrite exercises a powerful constraint on the course of public decision-making. A decentralized system, therefore, does not collapse into a market economy in the way that Locke's ideal veto did. If I hold out for the highest price I can get in the market, and admit that this is what I am doing, I may well be able to get a very high price for my cooperation. But if I am admittedly being awkward in political debate or if people suspect that the arguments I adduce are mere rationalizations designed to cover up ulterior motives, I shall forfeit respect and lose my effectiveness. The whole tenor of public debate is against unjustified self-interest. Therefore the more bodies that need to be persuaded of the merits of a scheme before it can go through, the more difficult it will be for proposals to be adopted which are not supported by some moderately good arguments. Instead of a set of switches in series one of which an ill-natured man might switch off so as to hold everybody else to ransom, we should see a decentralized decision-procedure as a series of rectifiers which allow current to go in one direction, not the other. Only reasons, not bargains, will get a measure approved all along the line. And therefore a decentralized system will favour not merely intense interests as opposed to diffused ones, but disinterested rational ones as opposed to exclusive or selfish ones.

Men are rational and altruistic, but only imperfectly so. It would be naïve to suppose that a decentralized system will rectify all the self-regarding currents of human affairs that flow from our inevitably interested motives. The d.c. analogy is too *simpliste*, and the give and take of discussion and debate finds a more appropriate analogy in alternating current, where different circuits with different characteristics will allow certain frequencies to pass but cut out everything else. The number of decision-makers and the form of the proceedings, like the capacity and inductance of a circuit, have an important influence on the ease with which they may be activated and the sort of results they will produce. As we have already seen, participation is often easier and more effective if the number of decision-makers is kept small so that those who are inexpert at mass-communications are not handicapped, and those who have to decide will be able and anxious to go into the question very fully; but great issues cannot be adequately handled except in a grand debate, where arguments must be addressed to many since the consequences will be felt by many. Only if our forms of participation are arranged with care, in view of the questions to be decided and the considerations to be borne in mind, will the limited rationality and altruism of those who take part be able to winnow out the grain of good sense from the chaff and verbiage of special pleading and irrelevance. Only a complicated system can accommodate our differing requirements for a political system, giving many opportunities for initiative while enabling those with very strong objections to stonewall measures affecting them for a considerable time. It imposes costs. The filtering effect is achieved at the cost of a lot of time spent by public-spirited participators listening to a welter of arguments, and sifting out the good from the bad – my having a say in decision-taking is a sore trial for those who have to listen to me, and I must expect my own patience to be taxed in turn so that others may have their protests and suggestions attended to and assessed by my disinterested and moderately rational mind. Decisions will take longer to make, and will have some tendency to go the way the activists want. But provided we do not go too far, it is a merit to be responsive to intensity of interest. We must, indeed, take care not to let the activists elbow out others, equally worthy of consideration but less demanding. If minorities have rights, majorities, even silent majorities, have them too. Perhaps the American system has been too sensitive to the demands of articulate and well-organized pressure groups; but equally the British one has been too insensitive. We have to strike a balance, democracy, as it is often understood today, pulling us one way, participation the other. We want everyone to have a say, without having to spend much time, effort or thought – else we effectively disfranchise the majority who have little appetite for political activity. But if we allow the apathy of the 'lumpenvotetariat' always to blanket the aspirations of active participators, we shall dampen their enthusiasm, alienate their affection and invite violence. Intensity of feeling ought to weigh with us; not as a conclusive argument, but as a prima facie one. We cannot always give way to the minority, however ardently they desire it. But in so far as they can produce a show of reason on their side, and are not merely out to feather their own nests, we should make it our policy to defer to their feelings quite a lot.

13 The Dangers of Democracy and Its Defence

The passions of the people are powerful, and can easily run awry. Democracy can be disastrous, both for the individual and for society at large. So can aristocracy, so can autocracy. It is well to be aware of what can go wrong under a democratic government, but to remember that all forms of government can go wrong. Government is inherently dangerous, and the dangers of democracy need to be assessed in comparison with the dangers to which other forms of government are exposed. As Churchill once said in the House of Commons:

Many forms of government have been tried, and will be tried, in this world of sin and woe ... No one pretends that democracy is perfect or all-wise. Indeed, it has been said that democracy is the worst form of government – except for all those other forms that have been tried from time to time.*

Like all forms of government, democracy can be unfair. The fact that a decision has been approved by a majority does not mean that it is right or just. If a tyrant may be arbitrary, a mob may be capricious. The very circumstances of a democratic decision-making procedure militate against careful consideration and full attention to the facts. Mass meetings are easily stage-managed, and often it needs greater courage than anyone possesses to stand out against the movement of a mob. Once mob-rule is established, to protest the innocence of one man unjustly arraigned before the people's courts is to expose oneself to the danger of being lynched. And although despots can be equally malevolent, they have fewer eyes and ears and, most of all, hearts. Stalin and his secret police seemed ubiquitous, but Pasternak and Solzhenitsyn could find some people they could confide in. Even

* *Hansard*, 11 November 1947.

in the Soviet Union, the secret police comprised only a minority of the people. Not everyone was an informer, and it was possible to think of Stalin as a monster. One is much more isolated in a crowd. To be unpopular with a mob is to have every man's hand against one. Every eye is hostile, every ear unsympathetic. And it is far harder to believe in oneself, when one is not merely a dissident from the regime but is every man's enemy. It is difficult to make a rational choice between horrors, but the French terror may have been even worse than the Russian purges just because it was more an expression of the will of the people. Democracy, because it can come closer to pure consensual unanimity, is for that reason more dangerous. Other forms of government, being more obviously artifices, are more easily criticized, and in the long run, when in error, easier to resist.

Danger can also arise from a different quarter, not from the people agreeing too readily to do wrong but from their being too divided to agree on anything. If there is a division of opinion and the question is put to a vote, there is a measure of artifice in translating the voting figures into a decision. Some people will have voted against, and then find that they collectively are deemed to have decided in favour. If the matter is one about which they do not greatly care, they will not mind; and if, having been involved in the debate, they found the arguments on the winning side telling, although not decisive, they may well accept the decision with a good grace; and if, though worsted on this issue, they have been successful on others, they may abide by the result. But if they are in a permanent minority, they may begin to question majority rule. I may be willing to go along with the majority of my fellow countrymen with whom I have some fellow-feeling, but if they consistently manifest in their decision-making a disregard for the canons of rationality and a readiness to flout the values I have espoused, I shall begin to wonder what lot or part I have with them. A permanent minority may become permanently alienated, and soon may seek to secede in geographical fact as well as emotional feeling. After all, the nation-state is not God-given. England in virtue of the English Channel, and France in consequence of the exertions of the French kings, came early to have a sense of national identity, and Germany unfortunately followed suit. But not all French-speakers feel French, and in Great Britain the Southern Irish, in spite of centuries of British rule, came to feel altogether apart from the other inhabitants of the British Isles. Once we elevate the principle of majority rule to the status of democratic dogma, we raise also the question *Majority of whom?* Irish Republicans do not regard the inhabitants of the British Isles as forming a community, but insist that the inhabitants of the island of Ireland do form such a community, and that it is as obviously right to kill Ulstermen to force them to respect the desire of most Irishmen that Ireland should be united as it was to kill Unionists to prevent them carrying out the desire of the majority of Britons that the United Kingdom should stay united. Equally in Ulster, the loyalists insist on their right, as a minority of the inhabitants of the Irish island, to go their own way and owe allegiance to the Queen and not to the Dail, but argue that within Northern Ireland the will of the majority should prevail, and that Roman Catholics in Londonderry or Belfast ought, on democratic grounds, to acknowledge their allegiance to the British Crown.

Democracy can offer no solutions to such problems. It has to assume them solved before it can begin to operate. It makes sense, within a homogeneous community, to refer disputed questions to a vote, just because the community is homogeneous, and the division on that vote is more a function of the question at issue than of the community as a whole. As this ceases to be true, so the democratic procedures cease to be relevant to eliciting appropriate answers to the questions under dispute. Rather than a democratic vote, which will inevitably reflect the interests of the majority community, and will, even more inevitably, be seen as oppressive and unjust by the minority community, it would be better to have the ultimate decisions taken by a single autocrat or a body of disinterested men who could be relied on to judge each question on its merits, and not to favour either side consistently. The Habsburg monarchy was able for a long time to maintain unity among a conglomeration of diverse nationalities; and the successor states, just because they are supposed to be democracies, have made acute the question of minorities – Tyrolese in Italy, Slovenians in Austria, Sudeten Germans in Bohemia,

Italians in Yugoslavia, Hungarians and Saxons in Rumania, to mention only some. The Supreme Court of the United States has often been able to prevent any majority obtaining a permanent upper hand over a minority, and, had circumstances been more propitious and its own judgements wiser, might well have avoided the Civil War.

Fears in politics are often more potent than facts. One of the greatest dangers of democracy is that it provides fuel to feed the fires of fear. If the ultimate decision rests with the majority, I am forced to fear not only the actual majority I know but the might-be majorities of the unknown future. I fear that I am being outbred by the Roman Catholics, the West Indians, the Pakistanis or the Chinese, and that although I live in a world of upright, rugger-playing Protestants, my daughters or grand-daughters may be compulsorily schooled in the errors of Rome or Islam or required by law to miscegenate with buck niggers or margarine-coloured chinks. If the ultimate way of deciding is by counting noses, then not only will other men's noses, otherwise inoffensive, be construed as a political threat, but I shall feel a further alarm, that cannot be rationally allayed, at their potential progenitive proclivities and powers. Under the Roman Emperors the Orontes flowed into the Tiber and produced nothing worse than an epigram from Juvenal; under the British democracy a much smaller flow has already conjured up populist visions of blood.

Even where a society is not already deeply divided, democracy may prove divisive. Democracy easily leads to parties and factions, and these, once established, will polarize opinion and preclude sensible solutions to current problems. For if I am deeply concerned about any one question, my rational recourse is to form a coalition with other interests, trading my support on the questions touching them for their support on the issue involving me. And a party thus formed will find it difficult to compromise, but having once secured a majority will need to railroad through the whole package deal. Similarly the other side will soon acquire its shibboleths, and neither side will be willing to give way on any issues, with the result that whichever side wins, the outcome will be generally less than could have been secured by reasonable negotiations or imposed by an arbitrator. Since the Revolution until recently democracy divided France into clerical and anti-clerical, quite needlessly. The fabric of society needs to be strong to stand up to the politicizing engendered by democracy; in many societies the bonds of unity are fragile and should not be exposed to unnecessary strain.

Democracy is also incompetent and inconstant. A large body finds it easy to will the end without willing the means. The ends are grand, and can be grandiloquently advocated; the means are niggling matters of detail, and the people get bored with them. In order to achieve political aims, one needs a firm political will, which is not easily bored nor readily deterred by difficulties as they emerge one after the other. As soon as the going gets rough, a democracy is likely to have second thoughts, so that although much is undertaken, little is accomplished. In contrast, the ruthless determination of a dictator is effective, and will succeed in delivering the goods. Hence, after a period of democratic vacillation, people will yield themselves to the forceful initiative of a dictator or clique, which will at least get things done. Above everything else, we require government to be effective, and it is not merely easy for the vigorous to wrest the reins of government from the nerveless hands of a democracy – the reins positively drop from the latter to the former. Authority does not need an antecedent or democratic patent, but is self-authenticating. Anyone who knows his own mind and is prepared to give a lead is likely to find a following. Effectiveness is more important than legitimacy in winning men's allegiance. And therefore democracy is always likely to lose out in the battle for survival, sometimes, as in the Third World, being violently overthrown by a *coup d'état*, more commonly, as in the West, suffering a seepage of power, which, while leaving it nominally a democracy, is continually diminishing the importance of the democratic aspect of government and placing the effective power in quite different hands.

Democracy is philistine. If many have to agree before a proposal is adopted, only those proposals which recommend themselves to a large number of people will be accepted, and the highest common denominator of a large number of integers will itself be small. Those measures that appeal to crude considerations held in common by the people at large will be passed, but those that appeal to the finer sensibilities will be lost. If we value artistic achievement – as surely we should – we must foster aristocratic aspects of government, and enable some people blessed with good taste to put their ideas into effect unfettered by any need to pander to the undiscriminating judgement of the profane and vulgar crowd. Even fifth-century Athens, which was a democracy and did produce artistic works of imperishable fame, did so only because the people had the good sense to be guided by the aristocrat Pericles. Where a democracy altogether rejects the aristocratic principle, and regards it as undemocratic for anyone to acknowledge anyone else as his superior in artistic taste, or will not suffer private patrons to exist because patronage, no matter how discriminatingly exercised, smacks of privilege, artistic creativity is stunted, and the whole of society is submerged in a tide of tasteless mediocrity. De Tocqueville perceived the incipient ugliness of the American way of life on account of the former principle, and we have witnessed the dreariness of communist countries on account of the latter. Artistic achievement depends on the spontaneous creativity of the individual, and therefore sits ill with full-blooded democracy.

Finally, democracy is often egalitarian and unjust. Both in ancient Greece and in modern Europe democratic institutions have had the effect of setting the poor against the rich, the idle against the industrious, the insipid against the inspired. The best form of government, as Aristotle and Alexander Hamilton well knew, was a mixed constitution diffusing the chief power among those best able to exercise it well. The effect of democratic doctrine has been to inject a note of egalitarian envy against every form of excellence, and to encourage the poor to soak the rich, and the stupid to bring down the sensible to their own silly level. Instead of getting steamed up over forms of government, we should settle for the system which provides better administration than any other, and, if we are lucky enough to have it already, be content to let well alone, and not take off on some question of high-flown principle.

Democrats often take criticism amiss. They see red when these or other objections to democracy are raised, and rather than answer the objections, describe those who put them forward as Fascists. It is a mistake. Dangers are best avoided by careful consideration, not by denying their existence. The cause of democracy is not served by establishing some form of democratic government in circumstances where it is bound to break down, or by abandoning all safeguards against its yielding intolerable results. As always in politics, it should be argued for in well-modulated terms and in a quiet voice, avoiding extravagant aspirations but ensuring that its modest claims can be made good. The most telling argument is a negative *ad hominem* one. Anti-democrats are keen to exclude others from a share of power, but less ready to envisage their own exclusion. The young blood from Christ Church is all in favour of aristocracy, and can produce good arguments why gamekeepers and shop assistants should not have the vote. It is useless to deny the force of his arguments – they are good arguments; better by far to agree that aristocracy is a good form of government, and suggest that only graduates of Leeds should have the vote, and only trades-union leaders should be in the Lords. More subtly, the socialist planner is impatient with the unwillingness of the people to be planned, and yearns for a single enabling act to give the government adequate powers to introduce Utopia. It needs only a little specious argument to show that Charles I, Lord Strafford and Archbishop Laud were the pioneers of the welfare state, and the cheek need not be noticeably tongue-filled as one moves on from the proposition that autocracy is the best form of government to the further one that Stuarts and Bourbons, rather than members of the S.R.C. or N.U.S., make the best autocrats.

Behind this dialectical ju-jitsu lie serious arguments. The first turns on the implicit assumption that political liberty is a good thing, and those who will not forgo it for themselves should not seek to forbid it to others. Those who inveigh against democracy commonly do so because the course of decision-making does not conform with their views of what ought to be done. They have views of their own on what should be decided, and regard it as right that their views should prevail. And that is an exercise of political liberty. It manifests their belief that it is proper for them to have opinions about what their society should do, and to take

steps to influence the decisions it takes. But if it is good for them
to have political liberty, it is difficult to see why it might not be
good for others to have it too. Of course, not everyone wants to
engage in public affairs, and not everything that anyone wants
ought to be done; but still men are social animals, and if they are
to be able to fulfil themselves they need to be able to make their
own contribution to the running of their society. Although by
itself the possession of the vote does not amount to much, a man
is more likely to be listened to if he possesses the vote than if he
does not, and so better able to influence the course of communal
decision-making. Given the right context, it can constitute a
significant part of political liberty. Political liberty is good because it enables a man to fulfil himself in an important and fundamental way. Democracy is desirable because it alone denies to
nobody this element of political liberty.

We may, secondly, make explicit the minimax argument of
chapter ten, and point out to the critic that although the defects
of democracy are real enough, under other regimes he might fare
even worse. True, other forms of government often can produce
better results than a democracy. The Roman Empire under Marcus Aurelius was better governed than the United States in the
nineteenth century, and the English gentry showed themselves better governors than the Athenian populace. But Marcus Aurelius
was succeeded by Commodus, and medieval barons were anything
but gentle. The merit of having part of the decision-procedure
democratic is that it provides a means of moderating the worst
excesses. You cannot kill all the people all the time. Although in
some circumstances democracy will be worse than other forms of
government, and although other long-established constitutions
may give us rational grounds for supposing that nothing very bad
will happen under them, if we incorporate democratic features
into our form of government, it helps to minimize the maximum
disaster that can be produced. The state, having at its disposal
coercive powers, is potentially very dangerous indeed, and we
should above all else pursue a prudential policy with regard to
Leviathan.

The minimax argument is important. It is based on realism
and leads to the definite recommendation that there should be

regular elections in which everybody should have the opportunity of voting the government out. It is a merit to be realistic. Political philosophy has been bedevilled, especially in the last few centuries, by visions of an earthly paradise to be achieved by political means. In the pursuit of pie over the next hill, whole peoples have marched down into the morasses of misery and massacre that lay in the intervening valley. And since vision has often occluded sight, the response of the practical politician has been to decry idealism of every sort, and pursue under the name of realism a policy of cynical self-interest or weak-kneed opportunism. The virtue of the minimax strategy is that it leads us to consider realistically what is liable to happen, and then to evaluate the possible outcomes and decide where within the available alternatives our priorities lie. We put in fuses. We cannot decide that nothing will ever go wrong, but only choose where the failures are to occur. And if we see ourselves as dealing in fuse-wire rather than the stuff that dreams are made of, we shall note one great virtue of having a democratic element in our decision-procedure, that it provides a safety-valve against many of the worst disasters.

The simple minimax argument, although within its own terms conclusive, does not go far enough. It is too general to give adequate security to the individual, and too external to engage his affections. It is nice to know that we cannot all be killed all the time, but what I really need to be assured of is that I shall not be killed even once. Only if Leviathan is wedded to justice can the isolated lamb lie down in safety with him, and prudential arguments will lead the individual to rate an attachment on the part of the authorities to justice and freedom as being no less important than their submitting themselves occasionally to re-election, and as no less constitutive of their being really democratic. Moreover, prudential arguments take too external a view of the state to be entirely satisfactory. They cannot engage our loyalties or express all our aspirations, and easily engender an unpleasing mixture of complacency and discontent. We shrug off criticism by observing that our system of government is not too bad, and then complain when it works less well than we might reasonably expect, viewing it from a less external standpoint. We have a lot to be thankful for, but a lot that needs altering. We have been spared the misfortunes that other peoples have suffered at the hands of their rulers, but although we have been very ready to tell foreigners to write home about our system's merits, the export model has not caught on, and even in the home market consumer dissatisfaction is evident. It may be 'super-pessimal', but often the logic of oligopoly leads to our being offered only a choice of evils, which although not as bad as they might be, are still quite bad enough. Our model is also very sluggish. We need sensitive controls if the state is to be responsive to our needs. Fuse-wire, although essential, is no substitute for switches.

More positive arguments for democracy and participation can be grounded in the nature of the state, which must not be viewed entirely from an external standpoint, as a machine or a thing, but should also be seen as an aspect of social life, a human phenomenon whose rationale reflects our own understanding of human nature. These arguments are far from conclusive. They do not prove that every country must adopt just those institutions which have evolved in Britain or the United States. Rather, they draw attention to certain fundamental facts about the state, and draw out a moral about the spirit in which its decision-making must be undertaken. I cannot arrive at a communal decision entirely in the first person singular, or it will not be a communal decision at all. I must to some extent approach it in the first person plural, and the logic of the first person plural imposes important restraints on the manner and the frame of mind in which decisions may be reached. At the very least some consent and some consultation is necessary, and only if we are sensitive to the opinions and considerate to the interests of individual members are the decisions we take fully communal ones which everyone can support and acknowledge as his own. Not that all our decisions could be absolutely communal, with everybody identified with them one hundred per cent. Not only does the enormous size of the state preclude it, but our human nature itself is inherently imperfect, and we cannot all be always of one mind with one another. It is because we are imperfect that we need social and political institutions. We cannot do away with them, but we can seek to redress the balance of imperfection. As we think about the state we form an idea of the frame of mind in which its decisions should be taken, and then we can establish institutional safeguards to foster that spirit in spite of human limitations. Our arguments do not constitute a direct defence of democracy but tell in favour of our decisions being taken democratically in the third sense of the word. And then particular procedures and institutions may be defended as ways of specifying how and by whom decisions should be taken if they are to be democratic in that third and fundamental sense.

The state has often been thought to be founded on force, but this, as we saw in chapter four, is a false perspective. It is true that the state, being unselective, must be potentially coercive, and to that extent non-participatory. But it is its being unselective, rather than its being able to use force, that is the fundamental feature. Although it must be able to use force, it cannot be always using it. It must very largely rely on the voluntary obedience of its members, and therefore is committed to some principle of participation, and it is reasonable to aim at having it a minimally coercive institution. Power rests much less on force than on authority, and authority is correlative with acceptance. Government depends, if not on the active approval, at least on the acquiescence of the governed, and although this democratic element may in some states be only minimal, it shows that just as everybody belongs to the state so the state belongs to everybody, and nobody may be altogether left out of account. Moreover, if it is to fulfil its essential purposes, the state needs information which only individuals can supply. In particular, it needs to know what people's priorities actually are. Although we can go some way towards looking after people's interests without consulting them, we cannot obtain complete guidance for all political action from the interests we can impute to people, but must sometimes ask them what their values are. However competent and dedicated a ruler I am, I cannot discover what decisions ought to be taken by simply secluding myself in my study and thinking about the public interest, but must also ascertain what particular people actually want. The public interest, although an important concept in our political thinking, is not a simple self-subsistent concept to be apprehended by ratiocination alone, but is characteristically ambiguous, and consequent on other concepts whose application we can only learn from the lips of other men. Public values depend on private values, and private values are not values at all unless sometimes some people avow them as their own. Only by asking people their opinion and paying some regard to their answers can the government fulfil its *raison d'être*.

Although the state is an unselective community, it is a community none the less. Community life is a joint enterprise. And although there is, inevitably and properly, a division of labour, the whole enterprise loses much of its value and significance unless it is seen as a cooperative activity of the community as a whole; and the more it can engage everyone's cooperation and support, the more likely it is to be successful. Communal decisions need to be ones that everyone can make their own. We cannot hope that we all shall be always completely identified with every decision taken by our community, or we should cease to be separate individuals. We cannot completely own, but need not altogether disown. Although, inevitably, we regard the state as being in some degree other than ourselves, an external authority we cannot entirely internalize, there are less complete degrees of identification which we can aspire to and ought to aim at. Not everything will be done as I would have done it, but still, if it was done well and for reasons I can appreciate, I may acknowledge responsibility for it and allow it to have been done in my name. To the principle of minimum coercion we may add the principle of minimum alienation as a condition of the health and well-being of the body politic. Only if such a condition is satisfied shall we be able to share Rousseau's sentiments for the society we live in, and only if it is largely organized on Locke-like principles with great tenderness towards the individual and great concern for freedom and justice, will individuals long continue to have little occasion to be alienated by it. A government is democratic not so much in that the people take all the decisions – that, in a large society, would be impossible – as in their not needing to disclaim the decisions taken by the government in their name and on their behalf. They can feel that they have taken all the decisions because they do not want to feel that they have not. It is decisions taken unfairly or illiberally, without due regard to the interests of those affected or the arguments actually adduced, that people naturally want to repudiate, and therefore it is in so far as a system avoids such decision-taking that it will be accepted as democratic. It is good that a government should be democratic in this sense because government can be properly understood only as a function of the community as a whole, and a community where communal actions are generally accepted by all is more of a community than one where communal actions are much resented, if not actually resisted by force. If a community is to be a minimally alienated one, traditional democratic institutions may be necessary but will not be sufficient, and the same arguments that can be adduced in defence of democracy can be called on also to support claims for less minimal forms of participation, especially in accordance with the canons of justice and freedom.

These arguments for democracy and participation should be set in a low key but with high overtones, echoing the mixed mode of our common human nature. We are selfish, but not entirely selfish, ignorant, but not totally ignorant, stupid, but not impenetrably so. If we were utterly unreasonable or sufficiently selfish, it is clear that no system would work, and if we were still very selfish but with a little common sense we would take Hobbes' option and agree all to submit to an autocrat with no conditions attached. Even if we were highly rational egoists, participation would be impossible and democracy disastrous. It is only because we have some fellow feeling and are prepared to share ideals as well as information with one another that democracy or any form of social life is possible. What I want is not entirely separable from what you want, and often all I want is that other people should have what they want, and even when we are conscious of some conflict, still we sometimes can manage moderately well on a basis of give and take. But only sometimes, and only moderately. We are not always altruistic nor all that reasonable, and so are seldom all of one mind. If we all were, then no decision-procedures would be necessary, and every decision, however taken, would be acknowledged by each of us as his own. If only some of us were, and the rest could recognize their rationality and disinterestedness, then Platonic meritocracy or Marxism would be acceptable forms of government. But however highly I think of myself, I have to admit that I am not omniscient, I am not infallible, I may not always mean well, and that therefore neither I nor my friends ought to be entrusted with absolute power absolutely. And if I think more about the matter, I see that I would not even wish it. Not only must there be opportunities for other people to tell me things, but I do not want, cannot want, always to be telling them things. Social life cannot be a one-way affair. Government is an aspect of social life. Therefore government is necessarily to some extent reciprocal. But the balance is easily lost. Some division of labour is forced on us by the limitations of our nature, and the logic of imperfect information in a large society enhances the authority of the establishment. We have to have forms and procedures which we recognize as authoritative, and unless we take special care, there will be a tendency to overlook factors which ought to be considered and to exclude from having an effective say people who ought to have one. We want to resist this tendency, because although our limitations are undoubtedly real, we see them as limitations which we should, so far as we can, transcend. Although we are insufficiently unselfish and imperfectly reasonable, these are imperfections, and we view each man as having potentialities and aspirations which go beyond the imperfections of his actual propensities and achievements, and as being therefore valuable and worthy of respect in his own right. This is what makes democracy both desirable and possible. We desire it because we discern in everyone some spark of something more than the merely animal; and again and again we have to rely on the fact that although people are often selfish, they are not always so, and although they are prejudiced and stupid, yet some tendency towards reasonableness still pervades all our intercourse with our fellow men.

We should not be starry-eyed about what can be achieved. Although the onus of proof is on those who would deny some form of participation rather than on those who seek it, we need to be sceptical about particular plans, lest they do more harm than good, by precluding other, less formal but more valuable, consultations, or by polarizing attitudes gratuitously. Forms, like votes, are by themselves not enough. They provide the skeleton, but need to be clothed with the flesh of real life. They are important – just as our bones provide the leverage which enables our muscles to be effective – but only because of their being the means whereby communal decisions may be reached which we shall not need to repudiate. Behind the formal decision-procedure lies the need that certain standards of reasonableness should be adhered to and a general consensus sought. We need not only political but social institutions to enable us to talk over difficult questions and think out acceptable answers, and we need to consider not only their form and composition, but how they actually work, and the frame of mind they both exemplify and engender. Democracy is less a matter of casting votes and counting heads, and more a willingness to listen to arguments and see the other chap's point of view. It is manifest not only occasionally at elections and public meetings but continually in many different aspects of our national life, in our anxiety to seek agreement all round and in our readiness to let anyone join in and have his say. We include people in rather than keep them out, and hope that after talking the matter over the decisions we shall take will be such that everyone can accept them and we all shall acknowledge them as our own. Individuals without any public standing can speak freely, and discover what other people think, what the arguments are and what support their own opinions have. Anyone who wants to can talk about public affairs without the fear of punishment or the futility of knowing that nobody will take any notice of anything he says. Not only are there no secret police to send him to Siberia if he presumes to meddle in matters of state, but there are people to talk to, an atmosphere in which speech flows freely, and channels of communication so that account is taken of what is said, and public actions accord with the assessments made by members of the general public in their daily discussion and debate. Although our fundamental concern is with the spirit in which our decisions are reached, it is our manner of reaching them that can most definitely be determined, and it is in this second sense of the word that our society can be most justly described as democratic. It is the parliamentary principle. Parliamentary government means, and still to some extent is, govern-

Further Reading

There are many dull books on political theory, but the following are interesting and important.

Classical works

Plato's *Republic*, translated by: F. M. Cornford, Oxford, 1941; A. D. Lindsey, Everyman; H. P. D. Lee, Penguin, 1970

Aristotle's *Politics*, translated by B. Jowett, edited by W. D. Ross, Oxford, 1921

Aristotle's *Nichomachean Ethics*, book 5, translated by W. D. Ross, Oxford, 1915

Thomas Hobbes, *Leviathan*, parts 1 and 2, Penguin, 1968

John Locke, *Second Treatise on Civil Government*

David Hume, *Of the Original Contract*

J-J Rousseau, *The Social Contract*

(the three titles above are conveniently available in E. Barker, *The Social Contract*, Oxford, 1947)

Alexander Hamilton, James Madison and John Jay, *The Federalist*, edited by Max Beloff, Oxford, 1948

J. S. Mill, *An Essay on Government*, edited by E. Barker, Cambridge, 1937

J. S. Mill, *On Representative Government* (in *Utilitarianism, Liberty and Representative Government*, Everyman; or edited separately by R. B. McCallum, Oxford, 1946)

A. de Toqueville, *Democracy in America*, translated and edited, Oxford, 1946

Modern works relevant to democracy

A. H. Birch, *The British System of Government*, London, 1967

A. D. Lindsey, *The Modern Democratic State*, Oxford, 1943

B. de Jouvenal, *Sovereignty*, Cambridge, 1957

E. Barker, *Reflections on Government*, Oxford, 1942

S. I. Benn and R. S. Peters, *Social Principles and the Democratic State*, London, 1959

Brian Barry, *Political Argument*, London, 1966. Heavy going at first, but the last two chapters are important, and give a good statement of the case for elective autocracy.

H. B. Mayo, *An Introduction to Democratic Theory*, New York, 1960

A. H. Birch, *Representative and Responsible Government*, London, 1964

F. A. Hayek, *The Constitution of Liberty*, London, 1960

H. F. Pitkin, *The Concept of Representation*, Berkeley, 1967

J. C. Livingston and R. G. Thompson, *The Consent of the Governed*, second edition, New York, 1966

P. Singer, *Democracy and Disobedience*, Oxford, 1973

G. Sartori, *Democratic Theory*, Detroit, 1962.

Brian Barry, *Sociologists, Economists and Democracy*, London, 1970

R. A. Dahl, *A Preface to Democratic Theory*, Chicago, 1956

J. Plamenatz, *Democracy and Illusion*, London, 1973

Appendix: Evidence to Dobry Commission

In 1973 a commission was set up under the chairmanship of Mr George Dobry, Q.C., to review development control. I was asked by the Transport Reform Group to write a memorandum based on my own experience of public inquiries. It was not originally addressed to readers of this book, but may help show how the general principles argued for here apply in actual cases.

I am a member of the Transport Reform Group, and have been through the questionnaire prepared by Mr Dobry. I append to this submission brief answers where I can give them. Most of the questions, however, are of a technical administrative nature or concern areas of planning control where I have no useful contribution to make. My experience has been of the development of road schemes, and of opposition on the part of the public to them. I have appeared as an objector at numerous public inquiries, and have done a certain amount in helping amenity groups and resident's associations to prepare their defence. In a quite different way, I have been concerned as an Oxford don in making submissions to the Franks Commission about the way a university should be run so as not to exclude the majority of dons from having any say, and I have been recently thinking more deeply about the issues involved while writing a book on *Democracy and Participation*. It seemed the most useful contribution I could make would be to give my personal experience and reflections on one aspect of planning. It does not directly answer the questions asked, but gives a worm's eye view and shows how differently issues appear from the other side of the desk. The views I express are generally concordant with those of the Transport Reform Group, but are a personal expression rather than a group statement.

The pervasive impression I have formed is of the great disparity between the official and unofficial participants in point of expertise, information and financial resources, and the consequent difference in point of view. To take a trivial example: some days before going to an inquiry at Droitwich, I had to plan to call in at a copying machine after taking my son to school, with enough small change to obtain one copy of my proof of evidence for the inspector and another for the counsel of the Department of the Environment, and I carefully weighed the cost before making two additional copies; on my arrival at Droitwich the programme officer asked if he could have my top copy to take further copies from, and within ten minutes had run off as many copies as he wanted. This is only a very small example, but it is typical. To get something typed for me is quite difficult; to ring back the programme officer and then hang on while he is found is for me quite an expense; to find out whether a particular clause turns up in the 1959 Act or somewhere else is for me a considerable labour. Above everything else, unofficial participants are short of time. When a massive envelope from the Department of the Environment arrives on my desk I cannot give it immediate attention. Before turning to it, I have to deal with my own professional duties first, and give tutorials, prepare lectures, attend committees, write testimonials and read examination scripts. It may be a week or more before I can read and digest the material and think out an appropriate response. I think this, too, is typical. For reasons that will emerge, objectors at inquiries are often professional men who are therefore already very fully occupied and are always finding it difficult to make time for any other activity. And this, combined with other factors, results in unofficial participants having a radically different time scale from that of the officials.

It is easy to see the officials' point of view. They are responsible for solving innumerable problems and are constantly being criticized for dilatoriness and inactivity. When at last they have worked out a solution, any delay in order to give statutory notice or to hold an inquiry could well seem to them to be just time lost. It takes them no time to see what is wrong with many of the objections. Objectors are just obstacles to be obviated, and with as little delay as possible. And, since the official mind, once made up, moves fast, it is difficult to appreciate how very much slower the thought processes of the unofficial mind might be. The unofficials, unlike the officials, are unfamiliar with the problem and the proposals. It takes a long time to get into a problem or understand exactly what the proposals amount to. I have read notices in the local newspaper and been quite unable to make out what is afoot, and had to rely on journalists or activists to translate from officialese into English I could understand, and that takes time; perhaps only a day or two, but quite easily a week. Again, officials have their own channels of communication and can rely on receiving or transmitting information quickly. But in the outside world information travels very much more slowly. To take one example: it was only half-way through the time allowed for entering objections that I learned of the plans to destroy the environment of the village of Ide, near Exeter. Many years earlier I had written asking to be informed if any proposals were made, but this did not produce any official notification. I learned in the end because someone in the village wrote to me in Oxford. But it takes time for that to happen. Whereas in an organization it is reasonable to assume that people who need to know will be informed within two or three days, one needs to allow two or three months before even those closely affected by proposals will get to hear of it. Similar dilation of time scale occurs in the preparation of objections. When I get to hear of the department's designs I do not know who else is affected or who my allies are. Some may be corporate or official bodies, e.g. a parish council or a school, but these do not meet very often and have a crowded agenda; they might meet every other month, and might need two meetings before being able to agree what line to take. Often the decision of one body depends on what other bodies are going to do. If anything less than six months is given for potential objectors to consider whether they should object and in what terms, many corporate bodies are effectively deprived of any opportunity of really objecting. The same holds good, in a different way, for private objectors. It takes a lot of time to agree on tactics and coordinate efforts. Between April and October there is always someone away on holiday. It is very difficult to get more than six people together at less than a fortnight's notice. In the autumn of 1973, I formed a consortium of five people to put up the money to take counsel's opinion on the minister's decision to put a road through Ide, because of the many unsatisfactory aspects of the inquiry and ministerial decision. There were only six weeks in which to do anything. It took a week to go round and see different people to discuss what might be done, and another week before we could find a solicitor with time to see me. Six weeks may seem a long time to people within the department, and might be adequate for a well-heeled objector who had his own solicitor who could be counted on to give his business priority. But it is far too short a time for less fortunately placed objectors to have an adequate opportunity of initiating action. A comparable difficulty occurred in Oxford under the Frank's constitution over the time allowed for members of Congregation to challenge decisions made by Hebdomadal Council on behalf of Congregation as a whole. The official mind was always for reducing the period, not realizing how long it took for people not in the know to discover and understand what was proposed, and how much longer still it would take them to organize a coherent challenge. *It is an ineliminable feature of participation that it takes time.* For participation is by non-experts who are not clued up, whose minds work slowly, who do not know who else may be interested and who have few resources for speeding things up. Rather than streamlining planning procedures we should be slowing them down, so that slow-thinking members of the public shall not be left behind. Else we are effectively denying objectors any opportunity of making themselves heard at all.

Unofficial objectors are handicapped by the lack of information and expertise as well as shortage of time. Most people find it very difficult to find out things. I am lucky. Living in Oxford, I have access to excellent libraries; and being a don, I can often pick my colleagues' brains. I can spend a Saturday evening reading Hansard or Acts of Parliament and can discover what the current orthodoxy about water conservation or traffic prediction is. Most people have no adequate access to sources of relevant information and are immensely handicapped in the presentation

of their case. I was present on one occasion last year at a meeting
when the chairman of the Ide Parish Council was pointing out
to his Member of Parliament, Mr Maxwell-Hyslop, the incon-
sistency in the traffic figures given by Exeter City Council when
arguing for another road some six months later. 'Are you quoting
total vehicle numbers or p.c.u.s.?' asked Mr Maxwell-Hyslop,
and the chairman was silenced. I was similarly caught out by the
town clerk of Exeter at an earlier inquiry. I remembered having
read in the local newspaper a report that a traffic census in the
1960s had shown that eighty-five per cent of the traffic was local
traffic. I wrote to a journalist who had been on that paper to ask
for a reference, but he was unable to supply it. An H.M.S.O.
publication gave comparable figures for many comparable towns
and so with a slight hedge – I said it was 'according to one report'
– I quoted this figure in my submission. The town clerk was on
to it, and asked where I had got it from. I explained that I had
read it in the *Express and Echo*, but had not been able to find the
reference although I believed my memory was correct in view of
the figures given by H.M.S.O., which I then produced for in-
spection. The town clerk made merry with the way I invented
figures to suit my case. In October 1973, the City Council, arguing for a compulsory purchase order on Bull Meadow, explained
that eighty-five per cent of the traffic was local traffic. This
figure came from a survey carried out and published in the 1960s.
It was in a book I had tried to get in Oxford, but not known to
the librarian of the geography department there. If I had had
ample leisure, or had had adequate time or had had easy financial
circumstances I would have tracked it down. A few further
letters and I could have tracked it down in the Bodleian or the
British Museum. If there had been enough time before the inquiry I could have come down to Exeter and got hold of a copy
there. Or I could have sent a cheque for £3 or £4 and bought a
copy on the chance it would prove informative. I labour this
point to show how difficult it is for private individuals to obtain
relevant information in a relevant form, even if it has been published. And a great deal of relevant information is not published,
and often not disclosed even when asked for. In two inquiries last
year the Department of the Environment argued that new roads

from Pearce's Hill to Pocombe Bridge and from Pocombe Bridge
to Tongue End ought to be built on economic grounds, and
would yield a return of twenty per cent p.a. on the cost incurred.
In each case I asked for the figures on which the return was calculated and in each case was told that it was 'not departmental
policy to reveal the basis of the calculations'. Further probing
elicited both that the calculations left out a number of relevant
factors and that in one case they did not refer to the road under
consideration. Altogether, the proceedings fell far short of the
stipulation of openness laid down in the Frank's Report on
Administrative Tribunals.

Most people are unfamiliar with the procedure at an inquiry.
I was. After a sleepless night, in which I had rehearsed myself
over and over again, I found myself in a theatre, on one side of
the stage a phalanx of officials, labelled the Department of the
Environment, on the other myself, labelled the objector. I managed to stand up moderately well to the questions put to me by
the Department of the Environment, and then was set on by Mr
Bennett, the town clerk of Exeter. 'Would not I agree that I was
adopting a rather selfish attitude?' 'Did I know that . . .?' When
I attempted to answer I was confined by the inspector to Yes or
No answers. I appreciate the reasons. An inquiry could easily
degenerate into a debating club if rules of order are not enforced.
Nevertheless, the rules themselves can be played by expert advocates. 'Do you know that . . .?' although technically a question
enabled the town clerk to introduce his own matter without my
being able to controvert it. Other objectors, I am told by people
in the village, fared worse, and some women felt too nervous to
submit their objections in person, and had them read for them by
the inspector. If I had been able to employ the services of a skilful
advocate, there are many respects in which the presentation of
my case could have been bettered. But it would have been very
expensive. And it would have been no use. For no matter how
good the argument, the inspector is not bound to be guided by
it, and even if he is, the minister can ignore his findings. The
situation is radically different from that in the courts of law.
There, the proceedings are formal and the arguments technical,
and only a fool would choose not to be legally represented; but

against the expense of lawyers' fees can be set the real chance of winning the case. The law may be inaccessible to the layman's understanding, but judges are bound by it. Inspectors are not similarly bound, and seldom seriously dissent from the department's proposals. Objectors get the worst of both worlds as regards legal formality. The proceedings are not sufficiently informal for them to do justice to their case without the aid of an expert advocate; but not sufficiently formal for a good case, well presented, to be sure of success.

The present state of the law about public inquiries is unsatisfactory, and thinking about what it should be is confused. The Stevenage case (Franklin and Others *v.* Minister of Town and Country Planning, H.L. (1948) A.C. 87) still stands. So long as it remains the law of the land that a minister is entitled to make up his mind before the inquiry, the current view that inquiries are so much eyewash will remain widely believed. When I began to question the proceedings of the inquiry and decision about the Pearce's Hill–Pocombe Bridge proposal, I learned that the Council on Tribunals had never got around to laying down the rules of procedure for this type of inquiry and that, therefore, no matter what had gone on at the inquiry it would be difficult to argue that it contravened non-existent rules of procedure. The onus of proof at present is laid on the objectors. Ide Parish Council, it was said, had not produced *compelling* (my italics) argument against the department's proposals, and therefore the proposals should be approved. There is no adequate judicial review – a citizen of the United States is far better protected against being done down by his government than is a citizen of the United Kingdom by ours. These and many other inadequacies are due to a lot of woolly thinking about the relation of citizens to the government, what the aim of administrative law should be, and how it may best be achieved. Officials characteristically see themselves as serving the public interest, and assume that this is some definite quantity which can be measured and ought to be maximized, and that those who object to their proposals are motivated by selfish interests which ought not to be allowed to obstruct the promotion of the public interest. Again and again I have come across instances of counsel trying to make out at inquiries that objectors were selfish and should, therefore, be ignored; and suggestions that there may be more than one aspect of the public interest are incomprehensible to economic experts who do cost-benefit analyses on just the opposite assumption. A comparison with the criminal law is illuminating. In the criminal courts it is never argued that the defendant is selfish in wanting to retain his liberty or his reputation, and that therefore his defence is to be discounted. On the contrary, it is thought highly desirable that everyone's liberty and reputation should be defended, and it is only with great reluctance, upon clear proof of a definite crime, that the courts will deprive a man of either. Again, in the administration of the criminal law we readily recognize that the public interest has many facets. It is in the public interest that crime should be suppressed and law and order maintained, but we do not argue from this that the police should therefore be given power to imprison suspects or beat up individuals who are undesirable, effective though these measures undoubtedly would be, because we regard the liberty of the subject and the maintenance of justice as also being in the public interest and arguing in the opposite direction. Officials are, unfortunately, much less quick to appreciate these fine distinctions and have not developed any instinctive identification with the objector's point of view, and are not anxious that his case should, if at all possible, be successful. But only if this is done and felt to be done will feelings of resentment and alienation be assuaged. No doubt Ide Parish Council was not very effective in organizing its case and perhaps every councillor in this day and age ought to know what p.c.u.s. are. But it is their lives that are going to be wrecked and they are not going to be reconciled to this by a procedure that accepts the Department of the Environment's casual assertions as established fact and dismisses all their arguments as not being absolutely compelling. In spite of much easy talk about compensation and putting people first, the effect of the department's plans is highly disruptive to some of the people concerned. According to the former Vicar of Heston, Middlesex, the arrival of the M4 in his parish was followed by a number of suicides. A documentary film 'I tried cottonwool but it made my ears go funny' by John Morris of 36 Brueton Avenue, Solihull, Warwickshire, is based on the effects of the M6. At the inquiry into Pearce's Hill–Pocombe Bridge road one objector got out his cheque book and offered to write a cheque for £50,000 to the department if they would abandon their plans – which would cost him more than that. Another objector at that inquiry pointed out that he would lose his livelihood, and was told by Brigadier Baldwin on behalf of the department that it was a normal business risk. With interests so vital and so large as these in jeopardy, the position of objectors is similar to that of those accused of criminal offences, but whereas, by the provision of legal aid, the structuring of the rules of evidence and the requirement that proof should be beyond reasonable doubt, we give those who are thought to have done wrong every opportunity to show that they ought not be deprived of their liberty or property, we show no such tenderness towards those who are known to have done nothing wrong but happen to be in the way of one of the minister's plans, and we leave their livelihood, health and happiness to the casual unconcern of a busy bureaucrat. During the last year, I have, for the first time, heard normally respectable people seriously contemplating violence, and real hatred expressed for cabinet ministers. My objection to the Pearce's Hill–Pocombe Bridge road was taken up in the National Press and I received letters from many parts of the country. One came from a middle-aged lady in Worcestershire whom, I imagine, I might meet at a point-to-point. 'I should like to take a stick of dynamite to every one of their bulldozers' she wrote. Another, equally old and, perhaps, even more respectable – at least titled – lady reported how she and her friends had been discussing the possibility of putting sugar in the earth-moving machinery's petrol tanks. 'I hate Mr Rippon's guts' I have often heard in the last twelve months. A godson wrote at Christmas full of joy at Britain's energy and economic crisis which was likely to make the government unable to carry out its plans for destroying the Itchen Valley. There is a very wide sense of resentment and alienation from the processes of government, and the underlying reason is that they seem unjust; real and grievous burdens are being imposed upon some individuals, inadequately justified by tenuous arguments as being conductive to illusory or unwanted goods. It is not that people are utterly selfish. During the war they were ready to make great sacrifices, because it was clear why they were being asked to do so. So, too, people now could be reconciled to sacrifices on their part if they were shown to be necessary. The trouble with the present planning procedures is that they do not, and as they are at present constituted cannot, achieve any measure of reconciliation because the onus of proof is the wrong way round. The damage done by the department's proposals is obvious, real, and keenly felt; it is not obvious that there will be corresponding benefits – the department does not prove that there is any need for its proposals, only asserts that there is – nor is it apparent that the benefits, if they exist, will outweigh the losses. Nobody in his senses would want to increase the Gross National Product at the cost of making life unpleasant for everybody; utilitarian arguments generally are inadequate to justify imposing severe deprivations on anyone.

The most fundamental change required is a change of heart. Policy-makers need to understand that the public interest has many faces, and that it is in the public interest that individual interests should be cherished, and that the public interest in securing a wide measure of agreement and in avoiding a sense of injustice and resentment is so important that other aspects of the public interest, such as prosperity and economic growth, ought to be compromised in order not to override it. Although public inquiries are not completely comparable with criminal courts, they are analogous in some important respects, and their procedure should be made appropriately similar. Where important individual interests are in jeopardy, the proceedings should be characterized by a manifest reluctance to invade these interests. Much more time should be given for those in danger to concert their defence. In other countries there is the equivalent of legal aid for those endangered by state activity. I believe this is right both on the score of justice and on other counts of public utility. Objectors are performing a public service by fighting proposals which are often foolish and often extravagant; they ought not to be out of pocket in consequence. Among other things they constitute a source of information which is invaluable, although perhaps unwelcome, to the government, just because it is independent of them. Governments always tend to rely too exclusively on their own information and to make mistakes on account of distortions in its collection and selection. In the inquiries in February and July 1973, I listened to the Dartmoor Preservation Association and the Exeter Conservation Society explaining that there was going to be a fuel crisis and the officials of the Department of the Environment blandly denying that they had any reason to suppose that there would be a shortage of fuel or any need to prepare a transport policy on the supposition that there might be. Treasury objections to applying public money to paying objector's costs should be met by the consideration of the millions of pounds that would have been saved if the country had prepared for the energy crisis even as late as February or July 1973. Those other objectors who pointed out that the extravagance of the proposals was likely to help bring on an economic crisis have also been vindicated by events; those who protested that to destroy good farm land was unwarranted in view of an approaching food shortage may all too soon be proved true prophets too. The Emperor will also always find it unwelcome to be told that he has no clothes, but it is none the less expedient that he should be told, and therefore, even though justice were of no account with us, we still would be wise to pay objectors' costs.

Other expedients would serve the same ends, either as alternatives or as supplements. There should be public officials, independent of the departments concerned and regarded as an extension of the Citizen's Advice Bureaux, whose task it should be to advise potential objectors and help them gather information. At present, it is largely a matter of luck whether a group of potential objectors includes among its number a don, a school teacher, a clergyman, a solicitor, or some other professional man who has some idea of how to find out the relevant facts and present a coherent case. Critics of objectors can in consequence say correctly that they are characteristically middle class. But this does not show that members of the working class do not want to object, but that in the absence of professional help *they cannot*. The way in which a government department works is baffling. Unless people are given a lot of help, they are lost. This help must come from an independent source. Although I have some-

times found officials of the Department of the Environment helpful and fairminded – the programme officer at the inquiries in
February and June 1973 – Ide Parish Council found itself led up
the garden path by officials of the Department of the Environment, who first suggested to them a line they might take and then
shot it down at the inquiry on engineering grounds. Another useful institution would be to have at the inquiry itself an independent advocate briefed as *amicus curiae* to help the inspector find
out the truth and ensure that justice was seen to be done. It is
impossible to prevent bully-boy tactics being employed by some
counsel – inquiries are the arena in which great interests conflict – but it would be helpful if the witness who had been unfairly treated could be re-examined to bring out the full truth.
Again, some procedural restrictions are necessary to prevent
objectors wasting time inordinately; but quite often further facts
should be brought to light after one particular objector has con-
cluded his case. An inquiry differs from a trial in there being
many parties to it and its not being so readily cast into simple
adversative form, and there is therefore more scope for an advocate not tied to any particular side of the case. Inspectors should
be of a higher calibre. Some seem to understand concrete stresses
and radii of curvature well enough, but seem not to register many
of the other points objectors make. More fundamentally and more
controversially, inspectors should not only understand arguments, but be guided by them. This is the respect in which the
analogy with the criminal courts is most important, but it needs
most careful handling. The underlying similarity of aim in both
cases is that the citizen should not be deprived of his cherished
interests by the government except for good reason. The difference lies in the degree of definiteness and cogency required in the
reasoning. Many procedural safeguards and rules of evidence
employed in the criminal courts would be out of place in public
inquiries. In recent centuries, a man can be convicted only if
he can be shown to have broken a *definite* law. It was not
always so, and cannot be so in public inquiries where policies
are only vaguely formulated and cannot be applied to individual
cases with the precision and rigour of the law. Much more must
be left to the inspector's discretion. But still he can be required

to approach the question with an open mind and address himself to the arguments adduced, and not to imperil any citizen's central interests unless a fairly weighty burden of proof has been discharged to show that this is undoubtedly what ought to be done.

The doctrine of ministerial responsibility will be argued against these suggestions. Ministers of the Crown, it is said, are responsible to Parliament, and therefore must not be fettered or prevented from ignoring all the evidence or overruling the inspector's recommendation, and doing whatever seems good to them. But the argument is invalid. Ministers often explain their actions by referring to the judgement of outside bodies, and they could do so in this type of case too. Alternatively, if inspectors acquire the reputation for integrity and intelligence that the judges enjoy, decisions of public inquiries might be no longer open to parliamentary questioning, like decisions of the courts. But in either case, it is important to recognize that ministerial responsibility to Parliament no longer provides an adequate safeguard against error and abuse. For one thing, there are too many inquiries and ministerial decisions. Parliament cannot supervise them all, and in recent years has shown itself increasingly unwilling to question any. Nor is the minister's own sense of responsibility enough. Ministers in recent years have tended to pride themselves on being 'tough', and take melancholy pleasure in pushing through unacceptable decisions in spite of popular protest. The natural tendency of ministers and their advisors alike is not to give way in any individual case, but perhaps avoid stirring up the next hornets' nest along their path. And ministerial responsibility, in so far as it is effective, reinforces this tendency. Criticism takes time to accumulate and is brought to bear on general policies rather than individual decisions. But it is the individual decisions that matter to the individuals concerned. Objectors are concerned to save their own houses and gardens and neighbourhoods and livelihoods from the government, and are only marginally interested in securing an alteration of the government's policy in other cases. What objectors want is that proper consideration should be given to *their* representations and *their* interests and that they should not have *their* lives blighted by some distant minister who has never listened to their arguments or seen for himself what havoc will be wrought by his plans, and who is known to have many other and more urgent things on his mind than the need to do justice to a few, politically unimportant, objectors. In so far as their efforts are effective, they want them to be effective in their own cases and not some subsequent ones. It follows that the decisions should be made by quasi-judges and not quasi-ministers, with an express responsibility to adjudicate fairly rather than administer successfully. Ministers of the Crown cannot discharge such a responsibility any more than can the Home Secretary himself decide who should be sent to prison. But it would be no derogation of the ministerial role to be relieved of functions they cannot adequately discharge. Ministers do not really take the decisions themselves, but incur the odium for decisions taken by other men on their behalf but not under their effective control. It would be far better both for Parliament and for Whitehall to remove a lot of contentious business which clutters up the system and is not carried out well by either Parliament or Whitehall. It would also be far better for individual citizens.

January 1974

Postscript

It is not often that an author is happy to be overtaken by events. But I, to some extent, am. I wrote this book in 1973, when Parliament had another two years to run, and the odds were that an election in 1975 would produce a comfortable majority either for the Labour Party under Mr Wilson, or for the Conservatives again under Mr Heath. The criticisms I articulate in Chapter 10 of the system of 'elective autocracy' were evidently weighing with many of my fellow citizens, and when Mr Heath went to the country in February 1974 neither he nor Mr Wilson was given a majority. The short Parliament of 1974 showed, contrary to the opinion of most commentators at the time, that it was no disaster for the government to be obliged to convince Members of Parliament by argument of the rightness of its proposals instead of relying on the Whips to muster sufficient lobby-fodder to get them passed. Many bad decisions were not made. Anyone who believes that minority government is a bad thing should meditate on Clay Cross, or better, go to Drumbuie, and there ponder the Offshore Petroleum Development (Scotland) bill of 1975. If we want to avoid retrospective legislation, running counter to the rule of law, promoted for private party ends, or if we want to have the House of Commons, rather than the departments of state, the place where important decisions are actually taken, we should take care in future to elect Parliaments in which no one party has an overall majority.

To this extent, then, I am happy that I was overtaken by events. In other respects, however, I have been borne out by them less happily. The great power and equal irrelevance of the parties has been shown by Mr Taverne's and Mr Milne's defeat in October 1974, and by the tortuous course of negotiations and re-negotiations with the EEC. Whether or not a man becomes a

Member of Parliament depends increasingly on caucuses in the constituencies: but it does not greatly signify who the Member of Parliament is. Those electors of Lincoln who ousted Mr Taverne on account of his support for the EEC must be reflecting ruefully how little effect their success has had, and how easily elective autocracy allows the autocrat to ignore the views of those who voted for him. To the future historian of Britain's European policy it will matter relatively little whether Mr Heath or Mr Wilson was Prime Minister, but to the future historian of the Labour party it will be very important, when considering its policy at any particular juncture, to remember whether it was in office or in opposition at that time.

I have not attempted to revise the book. By the time I had done so, it would again be out of date. I should need to rewrite Chapters 10 and 11, and to expand very considerably the discussion in Chapter 12. The tone would be different. I have become much more conscious of the high-handedness of the departments of state. Having come across more instances of petty tyranny on the part of immigration officials, tax inspectors and above all the Road Construction Units, I should now want to be more insistent still on the need to control the executive and to provide individual citizens with safeguards against decisions being taken to their detriment without real regard for their interests. I should write much more stridently now, as one who has witnessed the environment of Ide (p. 270 ff.) being destroyed, fields obliterated, farms severed and householders evicted, but this would not speak to the condition of the majority of my fellow countrymen, who are as yet unfamiliar with such things. I have therefore left the book as it was, but add this note of warning.

With the shadows over the country's future deepening, we shall be tempted to put off tackling problems of organization, as our attention is more and more absorbed in problems of survival. But it would be a mistake to argue that a concern with the processes of government is an irrelevant luxury in times of stringency. Britain's economy is weak because its society is divided, and our society is divided because our decision-procedures bruise, rather than conciliate, those concerned. Our economic and political institutions set decisions in an external perspective, as having been handed down by Them instead of being reached by us; we are not involved in them, and therefore, at best feel uncommitted to them, and, if they are adverse, are deeply hostile, and resentful of the system that produced them. So far as broad issues are concerned, we suffer because we have no national institutions for articulating and then accommodating the various differences that divide us. Our governments are weak, not because they are criticized in Parliament, but because they are not criticized enough, and therefore can neither adjust their measures to the temper of the people and the needs of the moment nor mobilize support by arguing effectively for them and countering really weighty objections voiced against them. Parliament, because it is not a mirror of the nation, cannot be a sounding board for the government either, and in emasculating Parliament the government has rendered itself impotent either to feel or to quicken the pulse of the people, and therefore cannot retain effective control over the course of events. What we need is strong government, strong not through being dictatorial and bureaucratic but through being sustained by popular support founded on understanding and respect.

So far as smaller-scale issues are concerned, much more thought needs to be given to the different sorts of decision – especially where the citizen is concerned to ward off highly adverse decisions, and issues of justice arise. Procedures at public inquiries give little cause for confidence. In January 1975 at a public inquiry at Epping a girl aged twelve gave evidence, saying what she felt about the forest. Counsel for the Department of the Environment cross-examined her in such depth, putting it to her that she and her mother were biased, that she was obviously upset. She was not allowed to have her mother, who was sitting behind her, help her understand a map she was being asked about. There are occasions when even the evidence of children must be subjected to searching examination in the interests of justice: but it is difficult to believe that this was one of them; and even the most ardent advocate of executive privilege will find it hard to reconcile what actually happened with the ruling made by the

Inspector the day before, when another objector was making his submission:

>... if you wish at any time to refer to any of your friends in order to verify the answers that you propose to give to any questions that are asked you, I shall always agree that that should be done.

There are no rules for the conduct of public inquiries on proposals to build motorways. The Council on Tribunals recommended that rules of procedure should be laid down, but the Department of the Environment has preferred not to act on that recommendation. No doubt there are disadvantages in having rules of procedure too tightly specified; and if inspectors were of the same calibre as judges, they might be able to see fair play as between isolated private citizens and powerful public authorities, and at least would not deny to one person one day the protection of a ruling made only the day before. Only if the rule of law is re-established, and government departments are constrained to show as much regard for the rights and interests of the individual citizen as they do for their own plans and programmes, will people recapture the sense that the government is their government and for them, rather than merely a government over them, and often against them. In the current demonology the great enemies of freedom and democracy are, according to the Conservatives, the trade unions, and, according to Labour, big business. Both are right, but both neglect the even greater threat to the citizen's liberty to order his private affairs and participate in public affairs posed by the activities of the officials of local authorities and the departments of state. Democracy, along with freedom and justice, is indeed in danger; but above all by reason of the uncontrolled power of government itself.

May 1975   J.R.L.

Index

More about Penguins and Pelicans

Penguinews, which appears every month, contains details of all the new books issued by Penguins as they are published. From time to time it is supplemented by *Penguins in Print*, which is a complete list of all titles available. (There are some five thousand of these.)

A specimen copy of *Penguinews* will be sent to you free on request. For a year's issues (including the complete lists) please send £1 if you live in the British Isles, or elsewhere. Just write to Dept EP, Penguin Books Ltd, Harmondsworth, Middlesex, enclosing a cheque or postal order, and your name will be added to the mailing list.

In the U.S.A.: For a complete list of books available from Penguin in the United States write to Dept CS, Penguin Books Inc., 7110 Ambassador Road, Baltimore, Maryland 21207.

In Canada: For a complete list of books available from Penguin in Canada write to Penguin Books Canada Ltd, 41 Steelcase Road West, Markham, Ontario.

Some Other Pelican and Peregrine Books

Some Other Pelican and Peregrine Books

The Arms Trade with the Third World
Stockholm International Peace Research Institute

Beyond the Stable State   *Donald A. Schon*

The Birth of Communist China   *C. P. Fitzgerald*

Comparative Government   *S. E. Finer*

Democracy at Gunpoint   *Andreas Papandreou*

Democracy in a Revolutionary Era   *Wheeler*

An Economic History of the U.S.S.R.   *Alec Nove*

The Economic History of World Populations
Carlo M. Cipolla

Some Other Pelican and Peregrine Books

Some Other Pelican and Peregrine Books